IMAGES
of America

AUBURNDALE

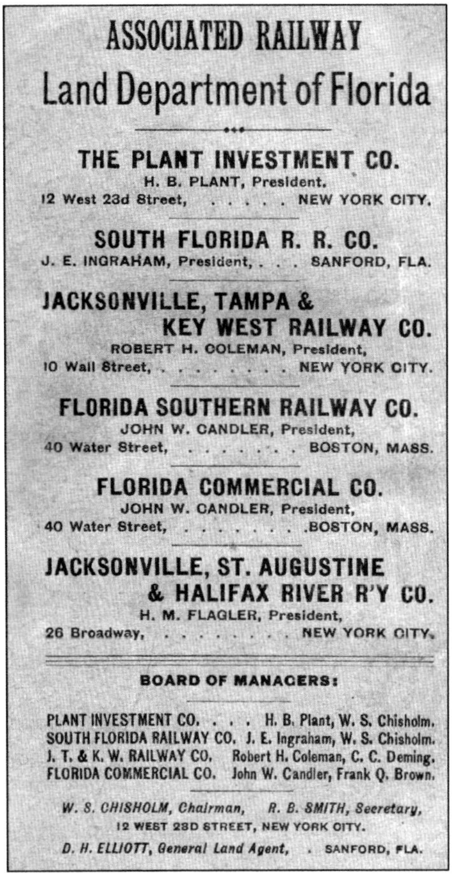

ASSOCIATED RAILWAY
Land Department of Florida

THE PLANT INVESTMENT CO.
H. B. PLANT, President,
12 West 23d Street, ... NEW YORK CITY.

SOUTH FLORIDA R. R. CO.
J. E. INGRAHAM, President, . . . SANFORD, FLA.

JACKSONVILLE, TAMPA & KEY WEST RAILWAY CO.
ROBERT H. COLEMAN, President,
10 Wall Street, ... NEW YORK CITY.

FLORIDA SOUTHERN RAILWAY CO.
JOHN W. CANDLER, President,
40 Water Street, ... BOSTON, MASS.

FLORIDA COMMERCIAL CO.
JOHN W. CANDLER, President,
40 Water Street, ... BOSTON, MASS.

JACKSONVILLE, ST. AUGUSTINE & HALIFAX RIVER R'Y CO.
H. M. FLAGLER, President,
26 Broadway, ... NEW YORK CITY.

BOARD OF MANAGERS:

PLANT INVESTMENT CO. . . . H. B. Plant, W. S. Chisholm.
SOUTH FLORIDA RAILWAY CO. J. E. Ingraham, W. S. Chisholm.
J. T. & K. W. RAILWAY CO. Robert H. Coleman, C. C. Deming.
FLORIDA COMMERCIAL CO. John W. Candler, Frank Q. Brown.

W. S. CHISHOLM, Chairman, R. B. SMITH, Secretary,
12 WEST 23D STREET, NEW YORK CITY.
D. H. ELLIOTT, General Land Agent, . SANFORD, FLA.

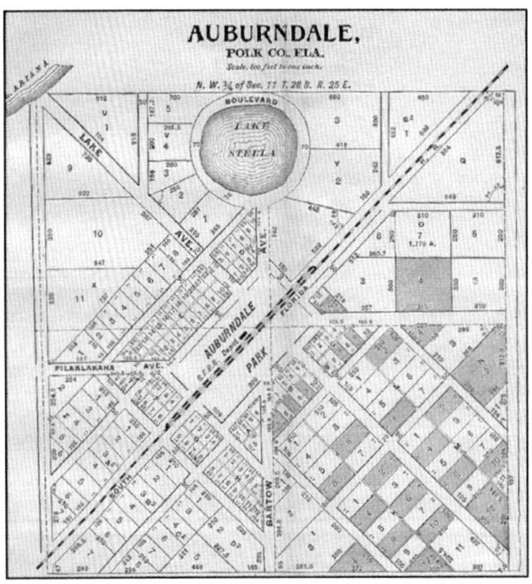

This map and text appeared in a "Florida Polk County Associated Railroad Land Department" booklet issued in 1890 to advertise land sales. The article described high, undulating lands on the southern shores of Lakes Ariana, Lena, and Mariana. It stated that these were all beautiful, deep, clear lakes. The waters were soft and good and abounded in black bass and many other varieties of fish. The elevation of the town was above tidewater (170 feet) and the surrounding lakes (30 feet), of which there were 200 within 10 miles. The article went on to state that the population of the town was 275, with four general stores, one drugstore, one school, one hotel, and one livery stable. Lots were offered at prices ranging from $100 to $500. (Photograph by Alice Elliot Kaszer.)

ON THE COVER: This 40-foot-by-18-foot pavilion on Lake Ariana was a gathering place for Auburndale residents. Many dances, boat races, and picnics were held here. It was built in 1903 on land donated by Captain J.R. Basiger. People often come from across Lake Ariana in boats to take part in the festivities or to shop in the stores. The community built a sidewalk from downtown to a set of cement stairs that led to the pavilion. It was torn down in 1938, when a new city pier was built. (Photograph by Alice Elliot Kaszer.)

IMAGES
of America

AUBURNDALE

Beverly June Scott

ARCADIA
PUBLISHING

ISBN 978-1-4671-1338-0

Published by Arcadia Publishing
Charleston, South Carolina

Printed in the United States of America

Library of Congress Control Number: 2014957051

For all general information, please contact Arcadia Publishing:
Telephone 843-853-2070
Fax 843-853-0044
E-mail sales@arcadiapublishing.com
For customer service and orders:
Toll-Free 1-888-313-2665

Visit us on the Internet at www.arcadiapublishing.com

This book is dedicated to the quiet heroes who braved the wilderness, endured the hardships, and steadfastly refused to give up their settlements along the shores of the lakes of Auburndale, Florida. Their legacy of survival against all odds and love of community continues to endure.

Contents

ACKNOWLEDGMENTS

I would like to thank each and every person who patiently put up with my questions and helped me find the answers. The staff of the Polk County Historical and Genealogical Library and the Polk County Clerk's Office in Bartow were extremely helpful and tolerant.

In 1911, a 19-year-old by the name of Alice Elliot Kaszer stepped off a train and adopted the new community of Auburndale, Florida. In her first three months in Auburndale, she took more than 200 photographs with her $1 Kodak Brownie camera. Alice learned to process her prints by mixing chemicals and exposing the film through the heavy drapes of her hotel room. She captured the history of a small central Florida town and preserved it for the generations. Alice printed many of her photographs on postcards that have traveled around the world. What was a hobby for her is a treasure for us. Unless otherwise noted, all photographs in this book were taken by Alice Elliot Kaszer.

The *Auburndale Star* was in business as a hometown newspaper for half a century. After it ceased publication, its information and images were left for the use of the people of Auburndale.

Introduction

In 1884, a train pulled into a brand-new depot bearing a sign that proclaimed "Auburndale." The depot was surrounded by pine trees, scrub oaks, and several clear, sand-bottom lakes. The only signs of civilization were the boxcars that had been set up on side rails as temporary homes for railroad workers and their families.

When the United States bought Florida from Spain in 1821, it was beautiful but desolate, humid, full of strange and unusual creatures, and considered most unhealthy—certainly not a fit place for persons of refinement. To encourage settlement, the US Armed Occupation Act of 1842 offered 160 acres of land free of charge to settlers who were willing to establish a home, stay for five years, cultivate five acres, and prove armament for protection. There were few takers. Florida was not considered prime real estate. However, by early 1870, Florida's reputation for being unhealthy had somehow made a complete about-face; it was now considered the place to go to cure numerous health conditions.

Meanwhile, in Chicago, William Van Fleet and Alfred Parslow saw a need. Parslow had just been awarded a $9,000 settlement for injuries he received in a train accident. Van Fleet decided that what central Florida needed was a railroad, and they, of course, should be the ones to build it.

By 1880, settlers were filtering into the central Florida area. The Civil War had left a trail of devastation in Georgia and Tennessee, and some settlers took advantage of the Homestead Act to get a new start in the green meadows of America's southern frontier.

Dr. John Patterson was a surgeon in the Civil War. He and his wife, Julia Ann, wanted to escape the destruction in their home state of Tennessee. They filed for a homestead on the east shore of Lake Ariana. They were soon followed by Reuben Fuller and his son Frank, who settled on a lake they named Sanitary. Reuben was a friend of William Van Fleet in Chicago and planned to make a lot of money when the railroad needed land for a depot. He and Frank laid out streets and platted lots for a town they called Sanitaria because they planned to build a sanitarium where they would offer natural cures for various ailments.

By the time the railroad reached Sanitaria, Van Fleet and Parslow had had a few misfortunes, ran out of money, and sold their railroad shares. This was bad news for Reuben. It seems the railroad agent and Reuben had different expectations: Reuben expected to be paid, and the new owners expected Reuben to donate the land for the depot. Reuben refused. A mile away, the Hartwell Howard and James Hampton families wisely agreed to the donation. The wife of one of the owners of the railroad named the depot Auburndale after her hometown, a small city west of Boston.

As the advantages of being near the depot became apparent, the residents of Sanitaria fled the failing town and relocated near the depot. The Howard and Hampton families became wealthy after they built a street along the south side of the depot and sold lots for businesses and homes. They donated the park around the depot and "all streets and alleys" to the people of Auburndale, never to be sold without the signature of every citizen. Dr. John placed logs under his Sanitaria store, hitched it to mules, and dragged it to Auburndale.

The Fullers' dreams faded away. Frank and Reuben Fuller abandoned their plans for Sanitaria and returned to Chicago, and the property returned to its natural environment. Eventually, it became part of Auburndale and was sold for taxes. The lake was renamed Mariana. Only a handful of old-timers still refer to it as Lake Sanitary. In an interview with a reporter years later, Reuben's daughter Loie said that her father remained bitter until his death because the railroad bypassed him by just one mile. In 1901, Alfred Dickey petitioned Auburndale to close the streets and avenues of Sanitaria.

In 1887, three trains a day stopped at the new depot to bring mail and supplies and to load citrus fruit for northern markets. For the first time in months, sometimes years, families were able to hear from relatives they had left behind. Goods were shipped in that could not be obtained locally, and winter visitors filled the hotels.

A row of unpainted clapboard shops sprang up on Main Street. Some store owners provided wooden sidewalks, but because of Florida's free-range law, customers sometimes had to step over a hog comfortably stretched out in a doorway.

Alice Kaszer and her mother, Mary, arrived in Auburndale in May 1911. On the train with them were Alice's two most prized possessions: a Kodak Brownie camera and a 1910 Buick. It is unknown why Alice adopted Auburndale as her new home, but Auburndale adopted her in return. When age and ill health forced her to curtail her photography career, she became a social editor for the *Auburndale Star.* The women of Auburndale made sure she had what she needed.

The little community thrived and all was well until one quiet Sunday morning in 1911. Almost everyone was in the Presbyterian church when a small fire was seen under a shop. Within minutes, Main Street was gone, never to be seen again, except in the photographs that a young Alice Kaszer had taken.

Main Street was rebuilt with "fireproof" red bricks, and once again all was well until a quiet Sunday evening when a group of poker players were careless with their smokes. The fire reached the Walker farm supply store, where dynamite, used to remove stumps to clear land, was stored. By morning, Main Street was gone again.

Merchants lost not only structures but also merchandise, cash, fixtures, mail, and personal items. Giving up or moving on was never an option. They would rebuild.

The personality of a town is established by its founders.

One

Railroads through the Orange Groves

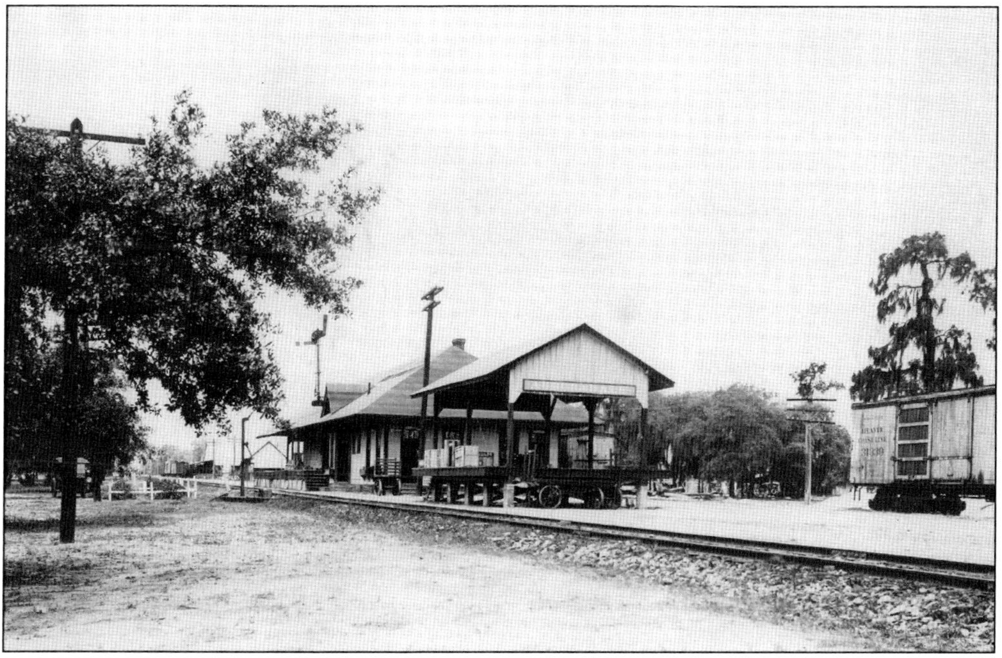

In 1884, the South Florida Railroad chose this isolated location in the wilderness of central Florida to build a depot. There was not another structure in sight. Because the depot was not in a town, Louis McLain, the engineer who designed the depot, contacted one of the owners of the railroad to name it. He deferred to his wife, who suggested it be named after her hometown, Auburndale, Massachusetts.

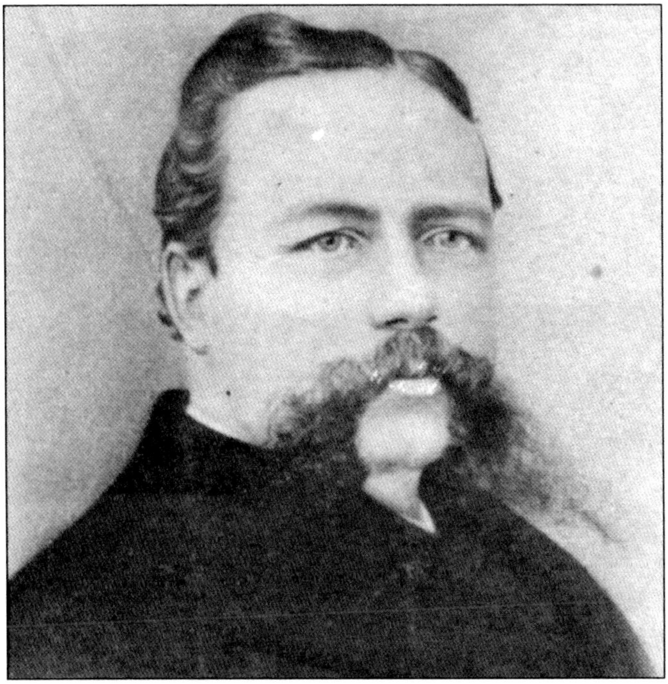

In 1879, William Van Fleet, pictured here, along with Alfred Parslow of Chicago, came to Florida to build a railroad from Sanford to Tampa. After many problems, they sold out to the South Florida Railroad, which became the Atlantic Coast Line. William and his wife, Medora, settled in Auburndale but soon moved to Bartow, where William and his father-in-law, Richard Rensselaer Foote, had interests in the phosphate industry. (Courtesy of the *Auburndale Star* Archives.)

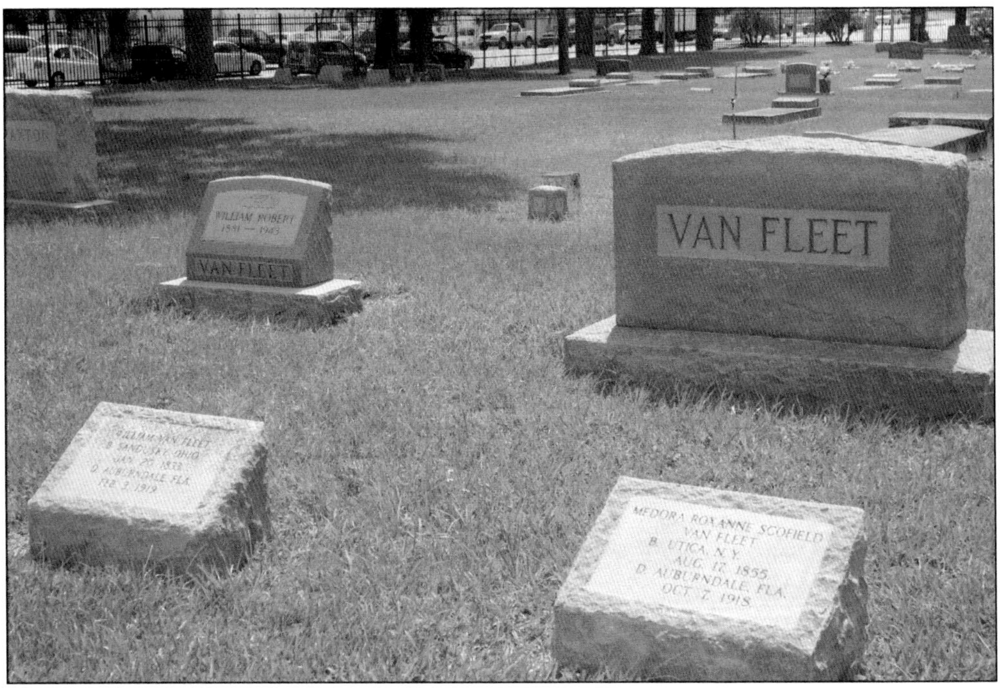

Many of the Van Fleet family are entombed in Auburndale Memorial Park. William and Medora's children—Lois Medora, Richard Rensselaer, William Robert, Martha "Mattie," Albert Eudelman, and James Alward—spent much of their youth in Auburndale with their grandparents Richard Rensselar and Martha Foote on their homestead on Lake Arietta. Their youngest son, James, graduated from West Point and retired as a four-star general. He is buried in Arlington National Cemetery. (Photograph by Beverly June Scott.)

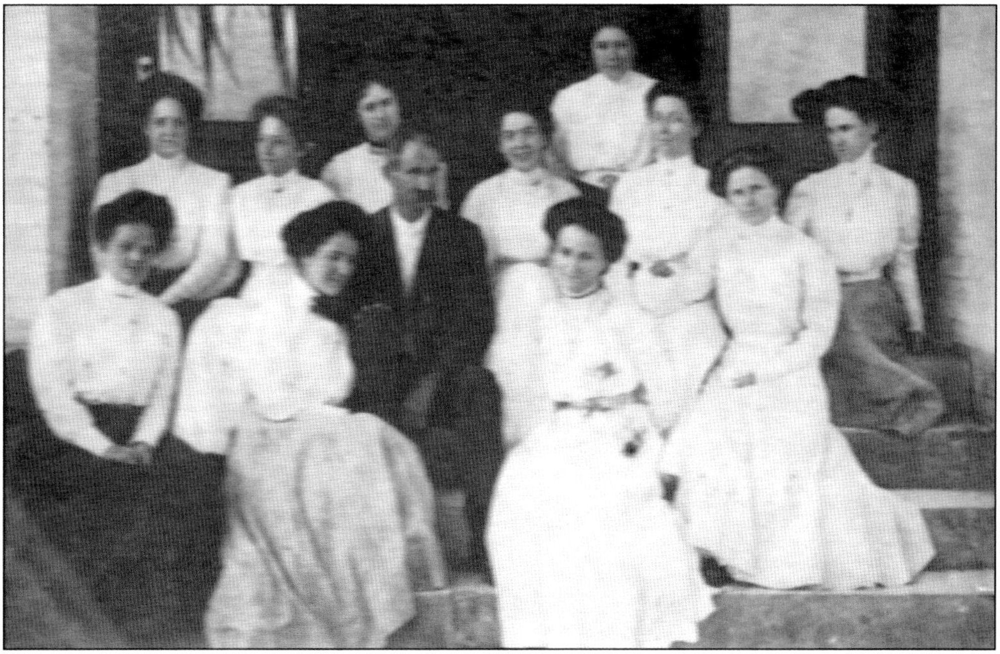

The two daughters of William and Medora Van Fleet are shown here about 1910. Lois Medora is in the first row, left of the man, and Martha "Mattie" is in the second row, right of the man. The other people in this photograph are unidentified. Mattie married Albert Dickey and was a teacher and principal in Auburndale schools for many years.

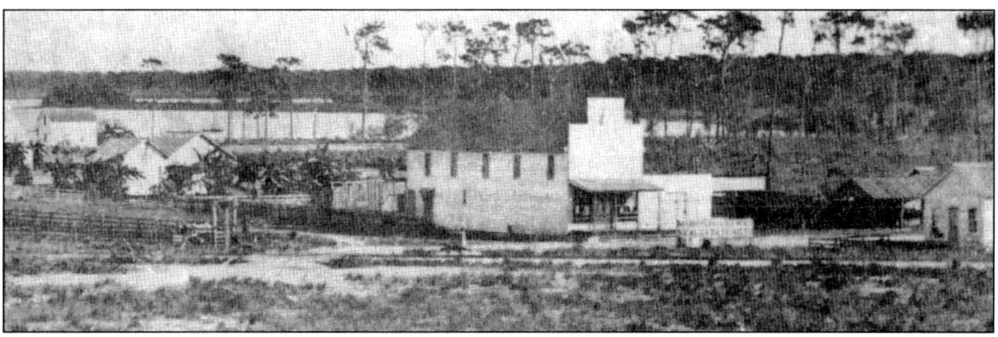

Reuben and Frank Fuller had plans for the little town they named Sanitaria, shown here in 1883. It was along what their friend William Van Fleet said would be the route of the new railroad that would connect east and west Florida. Reuben expected to sell land to the railroad for a depot, but the railroad had different expectations—it expected the land to be donated. Reuben refused. The depot was built a mile away and named Auburndale. (Courtesy of the *Auburndale Star* archives.)

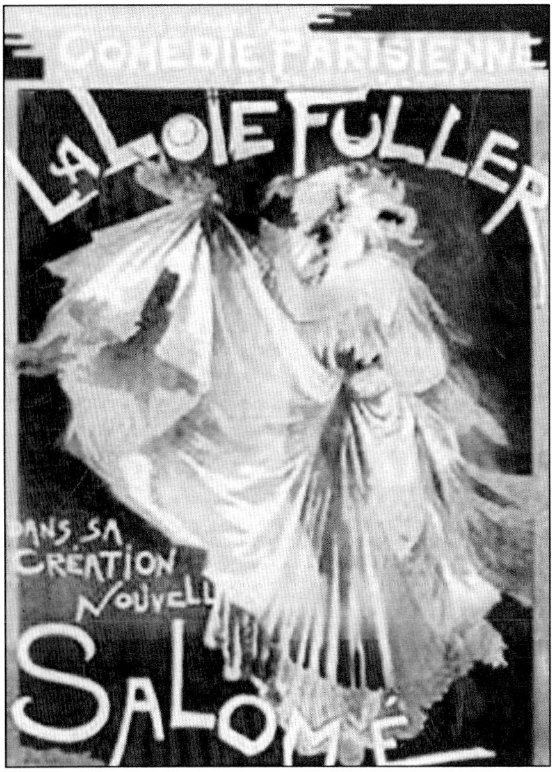

Louise Fuller, shown here in a French poster, was Reuben's daughter. Loie, as she was called, became world famous for her dances using flowing shawls and colored lights. Along with Isadora Duncan, Loie is given credit for inventing modern dance. She spent most of her adult life in Paris. (Courtesy of the *Auburndale Star* archives.)

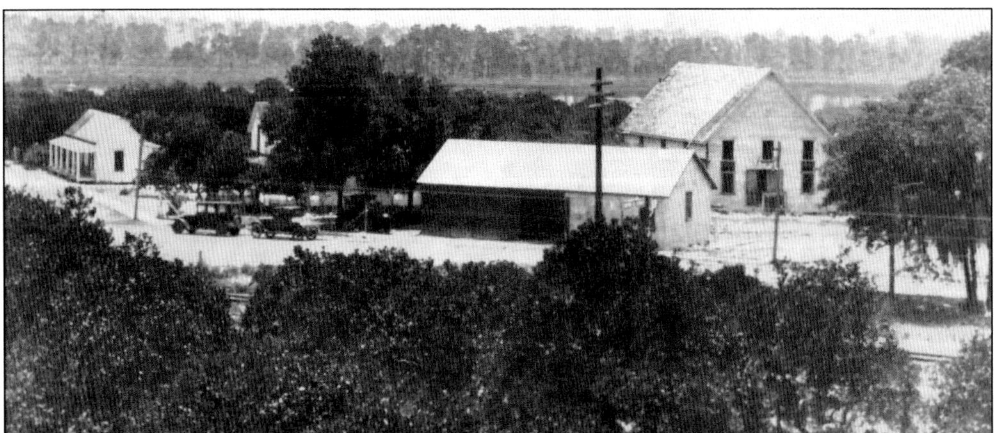

Reuben Fuller built the Sanitaria Opera House just for Loie. Sadly, Reuben said she never performed there. She did visit Sanitaria but returned to Chicago to pursue her career. Auburndale residents used the hall for social events. In 1893, the Social Club had a Calico Hop at the opera house. Admission was 25¢; a "sumptuous" oyster dinner was only 35¢. The opera house was torn down in 1946.

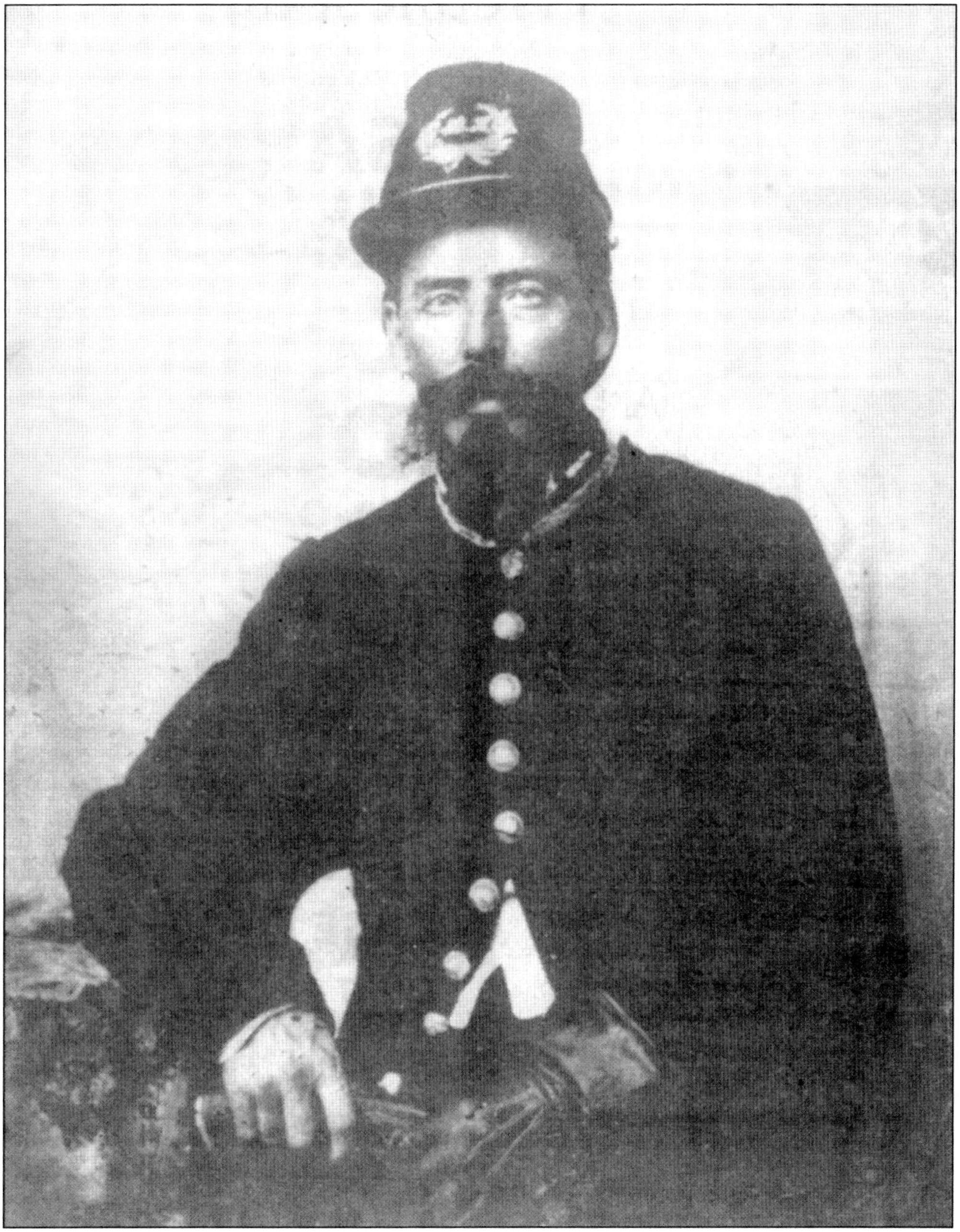

Capt. John Patterson was a Civil War surgeon. In 1882, he homesteaded east of Lake Ariana and built a store in Sanitaria. When Auburndale was chosen for the depot, he had his store placed on logs and pulled by mules to Main Street. After his death in 1903, John II ran the store. Dr. Patterson's granddaughter Margaret married Lawton Chiles. Their son Lawton Chiles Jr. was elected Florida governor in January 1991. (Courtesy of the *Auburndale Star* archives.)

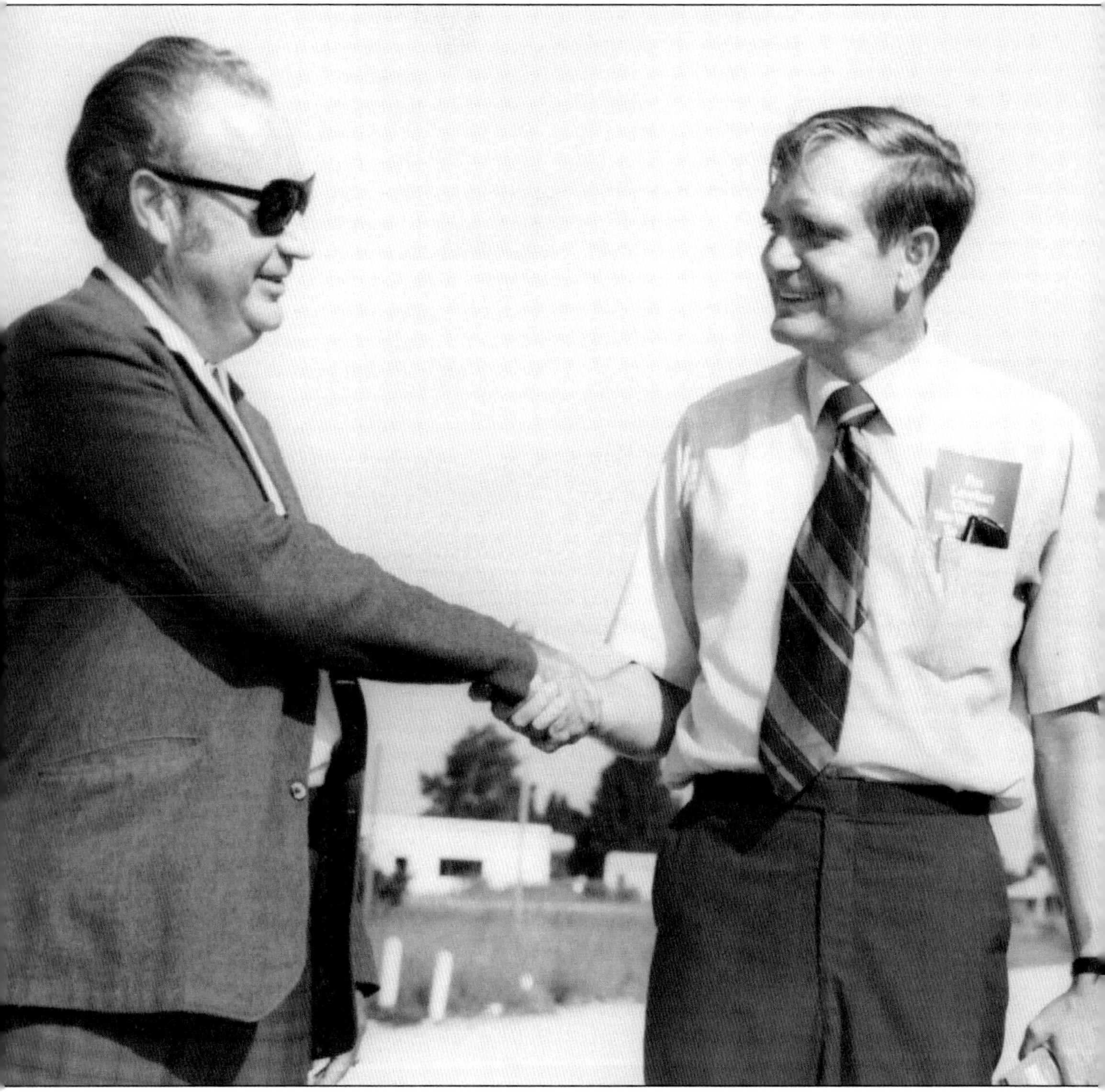

In his bid for a US Senate seat, Lawton Chiles Jr. walked the length of Florida to meet voters. He held this seat for 18 years. Here he (right) is being greeted by city manager Bruce Canova on his walk through Auburndale. Lawton, the son of Margaret Patterson and Lawton Chiles Sr., was the grandson of John Jr. and Annie Patterson and the great-grandson of Dr. John and Julia Ann Patterson. (Courtesy of the *Auburndale Star* archives.)

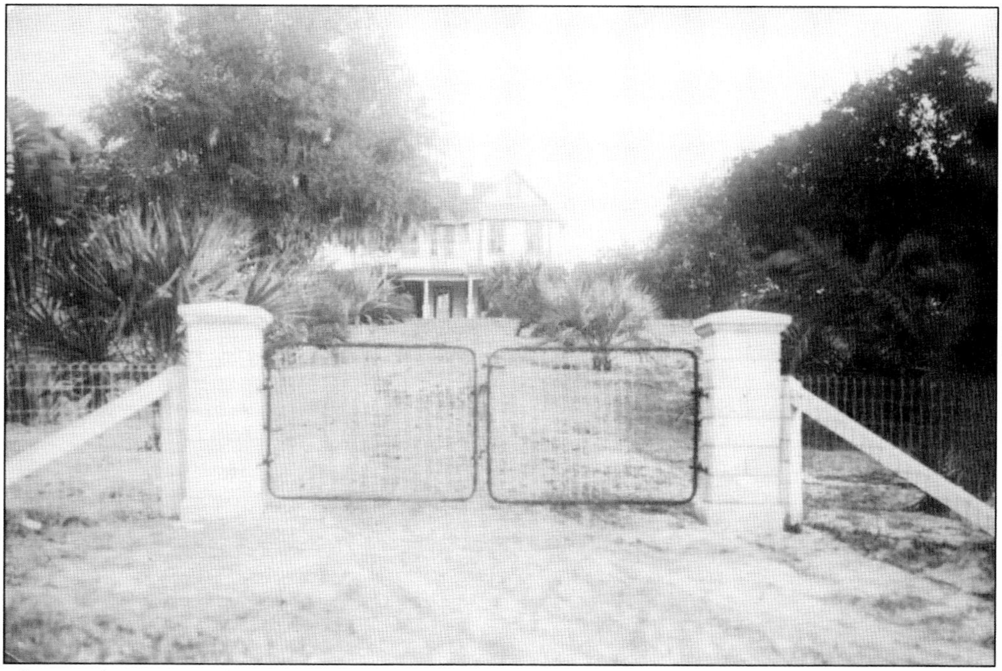

The stately Patterson home stood on a hill overlooking Lake Ariana. Dr. John practiced medicine here. He named the nearby Lake Juliana after his wife, Julia Ann, and another Lake Cardiac because it looked like a human heart. The name was changed to Heart, sometimes misspelled Hart. Dr. John and Julia lived here until their deaths. The house was vacant for years until it was destroyed by fire in 1970.

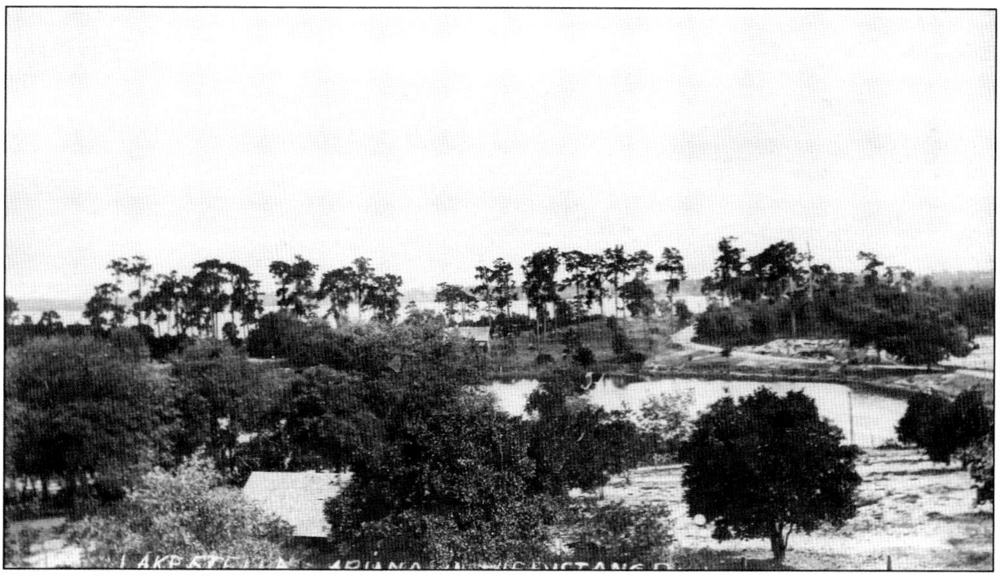

Lake Stella, shown here in 1911, was formed from a sinkhole thousands of years ago. Dr. Patterson named it after his hometown, Stella, Tennessee. During the Depression, one project of President Roosevelt's Works Progress Administration (WPA) was to dig a canal between Lakes Stella and Ariana. Later, a large clay pipe was laid in the canal and covered over.

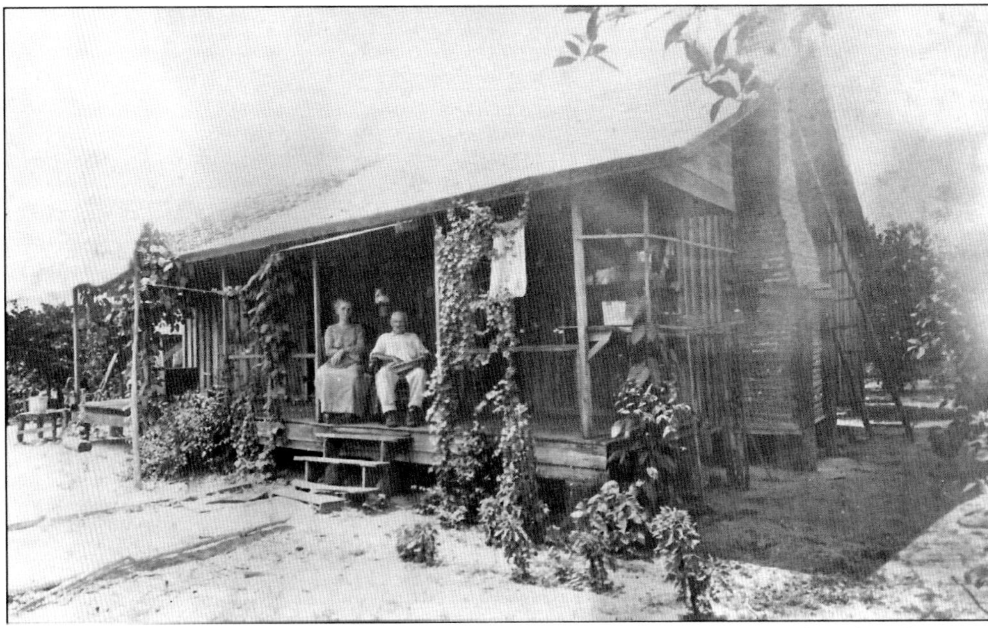

In 1915, Hannah and David Pearson took a few minutes to rest on the front porch at their farm west of Auburndale. Farms in this area were noted for bountiful harvests of strawberries. "Strawberry" Schools were closed from late fall to early spring and open during the summer so that children could help with the berry harvest.

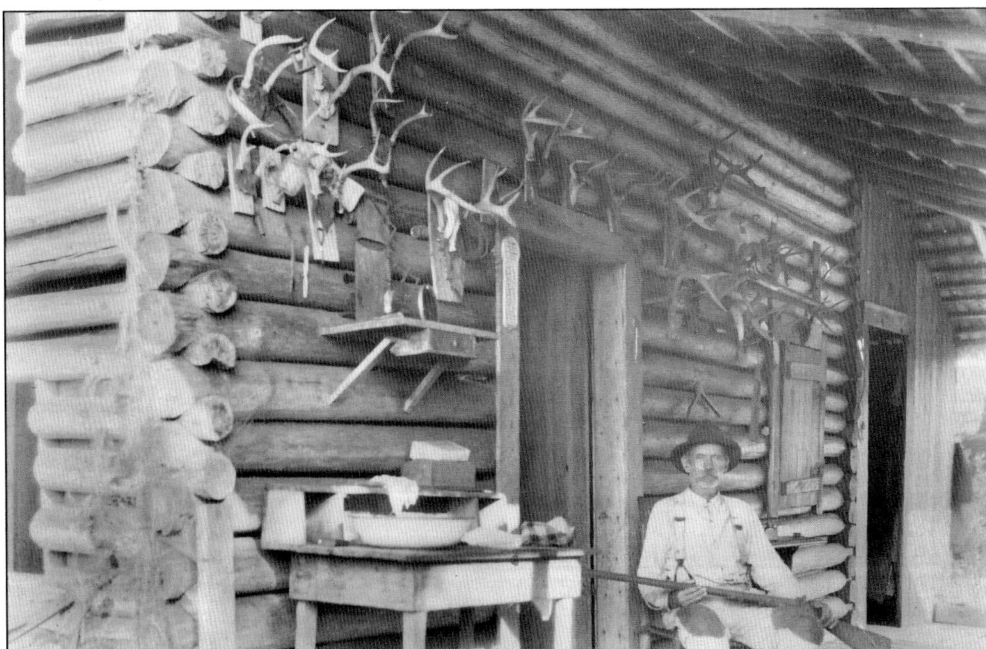

George Washington Fussell sits on the porch of his "cracker house" in the flat woods near Auburndale. Some of the first white settlers in Florida were men who rounded up and sold the wild cattle that inhabited the territory. Crackers were so called because they guided the cattle by cracking long whips over their heads to turn the herd. Crackers survived on what the land offered.

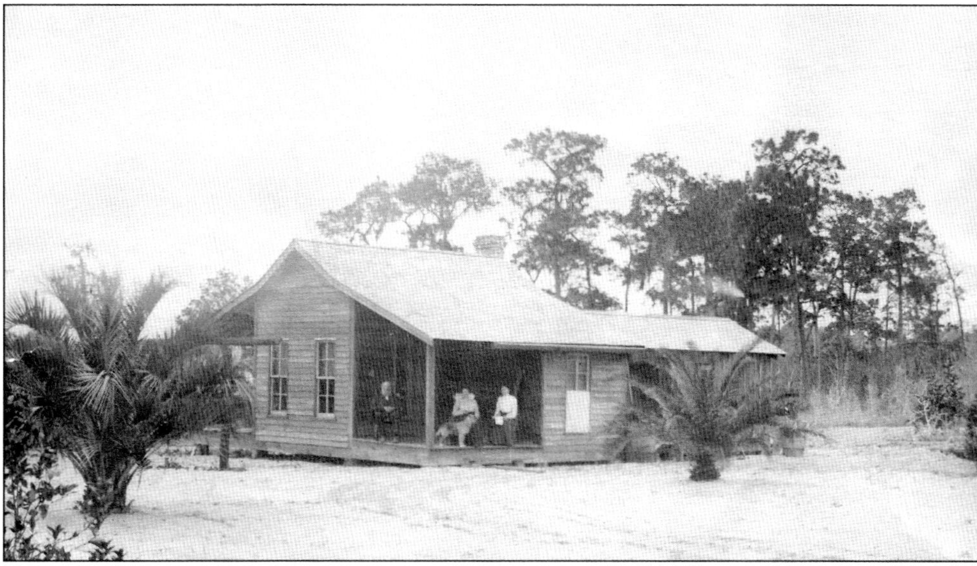

Duane and Abbie Turner came to Auburndale from Washington, DC. In 1890, the Turner cabin was located on the east shore of Lake Juliana. The cabin was made from hard heart pine, cut locally. This wood resisted decay, and few insects would touch it. Water was obtained from a lake or a hand-dug well. Meals were cooked in the fireplace.

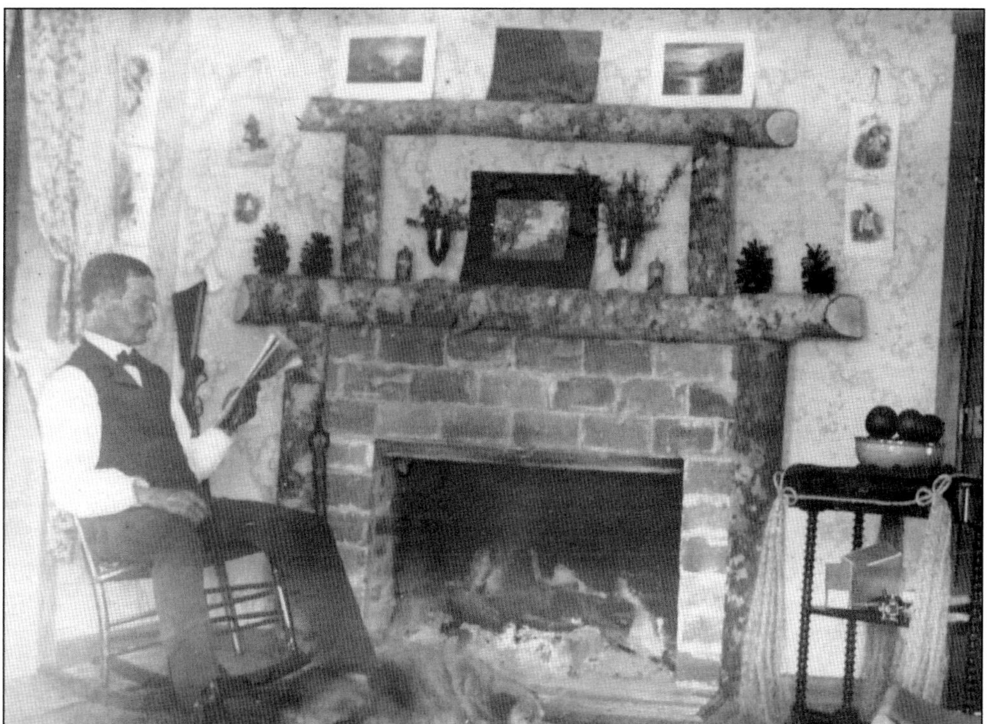

The interior of the Duane and Abbie Turner cabin was more richly furnished than most of the early cabins in Auburndale. Their furniture was probably brought with them. Duane Turner is shown here relaxing in front of the fireplace. He is dressed in the typical men's business suit of the time.

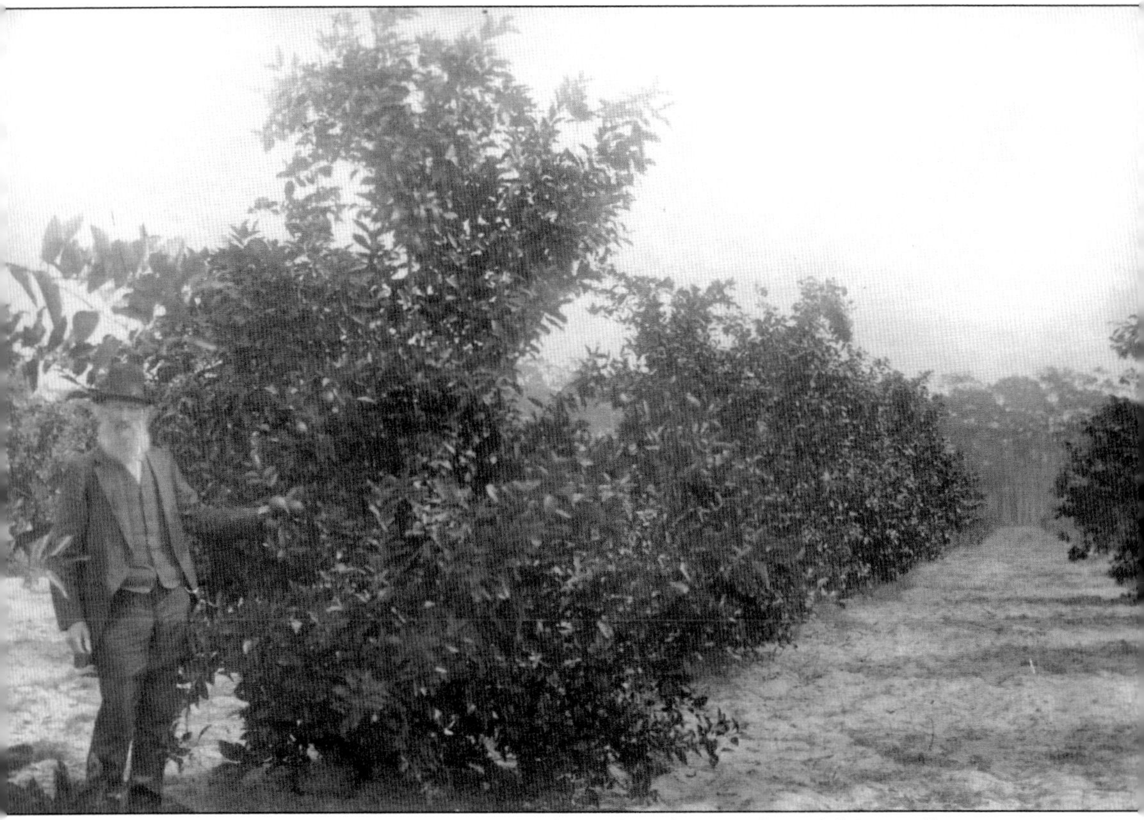

Abbie Turner's father is shown here checking their fruit. Auburndale's usually warm, sunny winters are ideal for citrus, and freezes are rare. Below-freezing temperatures for three hours will damage the fruit, and longer than that will damage or kill the trees. In December 29, 1894, the temperature began to drop, and by morning it was 18 degrees Fahrenheit. By evening, snow flurries settled on frozen oranges.

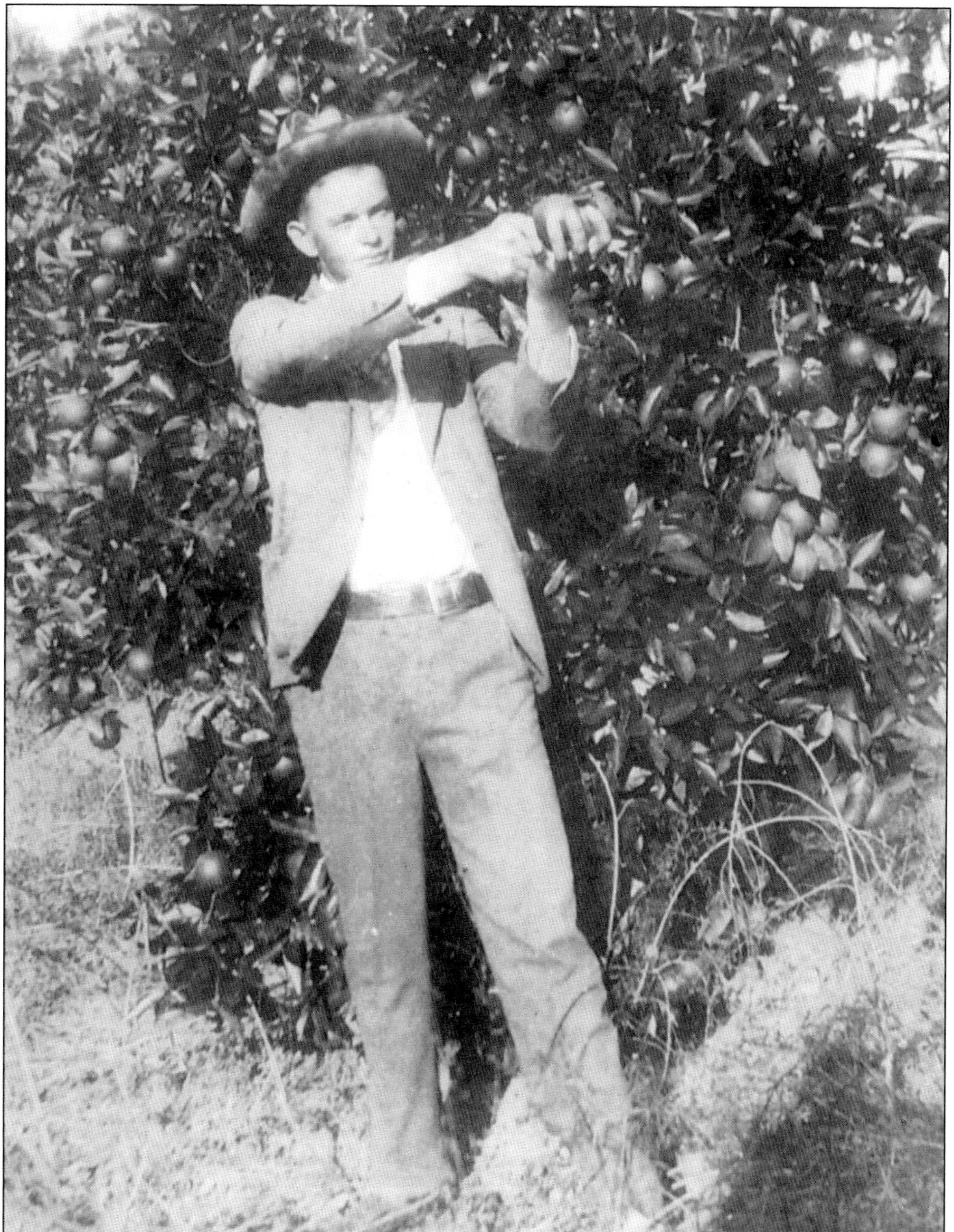

January brought warm sunny days with rain, and the trees sprouted new growth. On January 18, 1895, the temperature dropped and did not get above freezing for two days. Old-timers said it sounded like pistols were being fired in the groves as the freezing sap split bark open with loud pops. It would be 10 years before newly planted trees would reach the same production level.

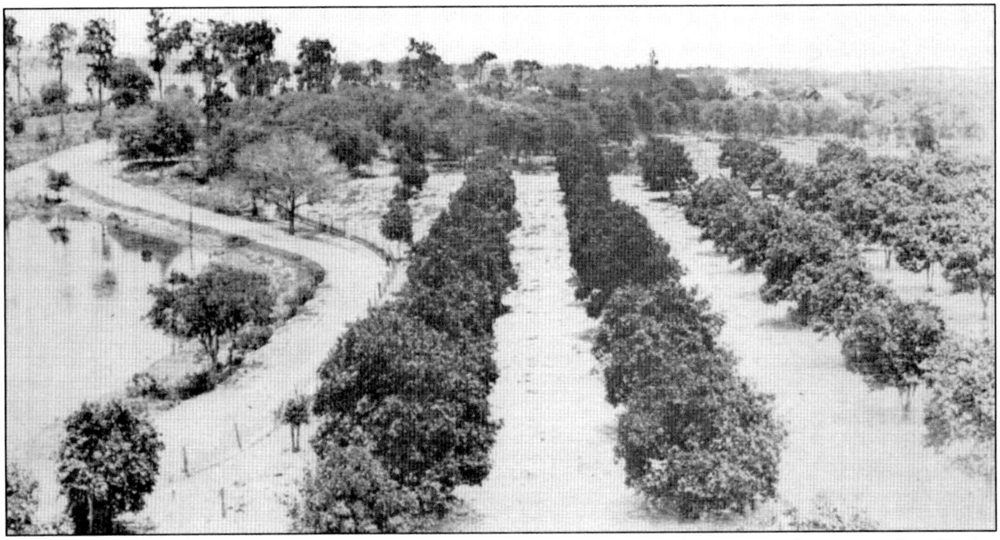

The bushy growth trees seen here about 1910 in the E.M. Baynard grove on the east side of Lake Stella show the recovery from the 1894 freeze. The John Patterson house and grove can be seen in the upper-right corner of the photograph.

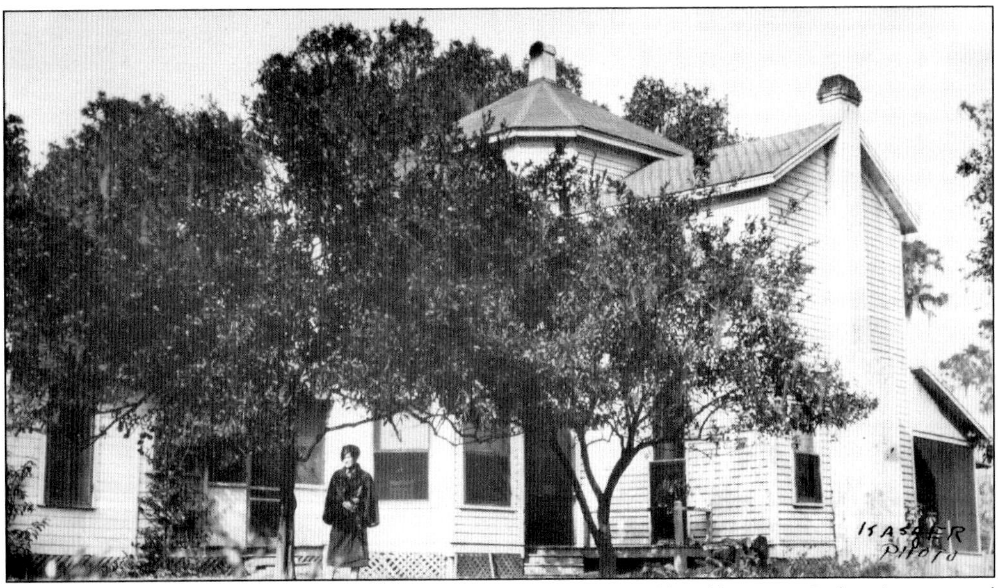

The Redfield home was located in the Gapway, a narrow strip of land between Lakes Arietta and Juliana. When Eugene Redfield died in 1908, the wake was held at his home, and he was buried on his land. Lydia, his wife, operated a boardinghouse and continued to oversee the groves until selling them to a large packing company. The home was then used to house grove workers until it was torn down.

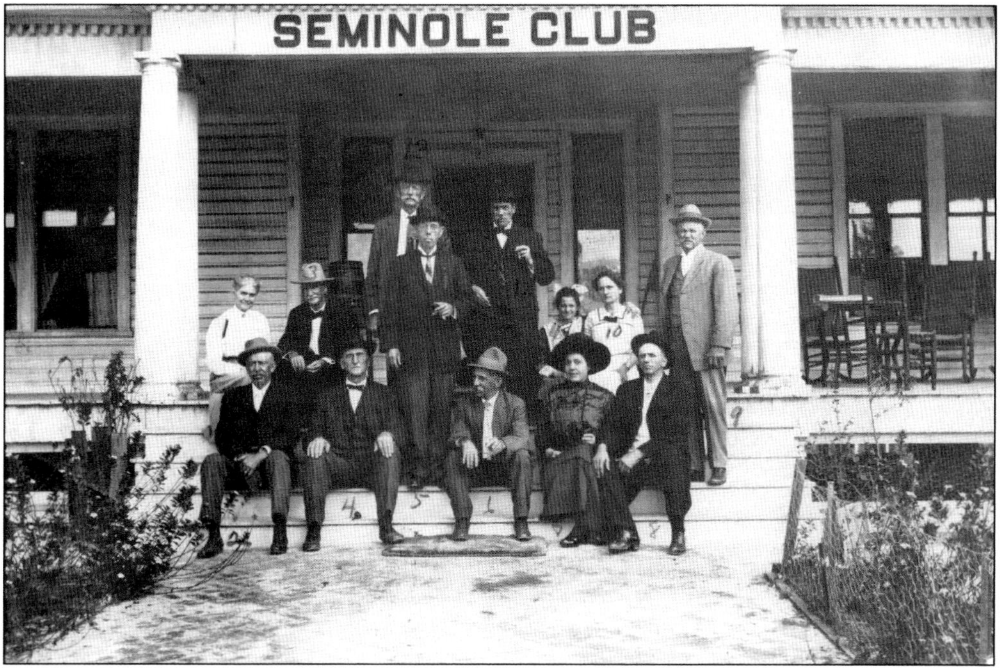

The 17-room Seminole Club opened in 1908 on the east side of Lake Ariana. The 600 members came from all over the United States. Dues of $100 bought the privilege to hunt and fish on the 12 acres controlled by the club. Members did not respect property lines, causing problems with residents. By 1910, Wesley and Helen Pricket were managing the Seminole Club. Their daughter Della married Harry Cline.

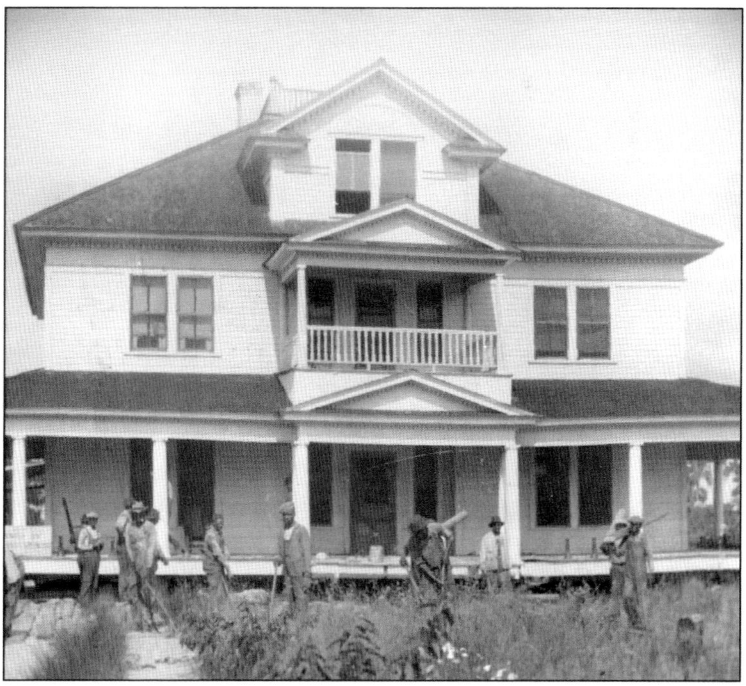

In 1920, the club was sold to Bill and Martha Gladden. They had the enormous structure moved down the hill closer to the lake. Operating the club proved to be too costly. In 1925, they sold the building but retained 10 acres. Mr. Gladden sold sand, used for home construction, from a hill rumored to be an Indian mound. The Seminole Club became a private residence. It was torn down in the 1970s.

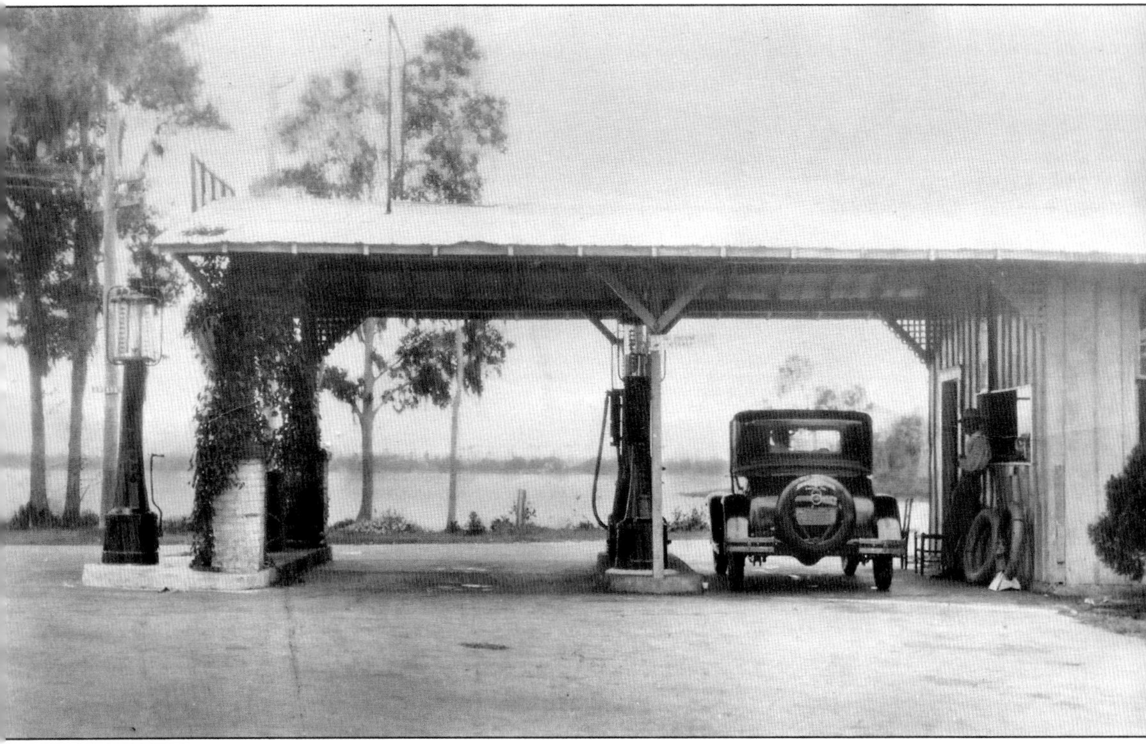

William Gladden built the Lake Shore Garage on part of the old Seminole Club property. He serviced and maintained Jere Stambaugh's fleet of grove trucks, as well as many of the vehicles used in the citrus industry. Lake Shore Garage was torn down in 1973. A convenience store is now on the site.

Two

Our Own Sweet Auburndale

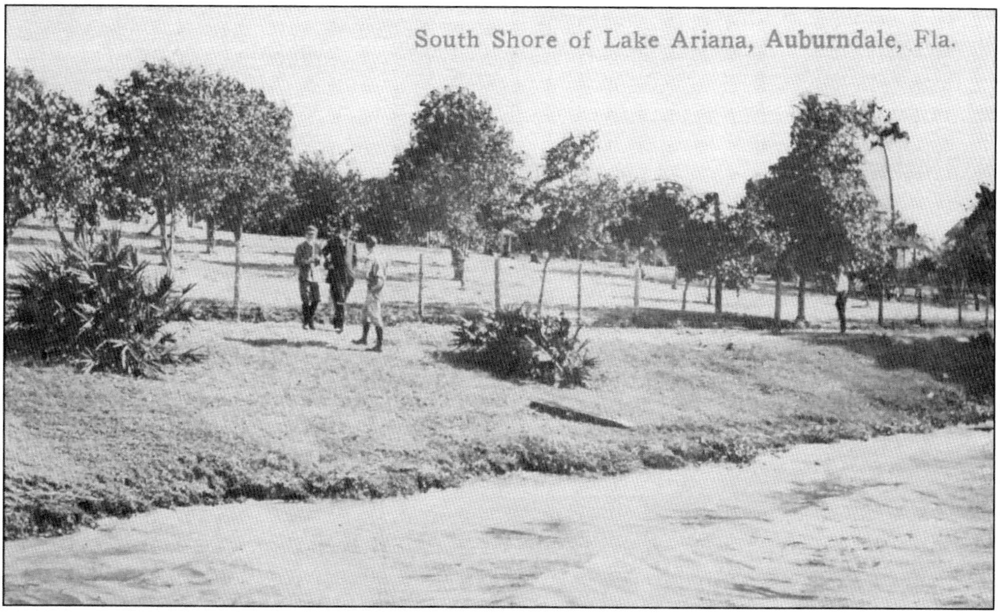

"Sweet Auburn, loveliest village of the plain, where health and plenty cheer'd the laboring swain." In his 1764 poem, Oliver Goldsmith told how Sweet Auburn was destroyed by residents' greed. This did not stop future swains from naming 10 US towns Auburn, not to mention naming three Auburndale, including "Sweet Auburndale" in Florida. The group in this 1911 image, enjoying a stroll along the shore of Lake Ariana, appears unconcerned about Oliver's prophecy.

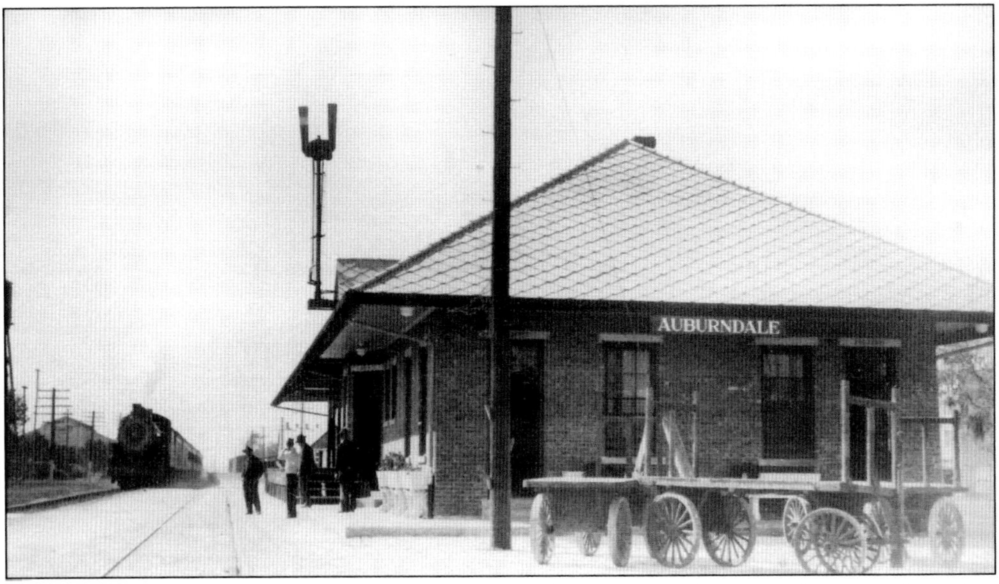

The Howard and Hampton families not only donated part of their homesteads for the depot but also deeded the streets, avenues, and the park around the depot to the people of Auburndale. The park can never have a commercial building in it, nor can it be sold without the signature of every citizen of the town. The depot was the hub around which the town was planned.

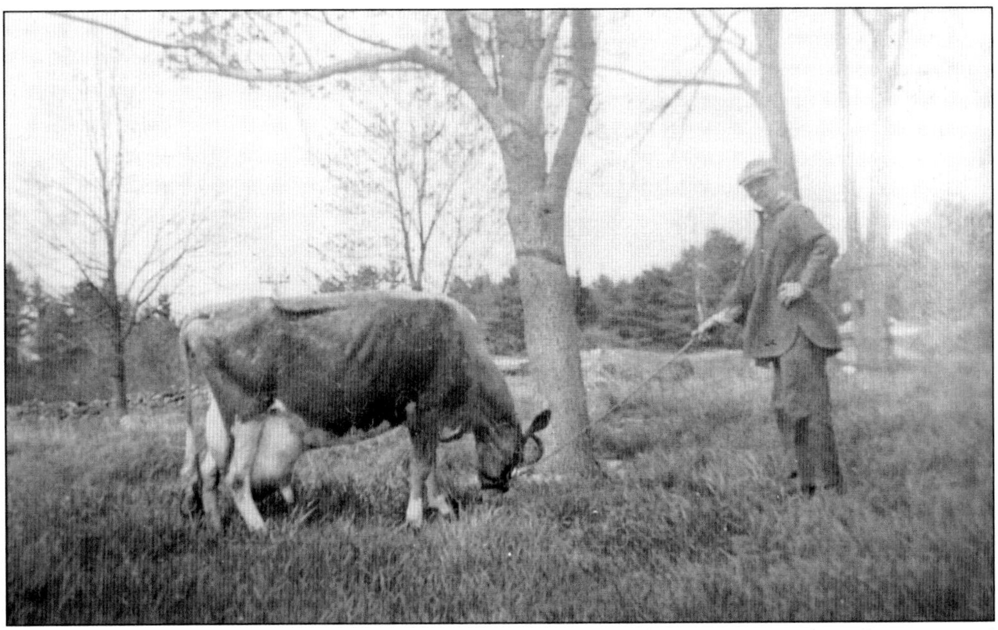

A young man brings his cow to the park to graze. Per Florida's open-range law, domesticated animals roamed freely. Every day, cows chewed their cud, chickens laid eggs under bushes, and pigs rooted in the bushes. If a farm animal was hurt or killed, the offender had to pay, providing of course that the culprit could be found and that the evidence had not already been eaten for someone's supper.

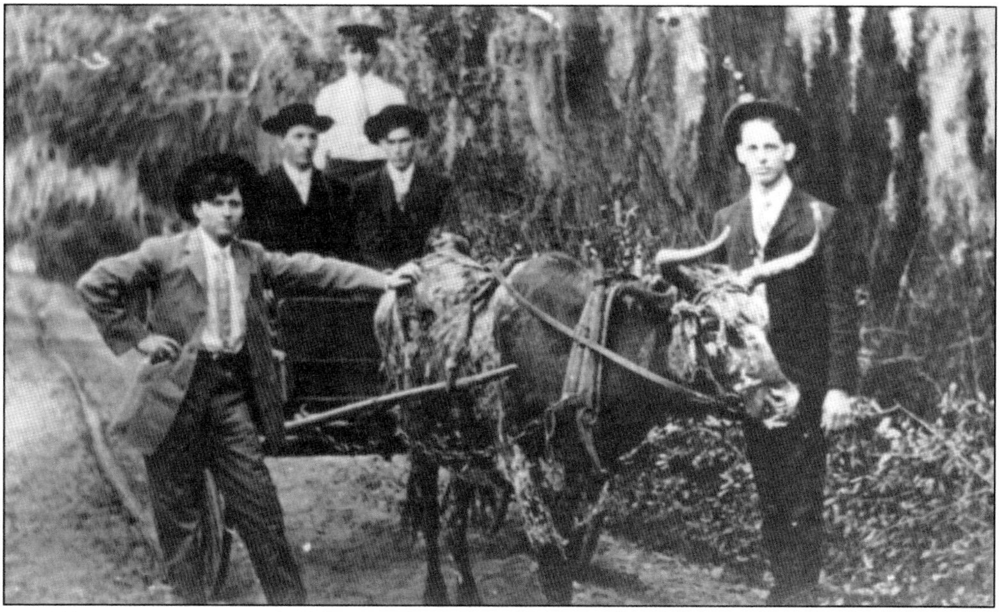

In 1911, transportation was slow, usually by foot, horseback, or ox cart. Roads were sandy and dusty in dry weather and mud holes that could swallow up wagon wheels were a problem during the rainy season. Here, Jim McCoy (left) and Felix Fussell take three unidentified visitors on a slow, and probably very uncomfortable, trip along the shore of Lake Ariana.

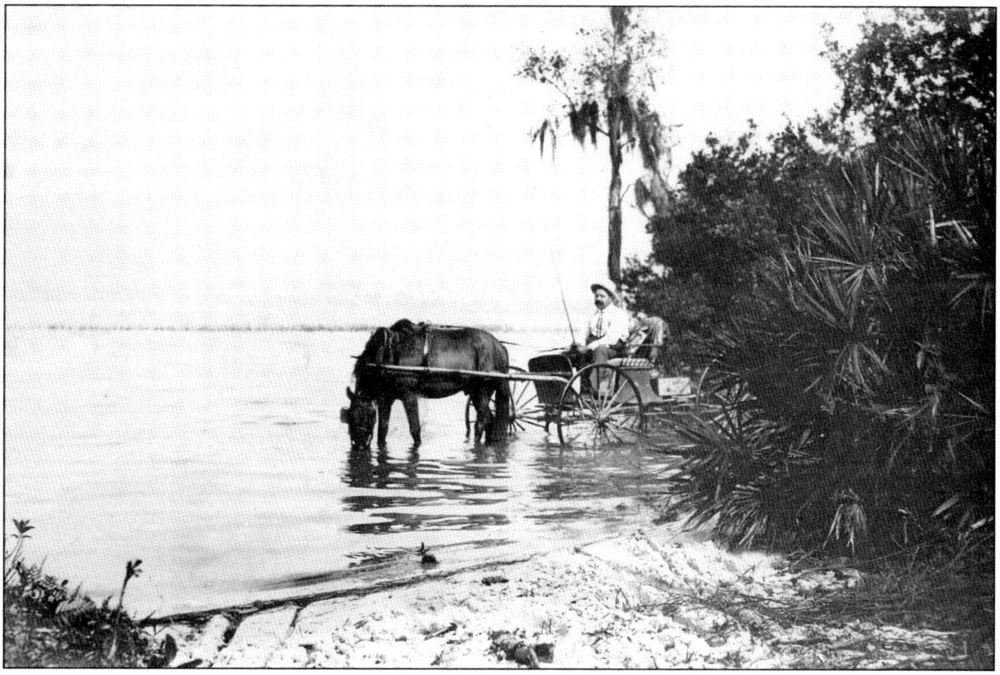

Every fall, the population of Auburndale increased as winter visitors arrived by train to enjoy the mild weather without snow. Some had residences, while others stayed at the Hampton House, the Patrick Hotel, or one of the boardinghouses. Recreation revolved around the lakes. Here, an unidentified man interrupts his buggy ride on the sandy trail around Lake Ariana to cool off, refresh the horse, and take in the scenery.

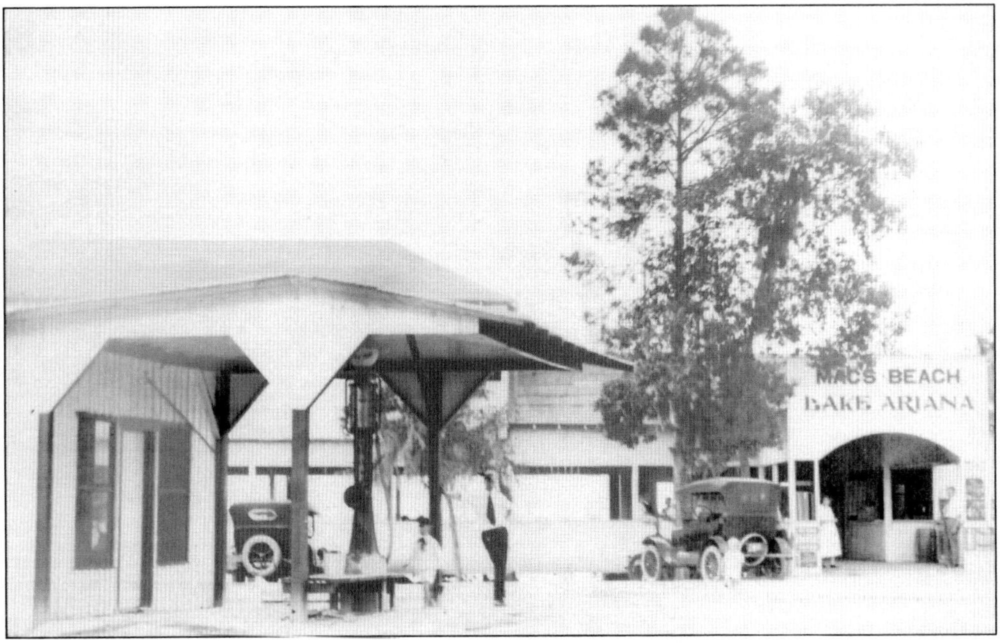

In the 1920s, brothers Hurbert and Glover McDowell built a pavilion over the water on the west side of Lake Ariana and charged 10¢ for swimming. The first floor had a snack bar, and the second floor was a dance hall. Mac's Beach quickly became a teen hangout and the location of many high school sock hops. After Mac's Beach closed, the city bought the property, razed the building, and put in improvements for the city beach.

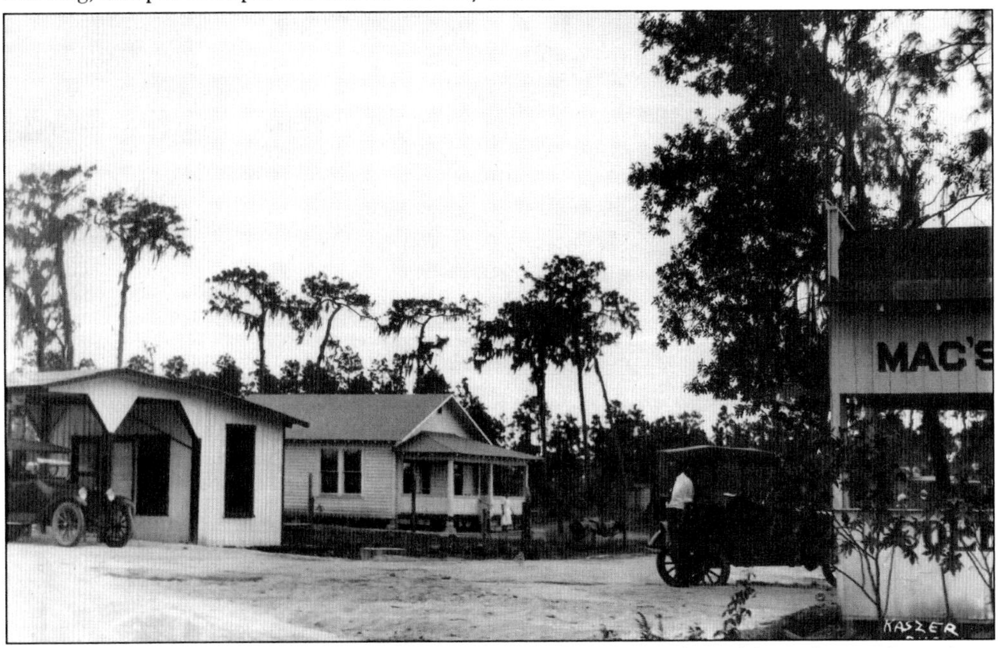

The McDowell service station was located across Lake Ariana Boulevard from the pavilion where the Dixie Highway turned to go to Lakeland. When the city expanded the beach, this part of the road was discontinued and covered over. The city's yacht club stands on this site. A fishing pier, a boat ramp, a clubhouse, a playground, and picnic areas were added.

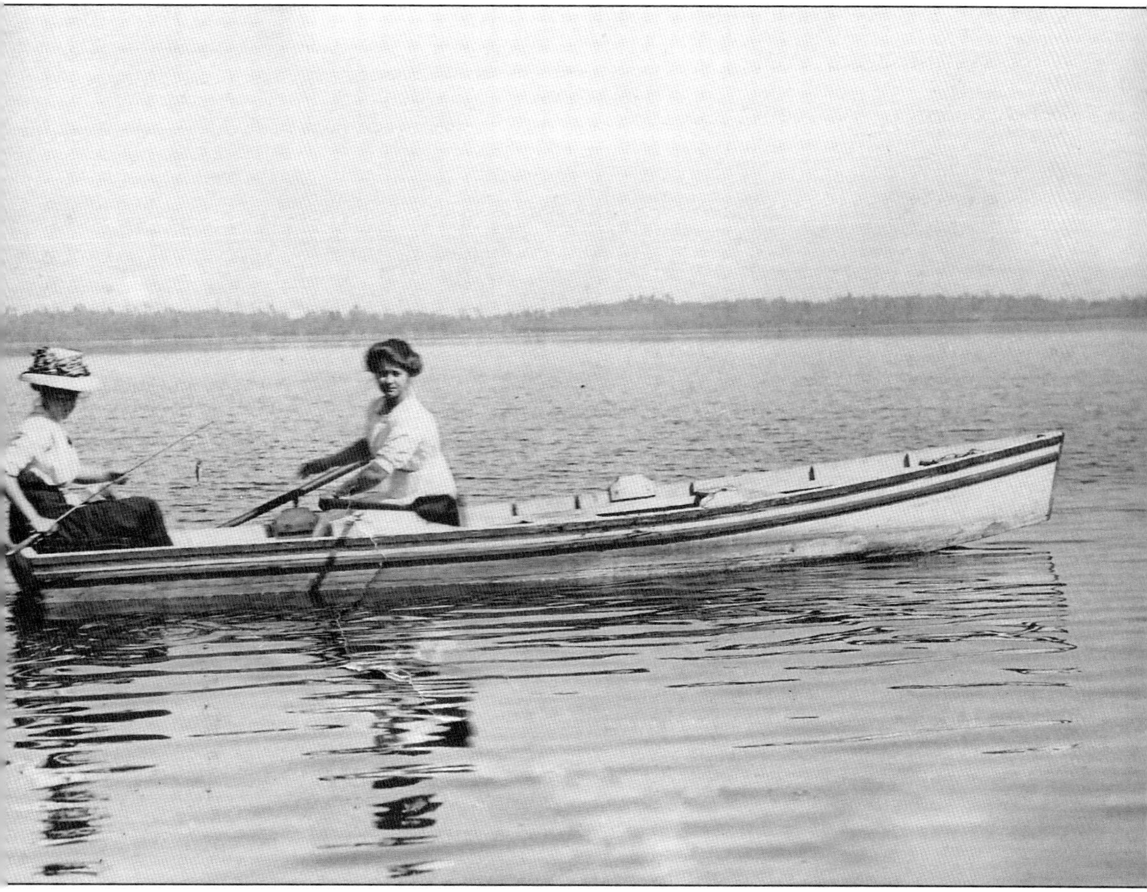

A summer afternoon was a good time to take a boat trip for these two unidentified young ladies; one is rowing while the other is fishing. Almost everyone in town had a boat. On Sunday afternoons, the lakes roared with the sound of gasoline-powered motors. Boat races were a usual weekend afternoon pastime.

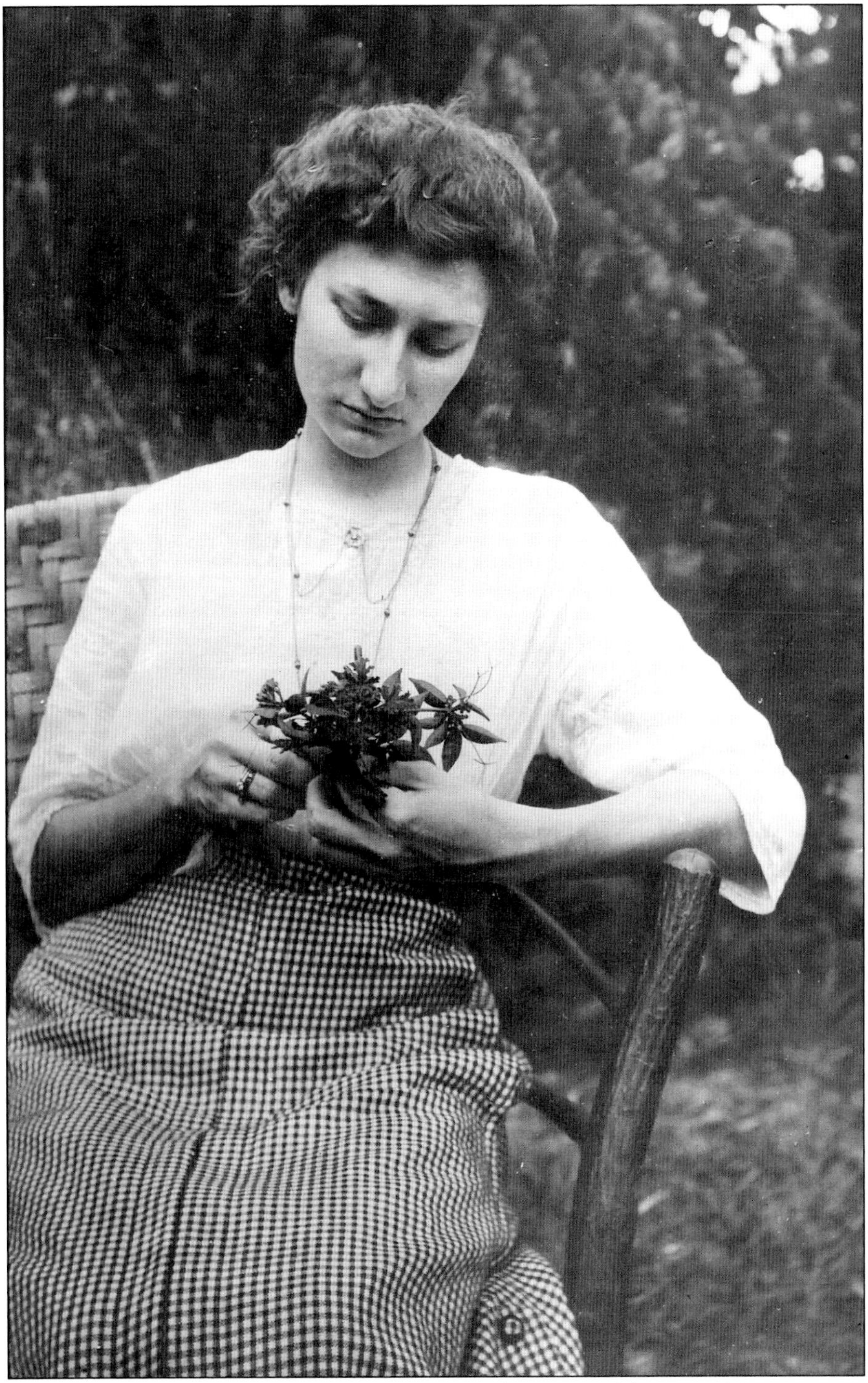

In 1911, Mary Kaszer and her 19-year-old daughter, Alice, arrived by train. Mary was a recent widow. The women adjusted well to local social life. Alice joined in the group of young people in Auburndale, and although it was rumored that she had a male friend, she never married. The 1920 census listed her marital status as "old maid."

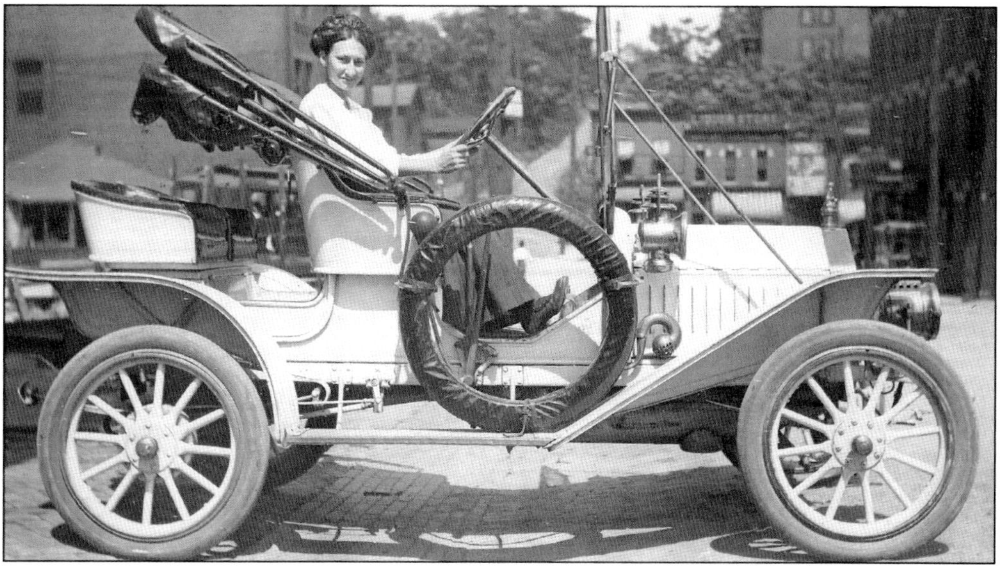

Alice brought her two most prized possessions, her Kodak Brownie camera and her 1910 Buick, the fourth automobile in Auburndale. Elmer Cline, Dr. Lewis Simmons, and A.C. Thorp were already motoring about town. Alice photographed the people, as well as their homes and families, and the row of clapboard buildings on Main Street. Her photographs forever preserved Auburndale and its residents in time.

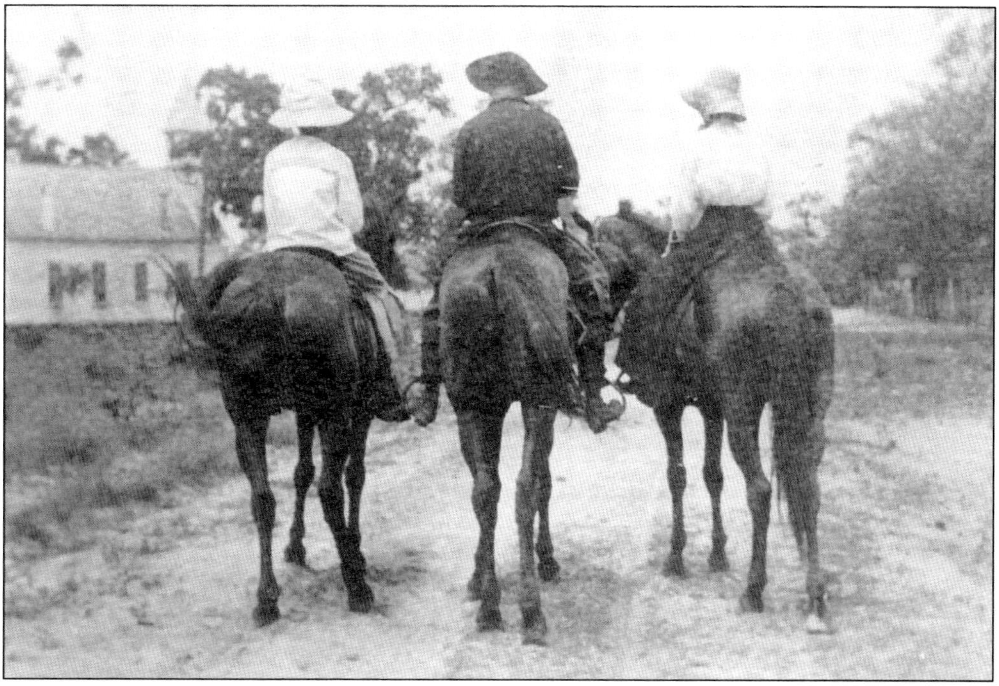

Pictured from left to right in May 1911, Alice Kaszer, Joe Wilkinson, and Pansy Eason take a leisurely horseback ride along Church Street. The Presbyterian church can be seen on the left. This was the first church in Auburndale. After a new church was constructed in 1925, this building was made into apartments and then torn down. Alice titled this photograph, "Two Queens and a Jack."

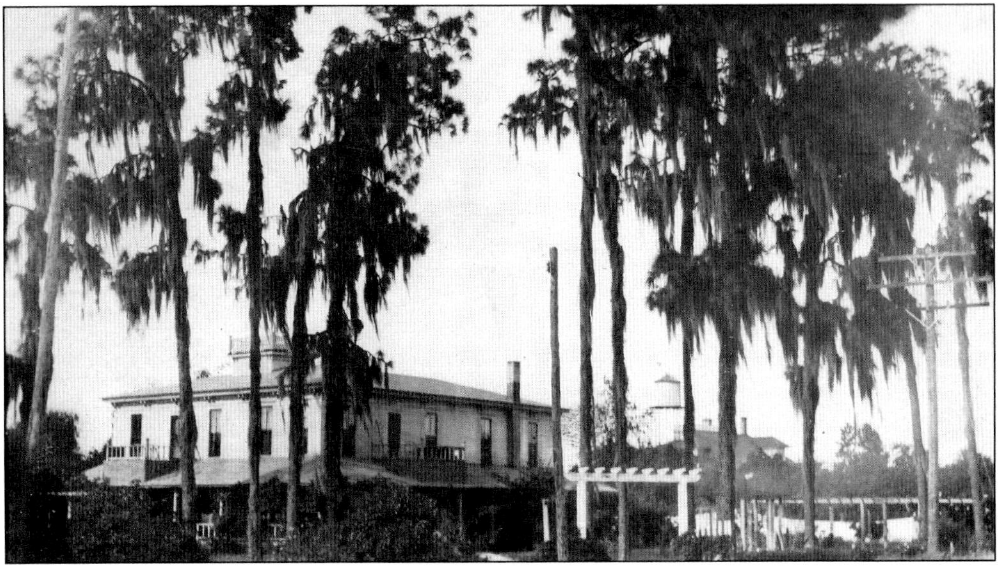

The Hampton Hotel, owned by James Hampton, was located next to the depot on the corner of Church and North Main Streets. Visitors to Auburndale could step off the train and walk a few steps to this grand hotel. After arriving in Auburndale in 1911, Alice and Mary Kaszer stayed here. Later named the Ariana, the Hampton continued to welcome patrons until it burned down in 1935.

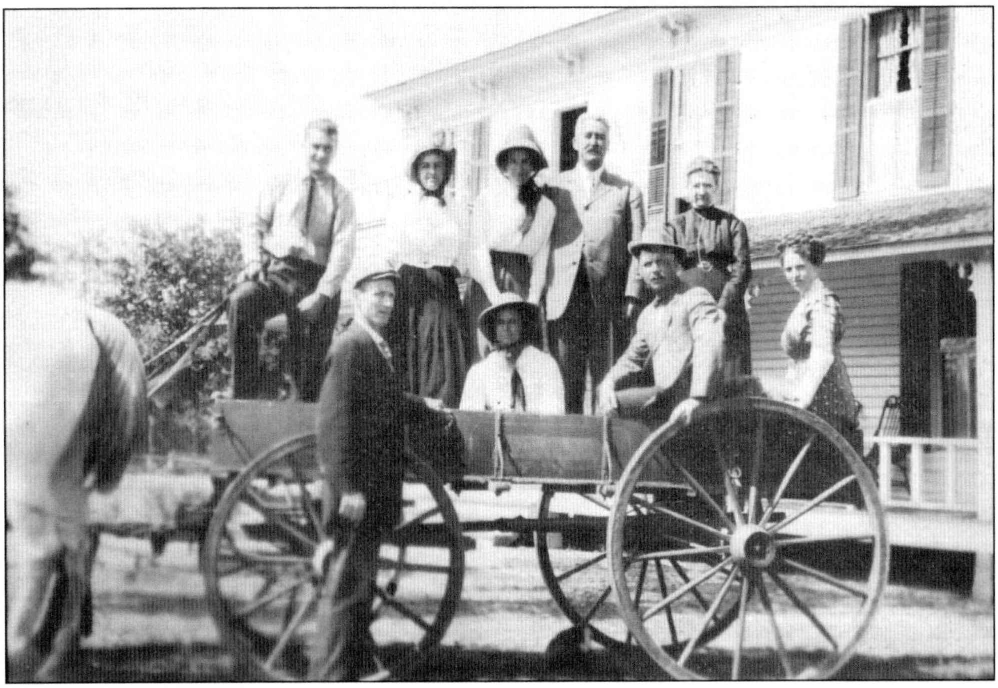

A wagonload of people waits in front of the Hampton Hotel for a tour of the town. By 1911, Auburndale was a flourishing community. It had not taken long for visitors to realize the advantages of spending winter months in this quiet, sunny location. Ladies would sit in rocking chairs on wraparound porches, while men fished in the surrounding lakes or talked business on benches on the park.

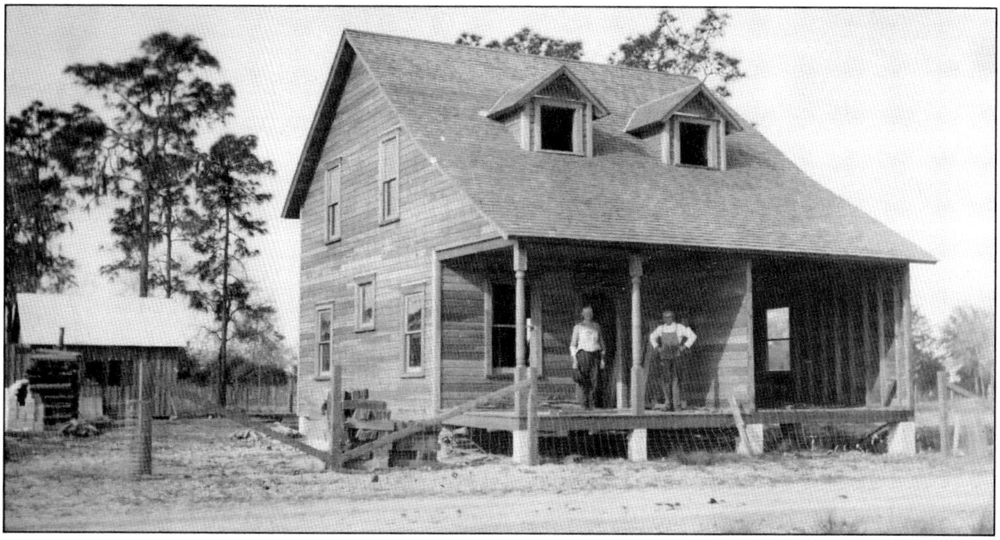

Alice and Mary Kaszer resided in the Hampton House while their new home was being constructed on the west side of the park. In this image, the house is not quite finished. Every morning, Alice felt it was her duty to inspect the work that was being done and instruct the workers on how to build a house.

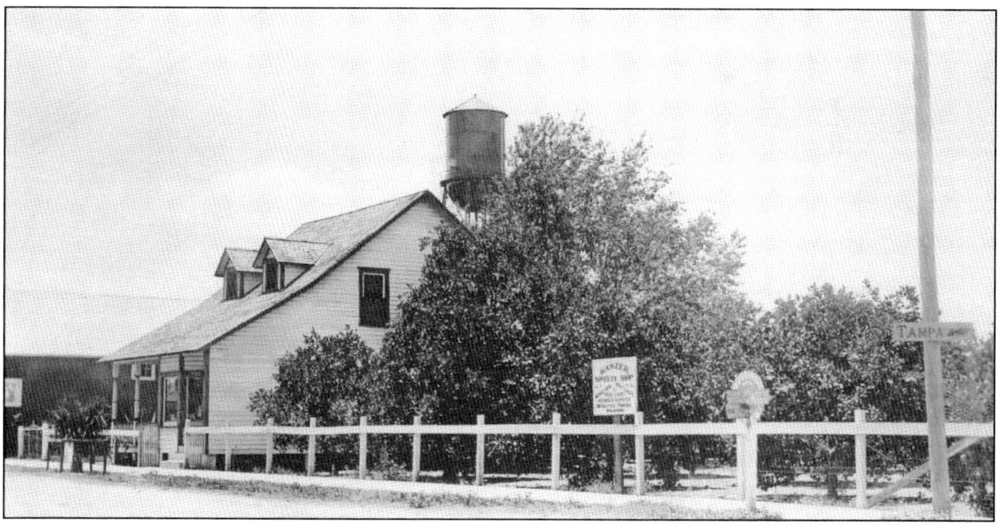

The front porch of the Kaszer house was enclosed and made into a shop for Mary and a studio for Alice. Mary made ornate hats for the local ladies. Alice was the only photographer in town. She processed her own photographs and made many prints into postcards that have been sent all over the world. Eventually, she acquired new cameras and equipment, but her first photographs remain sharp and clear.

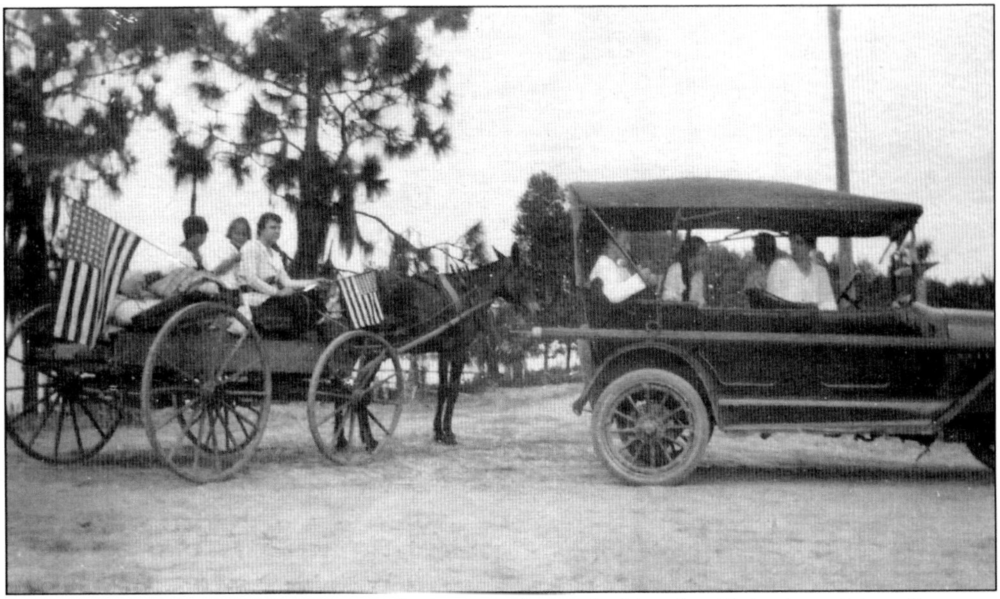

In this 1911 image, Alice leads a parade, apparently on the Fourth of July, down Main Street in her Buick. Even without the benefit of electronics, the youth of Auburndale managed to find ways to have fun. With only four vehicles in Auburndale, stopping traffic for a parade was not a problem.

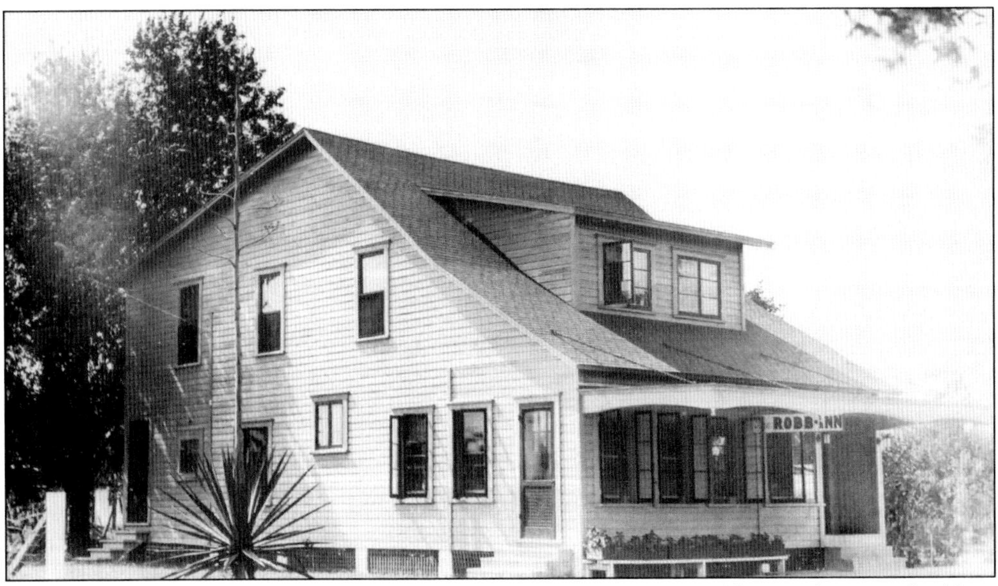

Upon the death of her mother, Alice Kaszer sold her house and moved her studio into a building on Lake Avenue. The house then became a restaurant called the Robb Inn. Later, it was bought by Tampa Electric and used for its office until a new office and leisure room were built. The house was eventually moved to a different location.

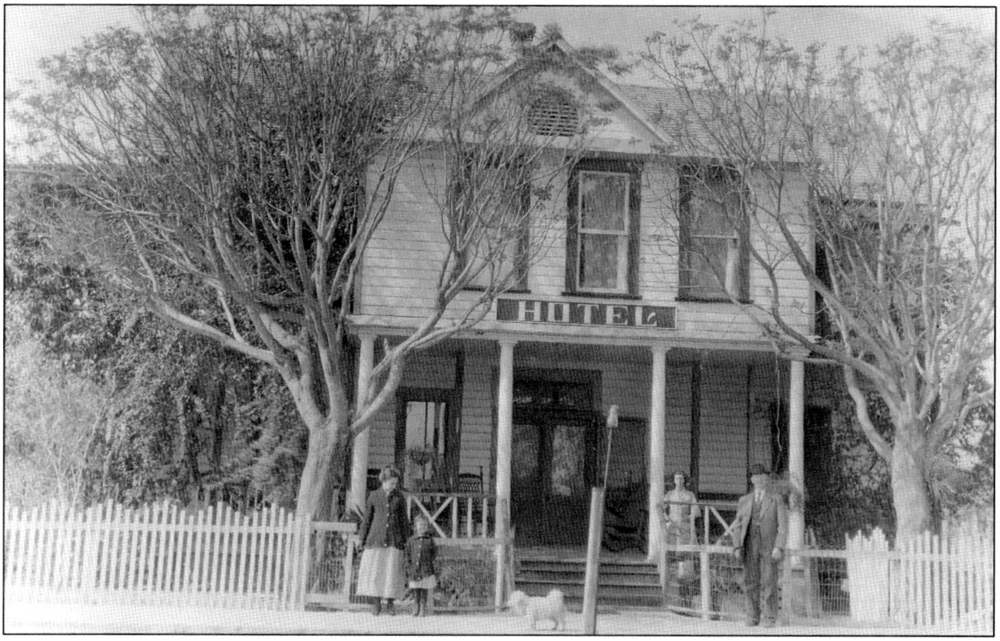

A.B. and Louise Patrick were host and hostess of the Patrick Hotel at the west end of East Park Street. The large, homey inn offered clean rooms, home-cooked meals, and a view of the park. The guests were within walking distance of the depot and the shops on Main Street.

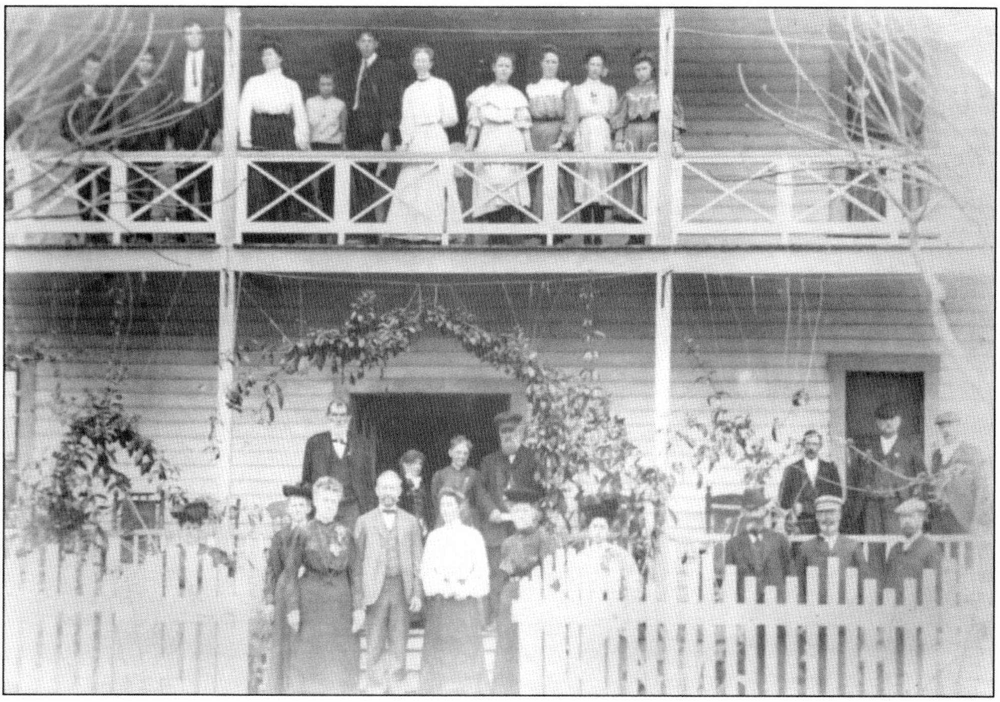

Guests, shaded by giant chinaberry trees, line the porch at the Patrick Hotel. In 1926, the Patrick caught fire and burned to the ground. The city had just purchased the new La France fire truck, but without running water, the old wooden building could not be saved. First National Bank was built on the site.

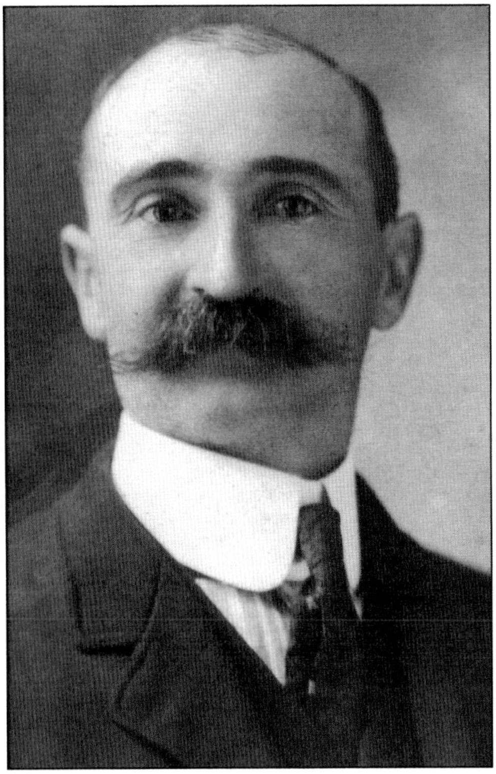

Ephraim Mikel "Mike" Baynard and Nettie Brook met in Auburndale in 1890. Mike was visiting his sister, and Nettie's parents had sent her to stay with her grandmother to protect her from the yellow fever outbreak in their home in Key West. They were married in 1893, and Mike commissioned their first home to be built on Lake Avenue. After 20 years, he decided it was not big enough. Mike wanted the biggest house in Auburndale—he got it. In 1913, they moved into their 19-room house on Lake Stella. More than once, Mike backed up his Packard from the garage behind the house, ended up in Lake Stella, and had to be pulled out. Nettie refused to get into the car with him until it was safely down the hill. Mike owned groves, a cattle ranch, and two business buildings and a hotel on Main Street. The Baynards had two daughters, Ruth and Elizabeth.

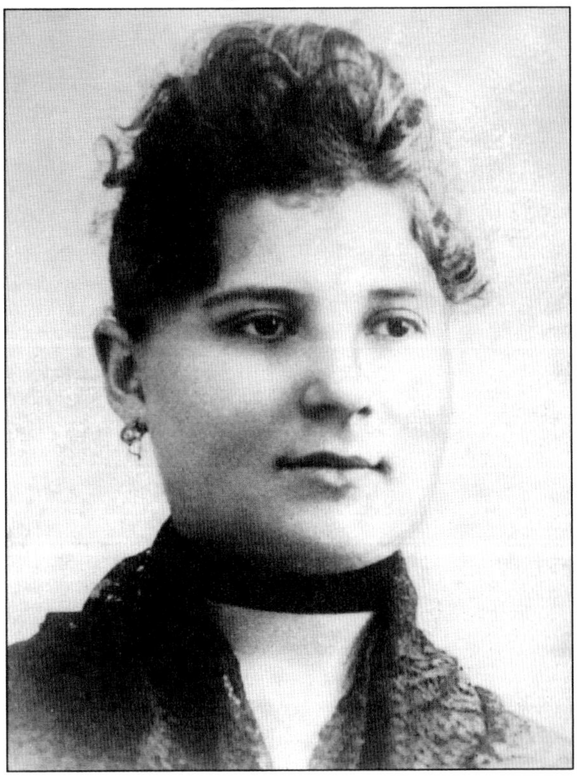

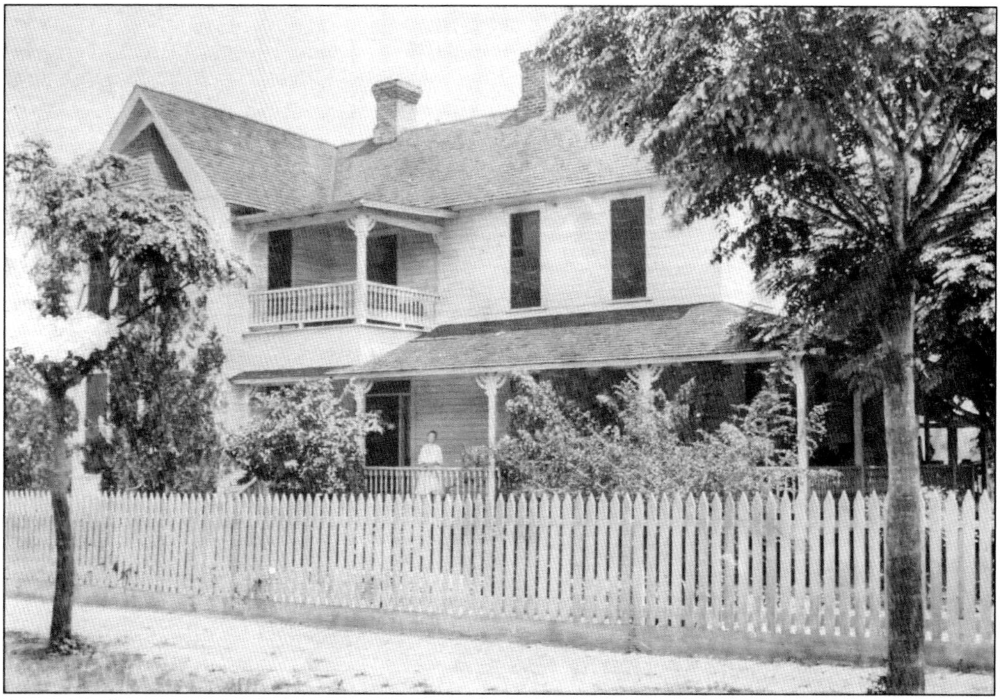

Completed in 1894, the first Baynard house was made from local pines, but some features—such as fireplace mantels, doors, and molding—were ordered from factories in the North. The kitchen was a separate building in the rear. Light came from coal oil lamps, and water was obtained from a hand-dug well. The city bought the house in 1985, restored it, and opened it to the public as a museum.

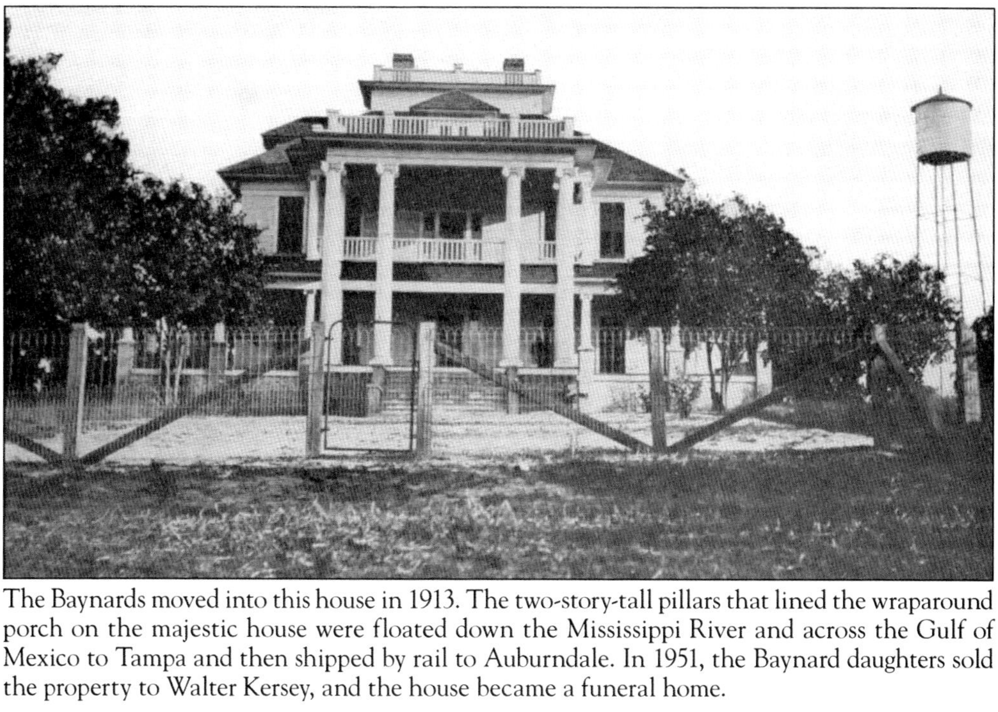

The Baynards moved into this house in 1913. The two-story-tall pillars that lined the wraparound porch on the majestic house were floated down the Mississippi River and across the Gulf of Mexico to Tampa and then shipped by rail to Auburndale. In 1951, the Baynard daughters sold the property to Walter Kersey, and the house became a funeral home.

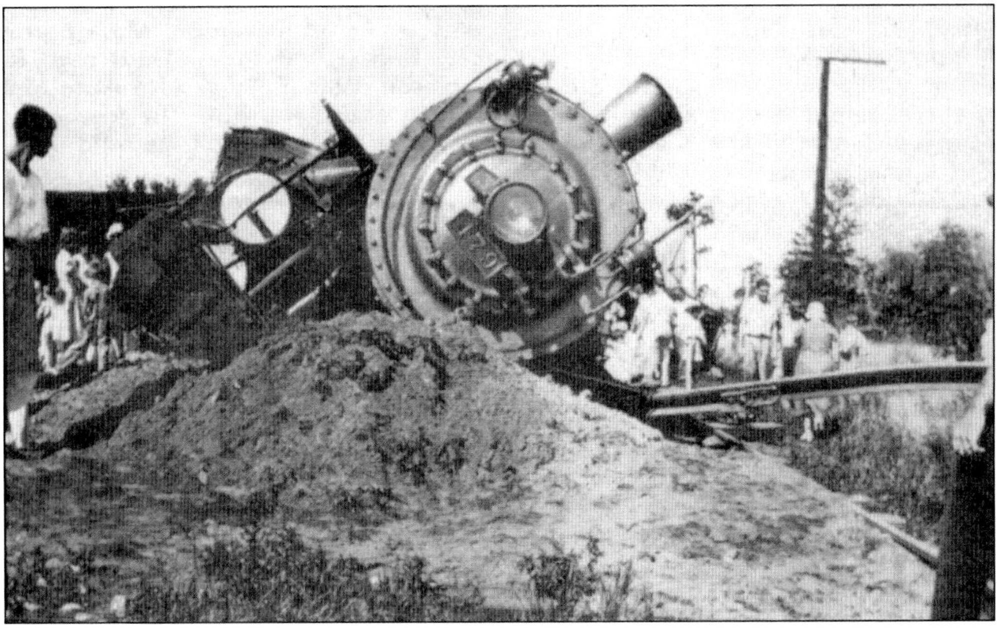

In 1933, ten years after Nettie died, Mike Baynard was killed instantly when his Packard was hit by a train at the railroad crossing within view of his home and the hotel where he and his wife were married. He was in his 70s and totally deaf. The impact caused the mighty engine to sidetrack, rise in the air, and come to rest on its side. The fireman was killed when the boiler ruptured.

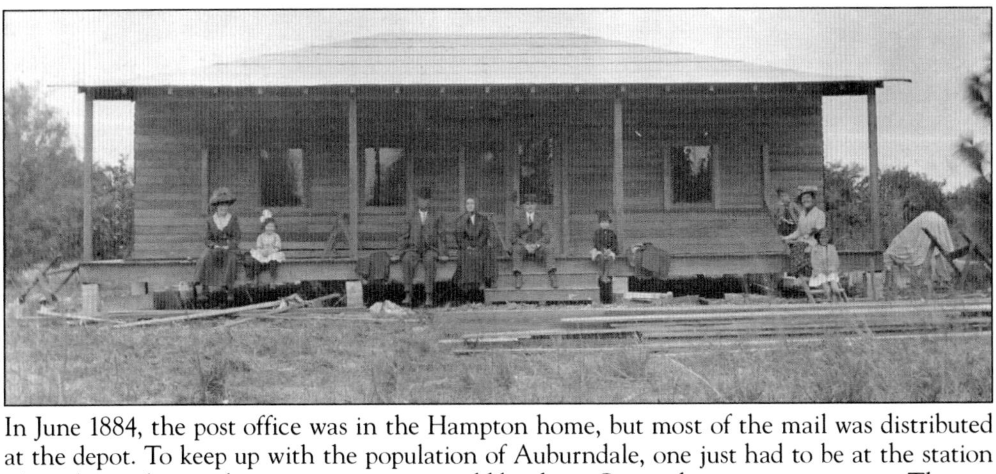

In June 1884, the post office was in the Hampton home, but most of the mail was distributed at the depot. To keep up with the population of Auburndale, one just had to be at the station when the mail arrived; everyone in town would be there. Succeeding postmasters were Thomas Watkins, John McDermott, Naomi Thorp, Alfred Zachary, W.S. Sands, James P. Jones, John McLain, Charles Meadows, Ralph Allen, Mansell Orchard, and Reginald Dickey.

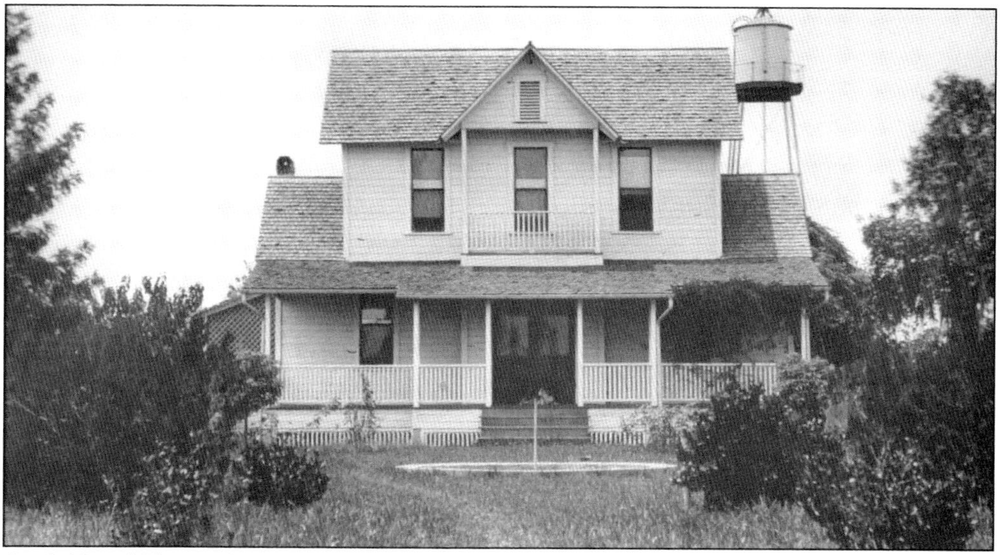

Amfield and Elmer Cline and their son, Harry, came from Ohio. In 1895, they built their home, "Buck Eye Villa," on the west side of Lake Lena. Elmer was a mechanic with a shop on Shelby Street. He owned the first automobile in Auburndale. He drove his one-cylinder Cadillac for 20 years.

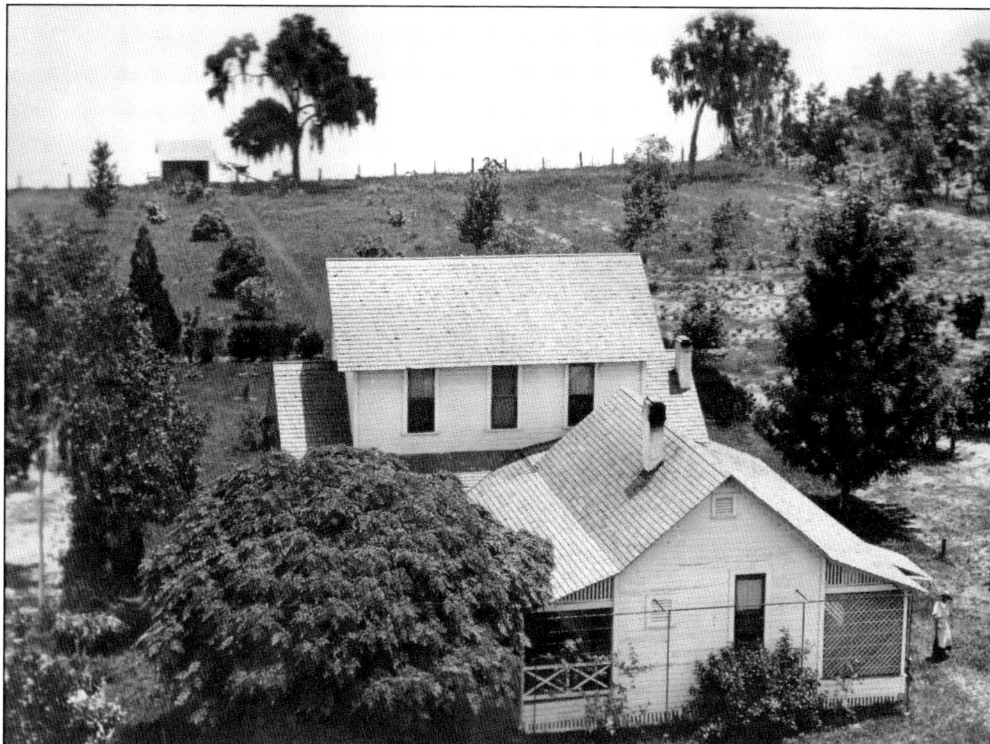

In 1948, the Cline house was moved to the north side of Lake Lena. The main house had two parlors downstairs and two bedrooms upstairs. The kitchen and dining room were in a separate building connected to the main house by a breezeway. The kitchen and dining room were moved separately and attached to the house at the new site.

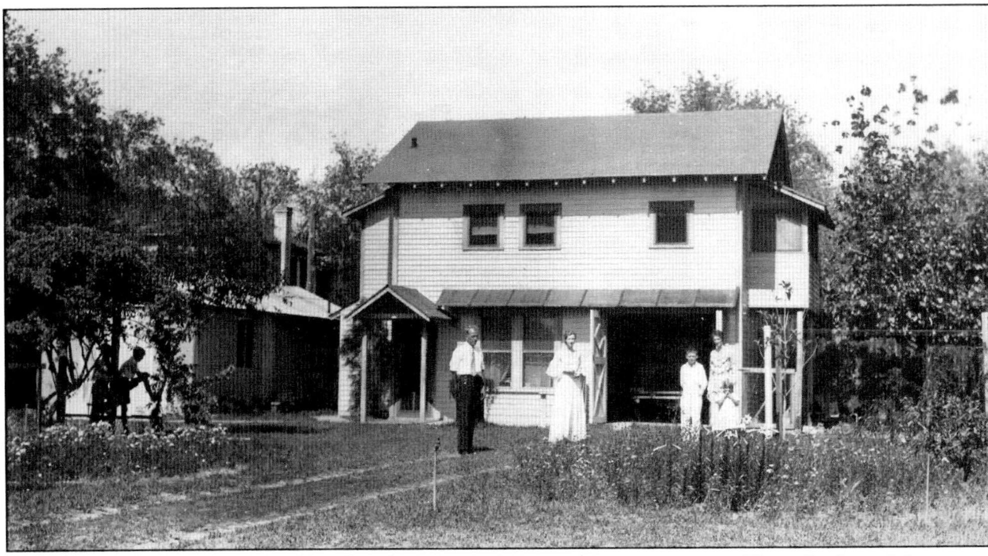

Harry and Della Cline lived in this home on Ariana Avenue next to Harry's shop. Harry was a man of many talents. He could build anything that needed building or repair anything that needed repairing. He installed the plumbing in most of Auburndale's early homes, and he was an excellent sign painter. But, he was never too busy to repair a child's bicycle.

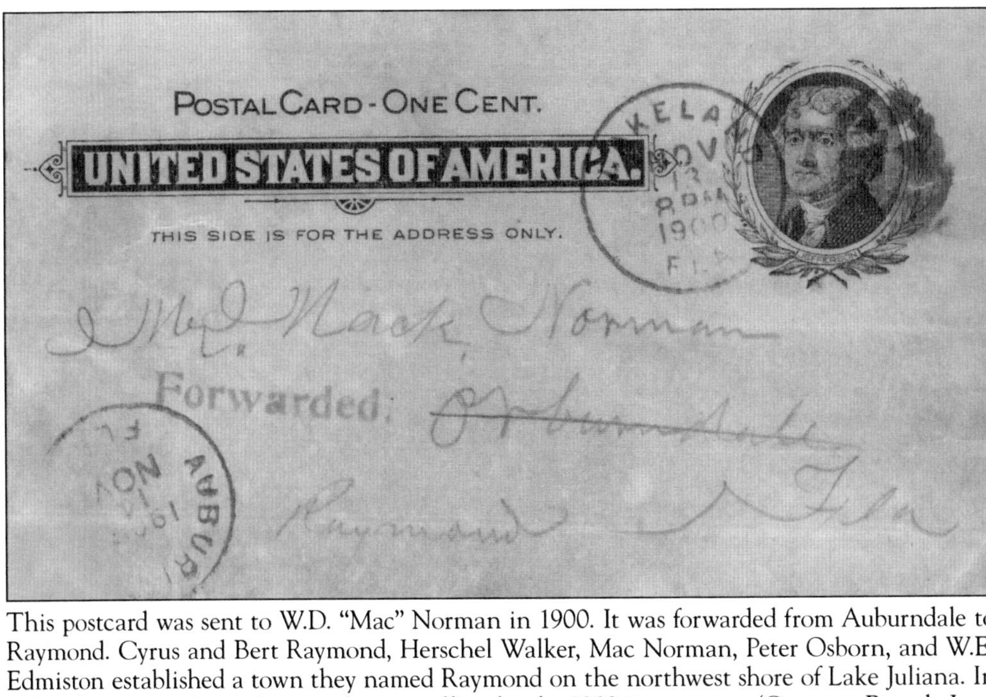

This postcard was sent to W.D. "Mac" Norman in 1900. It was forwarded from Auburndale to Raymond. Cyrus and Bert Raymond, Herschel Walker, Mac Norman, Peter Osborn, and W.E. Edmiston established a town they named Raymond on the northwest shore of Lake Juliana. In 1890, there were 40 residents and a post office, but by 1902 it was gone. (Courtesy Beverly June Scott collection.)

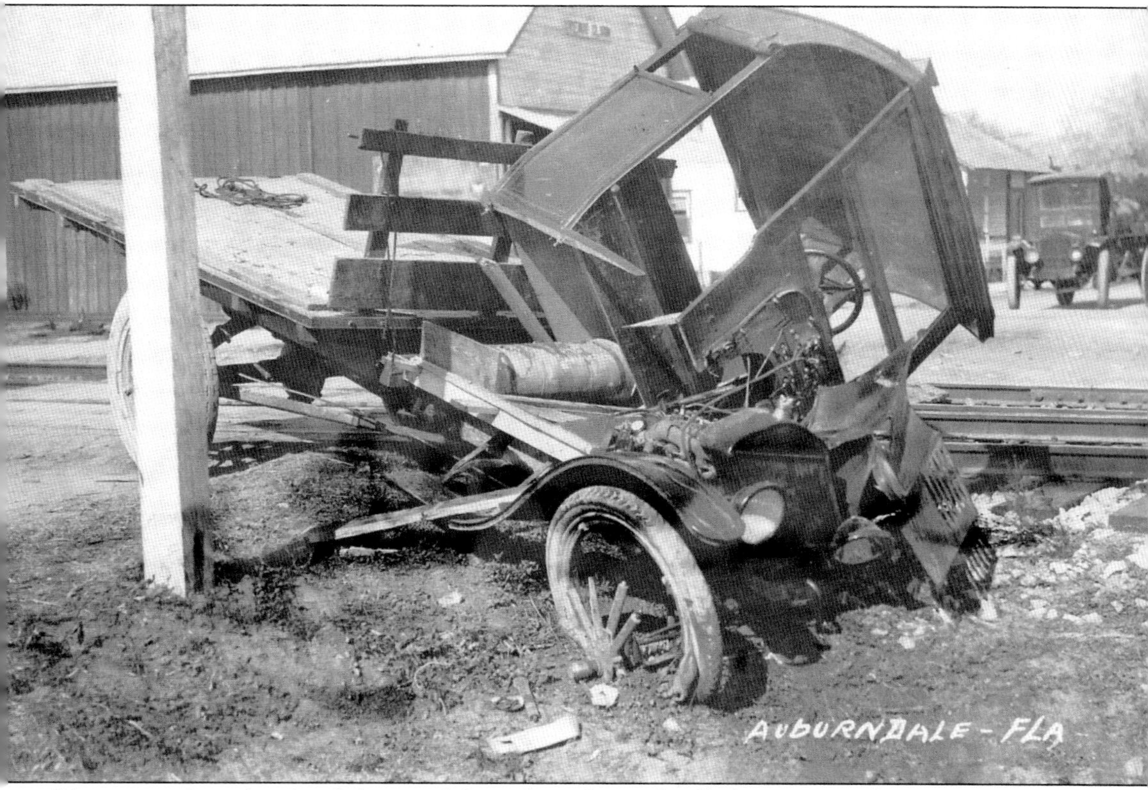

Oftentimes, the railroad and the cars did not share the road well; the train usually won. This car was destroyed in an accident with a train, but no one was injured. Remus Owen's Real Estate and Fertilizer Store can be seen in the background. This structure burned, and the Auburn Theater was later built here.

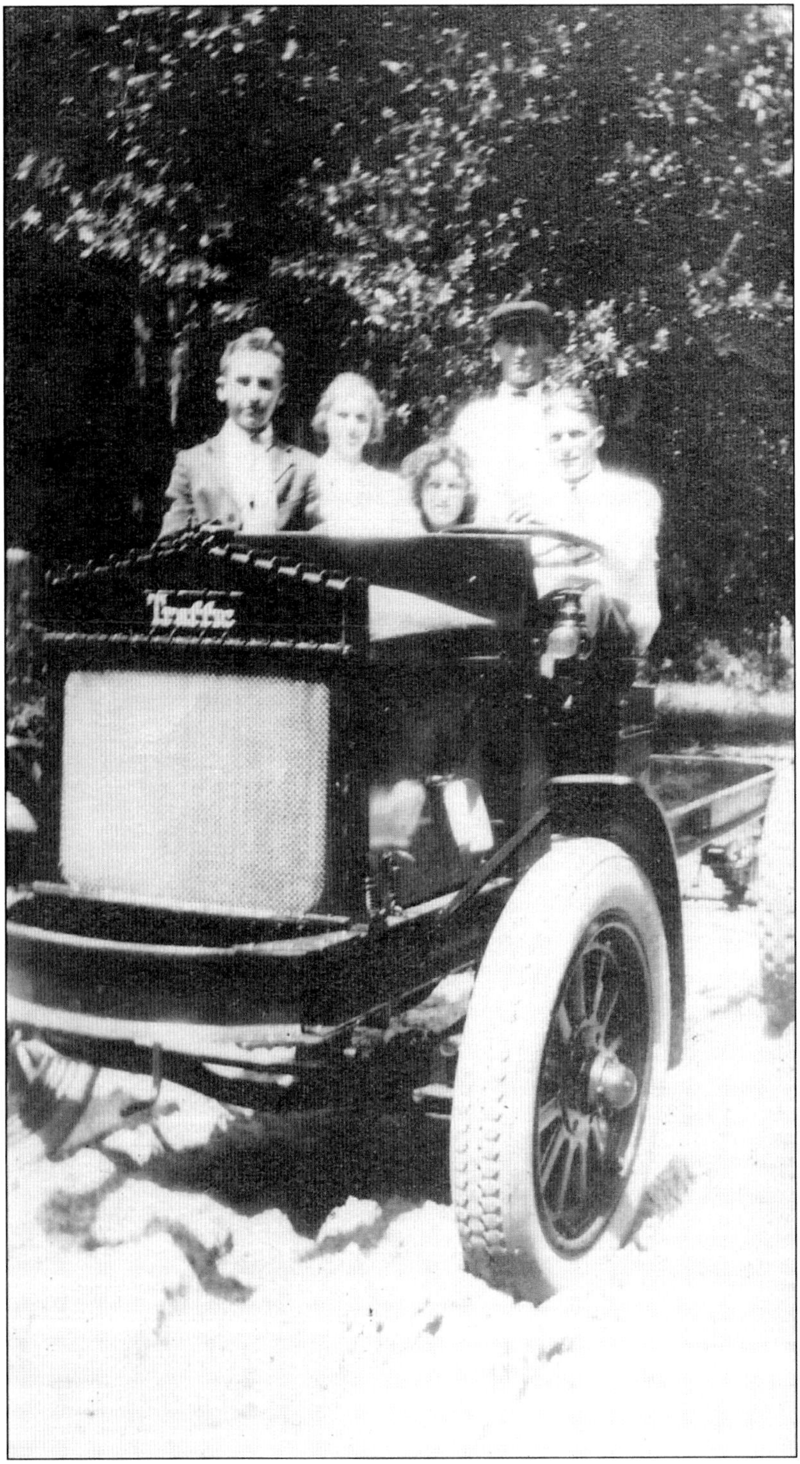

Marvin Cooley (left) and Slim Allen, brother of Carl Allen, are shown here taking some unidentified young people for a ride in an open-air truck. The Traffic Motor Truck was manufactured from 1917 to 1929 in St. Louis. It sold for $1,195 and could obtain speeds of 14 miles per hour.

Three

A Town Rises from the Ashes

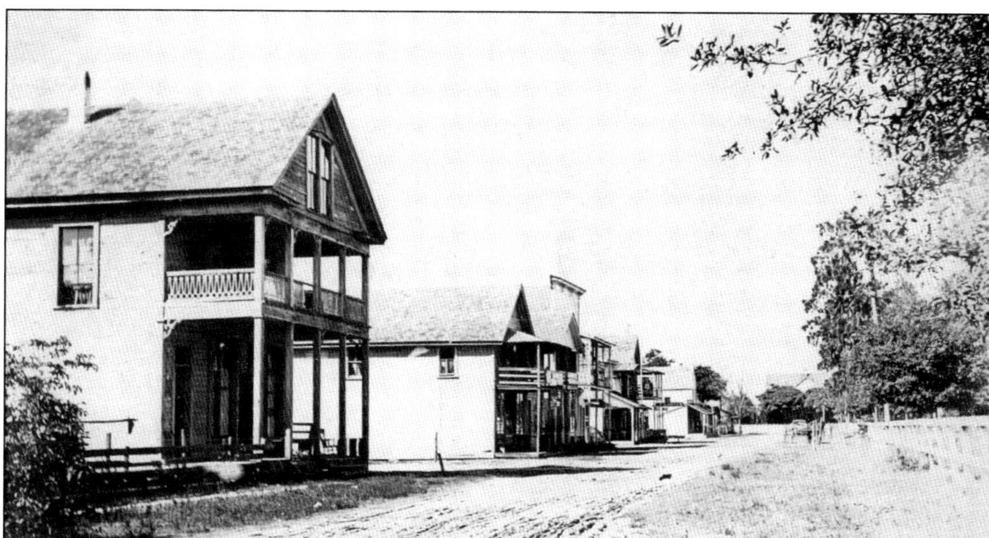

When Auburndale was incorporated in 1911, the year-round population was 411. A row of clapboard buildings lined Main Street across from the park. There were no streetlights, running water, or electricity. Looking east to west were the C.E. Wolfe Boarding House, the Auburndale Pharmacy (owned by E.M. Baynard), the Pattersons' store (the town council met on the second floor), the City Meat Market, the post office, McLain Bank, and Werner Jones's livery stable and undertaking parlor.

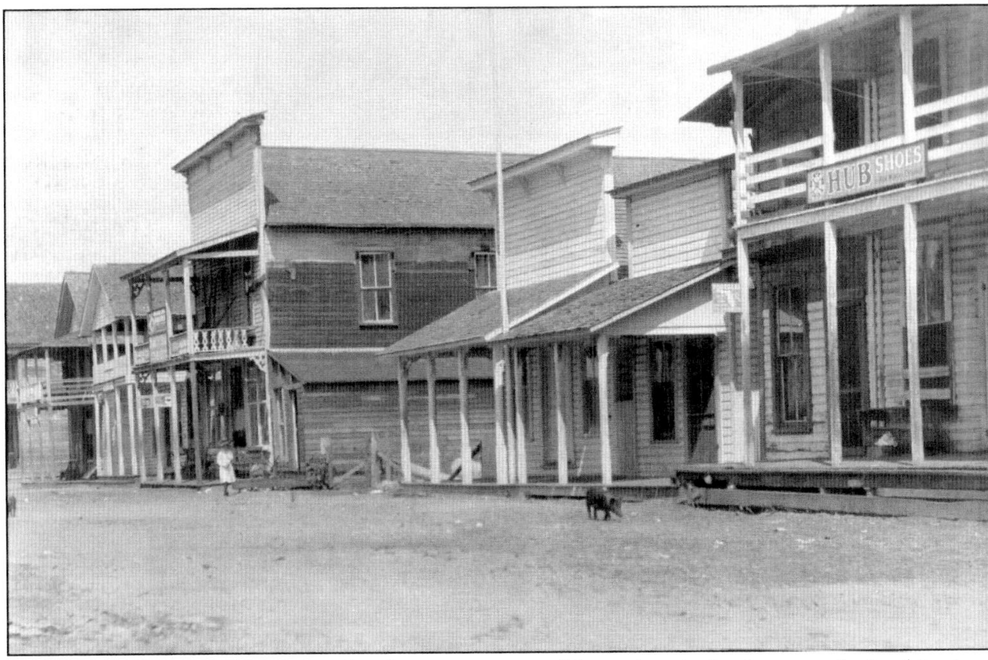

Farm animals roamed freely in the downtown area. (Note the pig in the street). At this time, Auburndale was still a community with no local laws. The first law passed after the town was incorporated in 1911 was to ban farm animals in the downtown area. The little girl pictured here is Nellie Norman, daughter of Mary and Mac Norman.

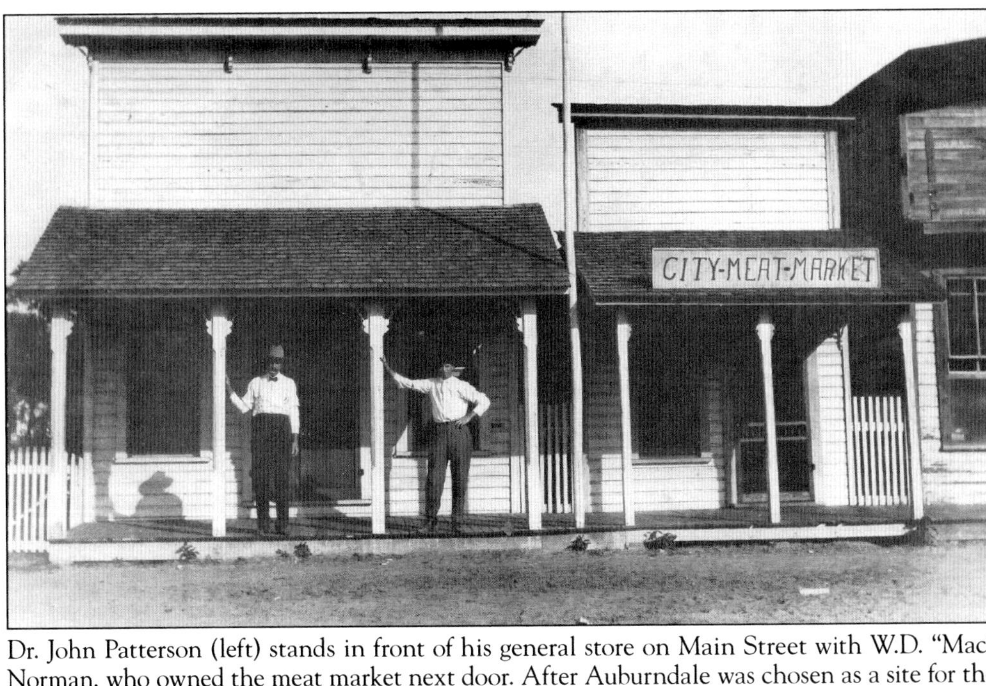

Dr. John Patterson (left) stands in front of his general store on Main Street with W.D. "Mac" Norman, who owned the meat market next door. After Auburndale was chosen as a site for the depot, this building was moved from Sanitaria to Auburndale by loading it onto logs, tying the logs to mules, and dragging it to Main Street.

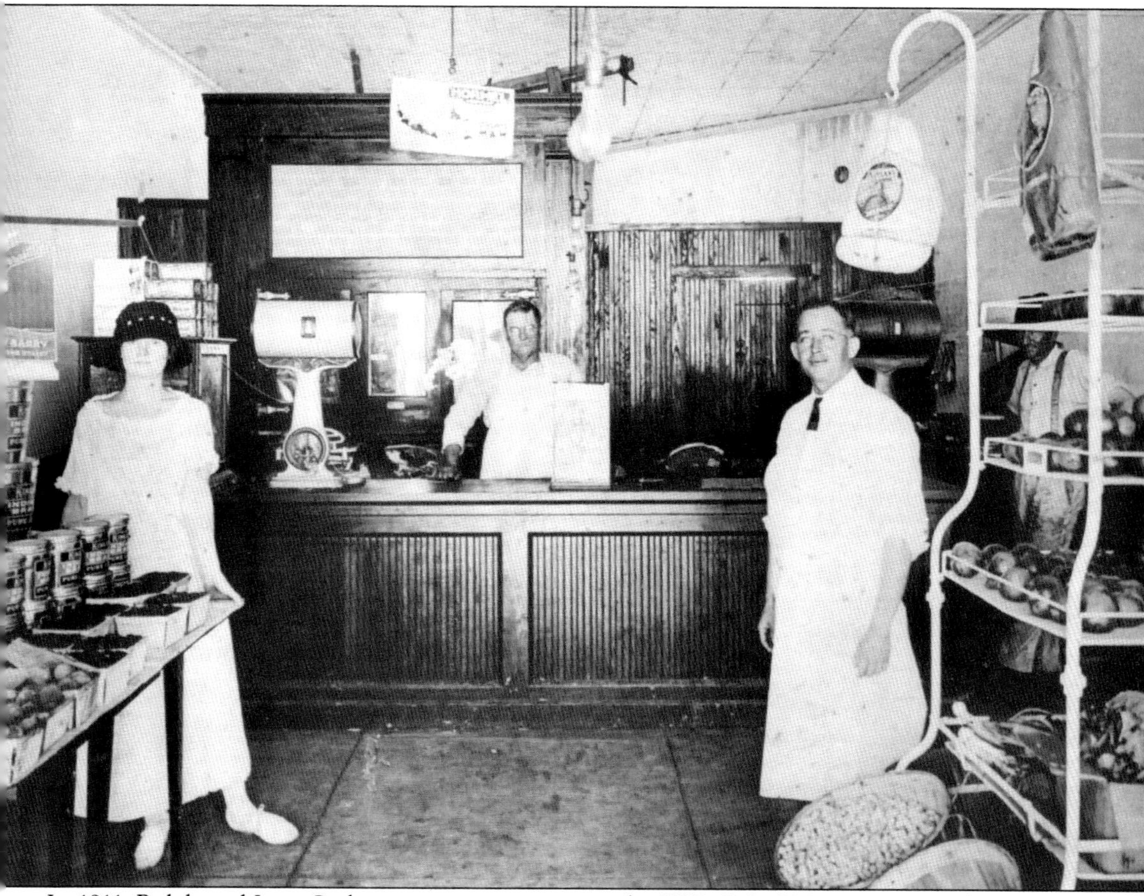

In 1911, Ralph and Irma Seckinger were customers in the W.D. "Mac" Norman Meat Shop on Main Street. Mac supplied Auburndale with fresh cuts of meat. Vegetables came from surrounding farms. Corn, a staple, was coarsely ground to grits, a southern breakfast favorite. It was ground fine to make cornmeal for bread. Sweet potatoes, turnips, and collards thrived in the cooler months. Sweet potatoes contributed to another product: moonshine, or "white lightning."

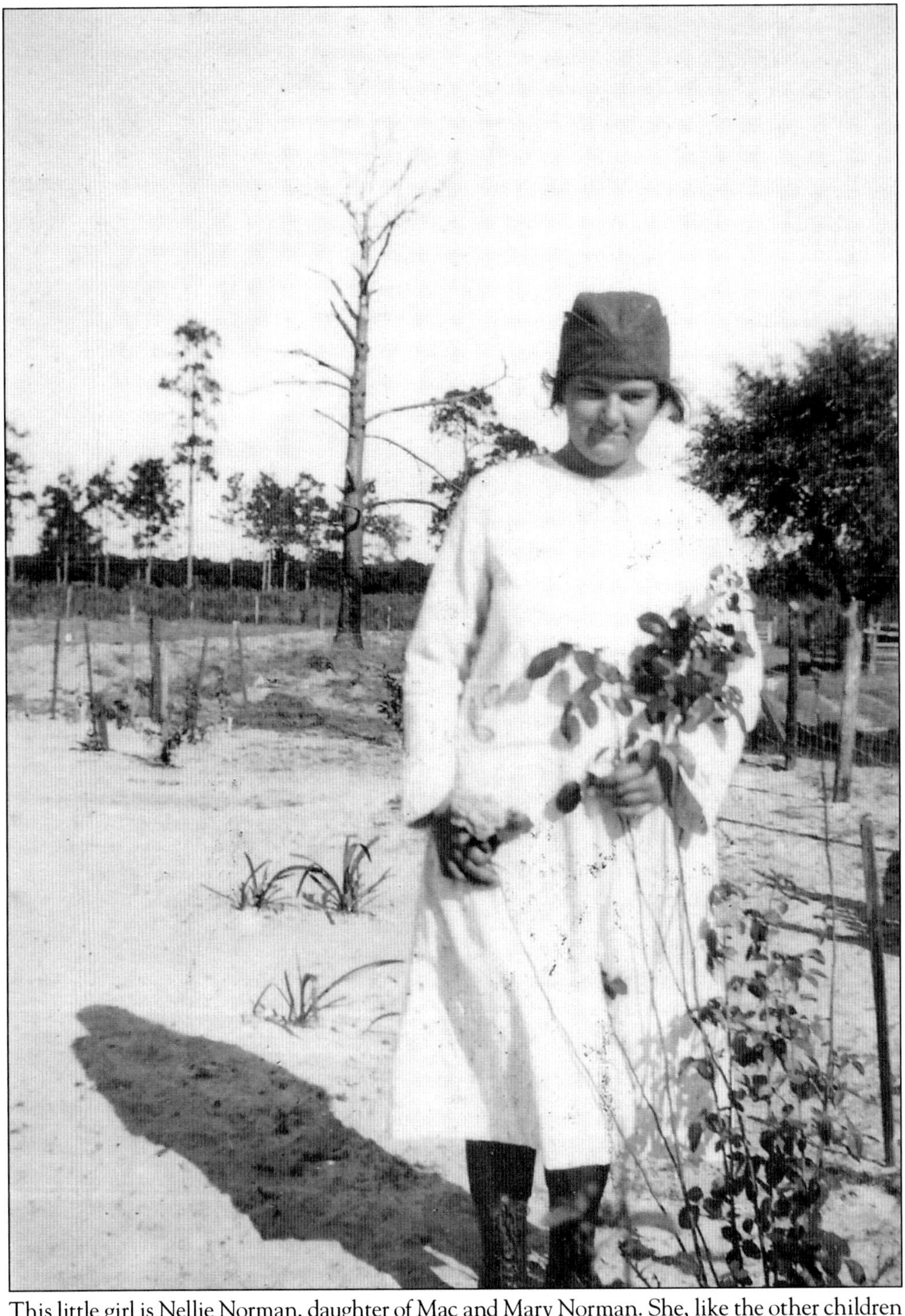

This little girl is Nellie Norman, daughter of Mac and Mary Norman. She, like the other children in the town, grew up playing in the park and on Main Street. Nellie spent her life in Auburndale. She had one daughter, Mary Lyons, who also grew up and spent her life in Auburndale.

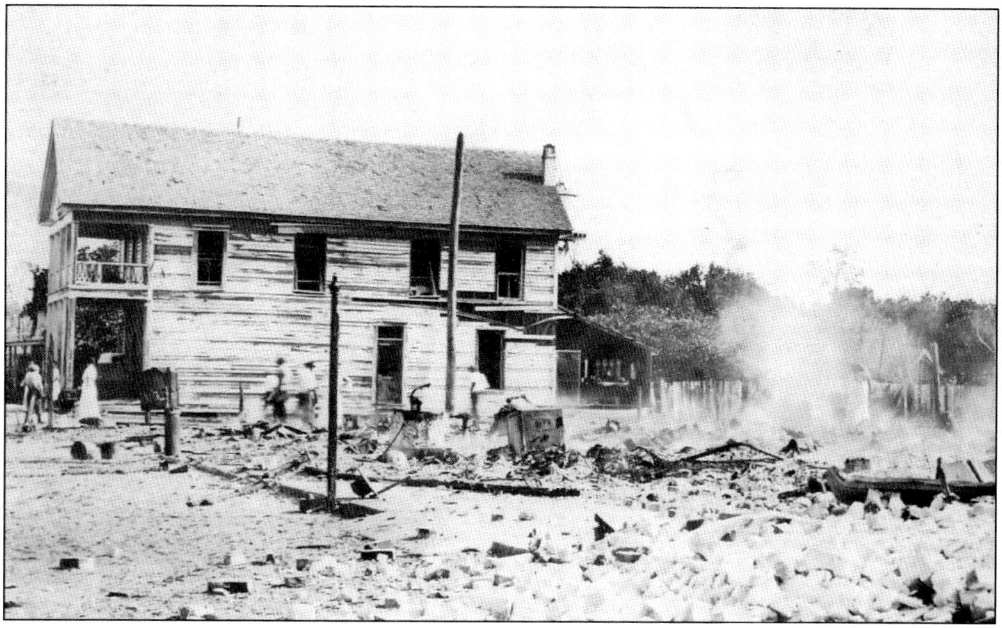

One Sunday morning just before Christmas on December 17, 1911, almost everyone was in church when C.E. Wolfe spotted a fire near one of the shops. He sent his young daughter Molly racing to the church, but town marshal Crosby got there first. He flung the door open and shouted, "Excuse me preacher, I don't mean to interrupt your sermon, but the whole damn town is burning down!" Within minutes, it did.

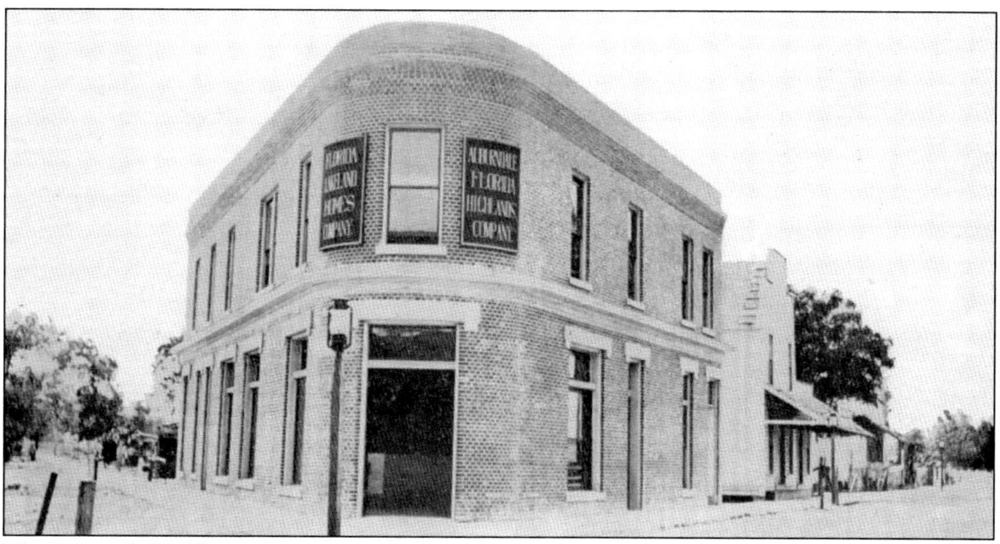

The "Triangle Building," the State Bank Building, was completed in 1912. The building conformed to the shape of the lot. In April of that year, the doors opened on a modern bank with $15,000 capital. John Patterson Jr. was the head cashier. The second floor was office space. This was the only building left standing on Main Street after the second fire in 1913.

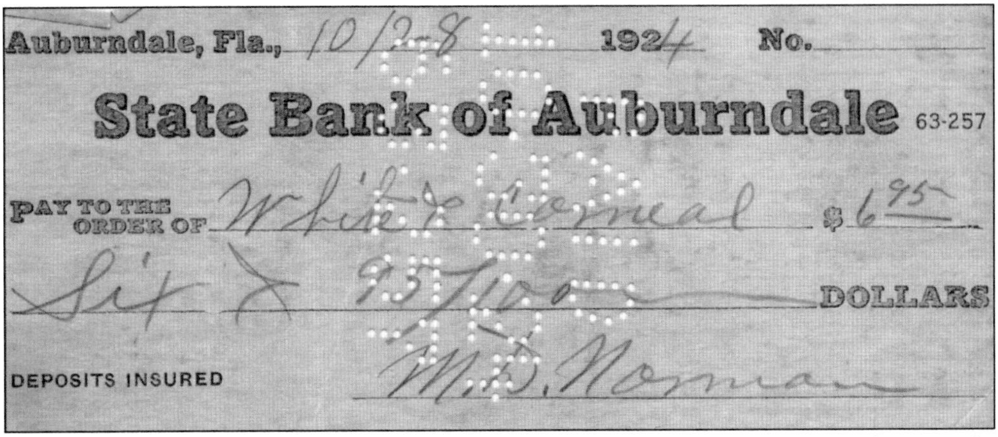
Auburndale, Fla., 10/28 1924 No.

State Bank of Auburndale 63-257

PAY TO THE ORDER OF White & Corneal $6 95/

Six & 95/100 DOLLARS

DEPOSITS INSURED

M.D. Norman

This check, drawn on the State Bank, was written by W.D. "Mac" Norman in October 1924 for $6.95. White and Corneal were owners of a lumber company on Lake Ariana, later named the Auburndale Lumber Company. The company opened in 1924 and supplied lumber for most of the early homes in town. (Courtesy Beverly June Scott collection.)

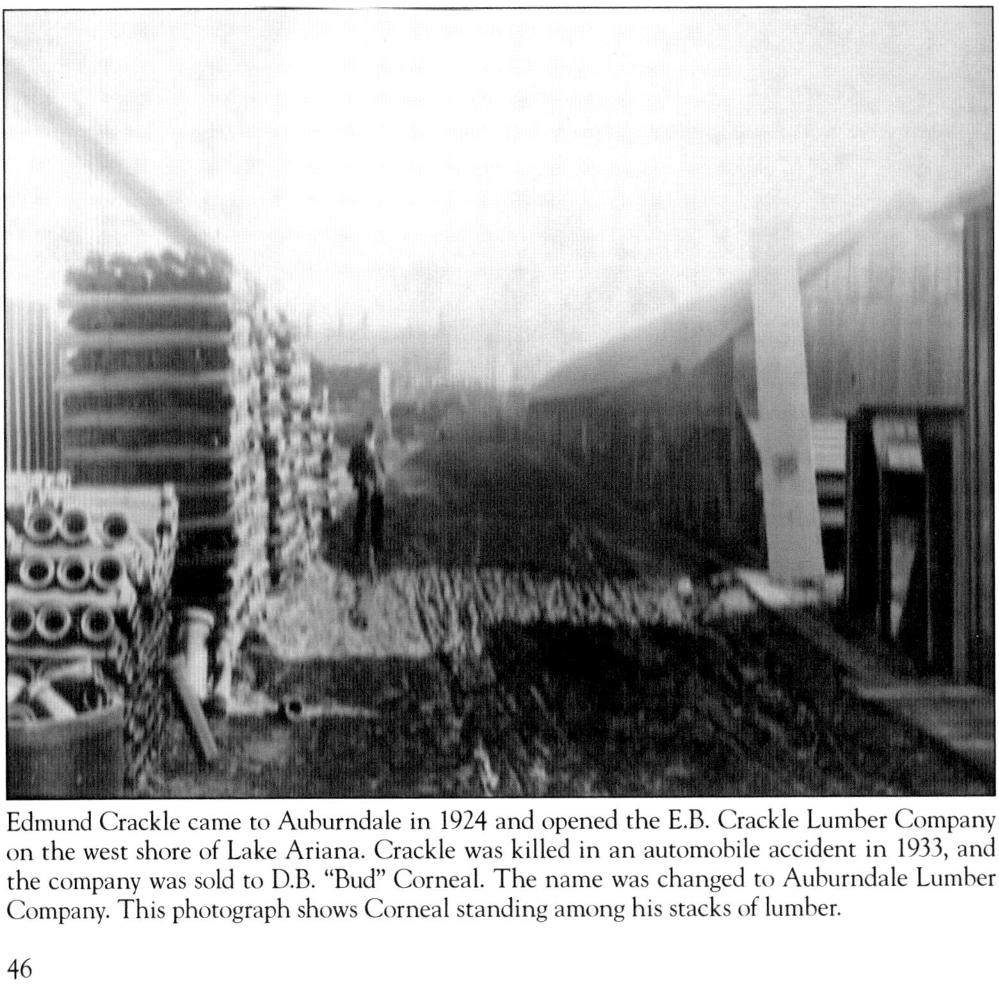

Edmund Crackle came to Auburndale in 1924 and opened the E.B. Crackle Lumber Company on the west shore of Lake Ariana. Crackle was killed in an automobile accident in 1933, and the company was sold to D.B. "Bud" Corneal. The name was changed to Auburndale Lumber Company. This photograph shows Corneal standing among his stacks of lumber.

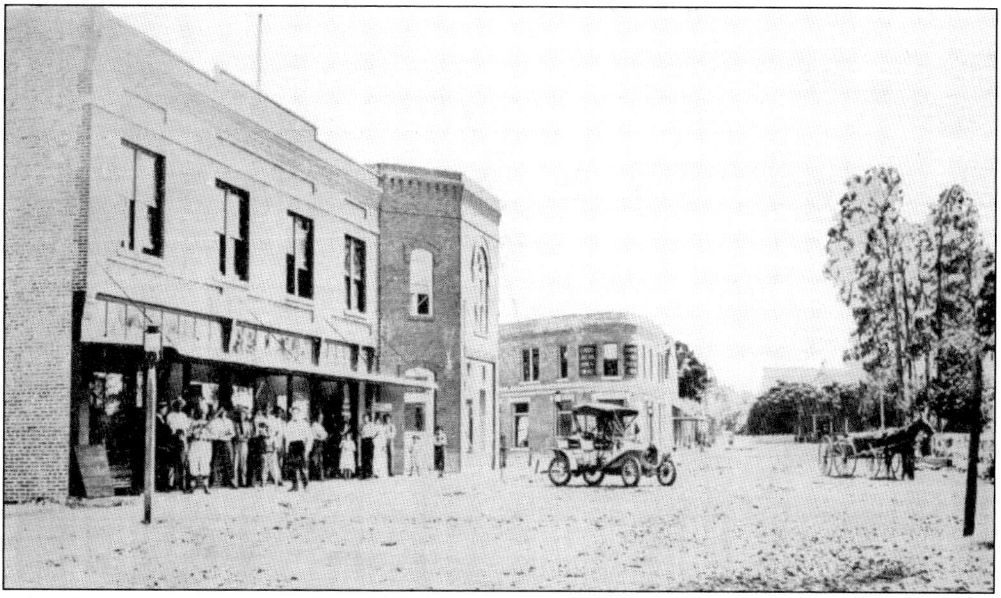

After the 1911 fire, Main Street was rebuilt using red brick. This photograph shows the Patterson and Jones Buildings in 1913. Many of the town's population are posing for this photograph. The car, a 1910 Buick, belonged to Alice Kaszer. Late on a Sunday afternoon, on November 23, 1913, a group of poker players in one of the buildings were careless with their cigarettes, and a small fire quickly became a large one.

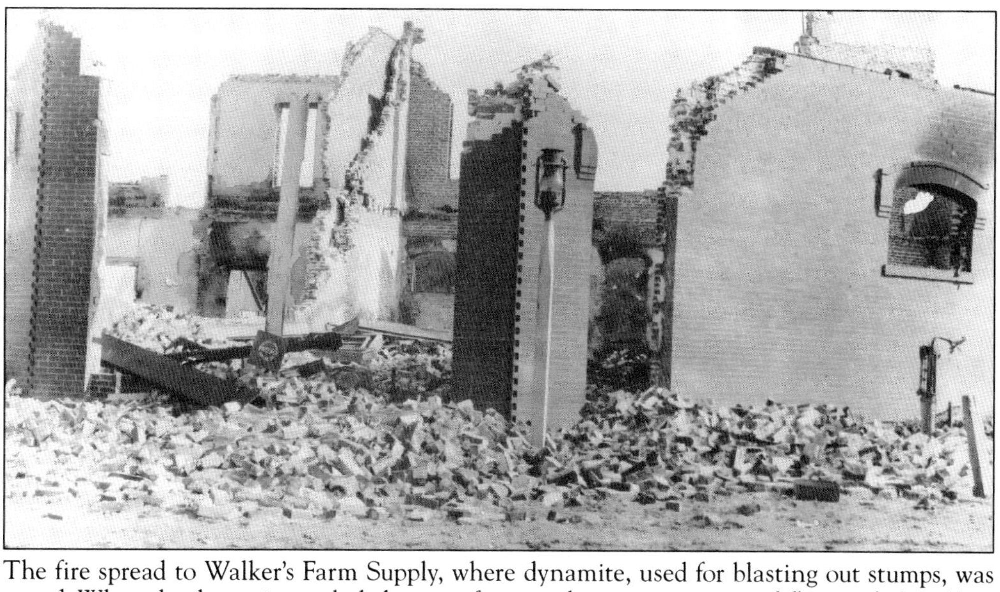

The fire spread to Walker's Farm Supply, where dynamite, used for blasting out stumps, was stored. When the dynamite exploded, it sent farm implements, pumps, and flaming bales of hay flying throughout the downtown area. The implements broke holes in brick walls, giving the fire access to the interiors of the shops. The brick walls collapsed from the heat, and once again, Main Street was a pile of ashes.

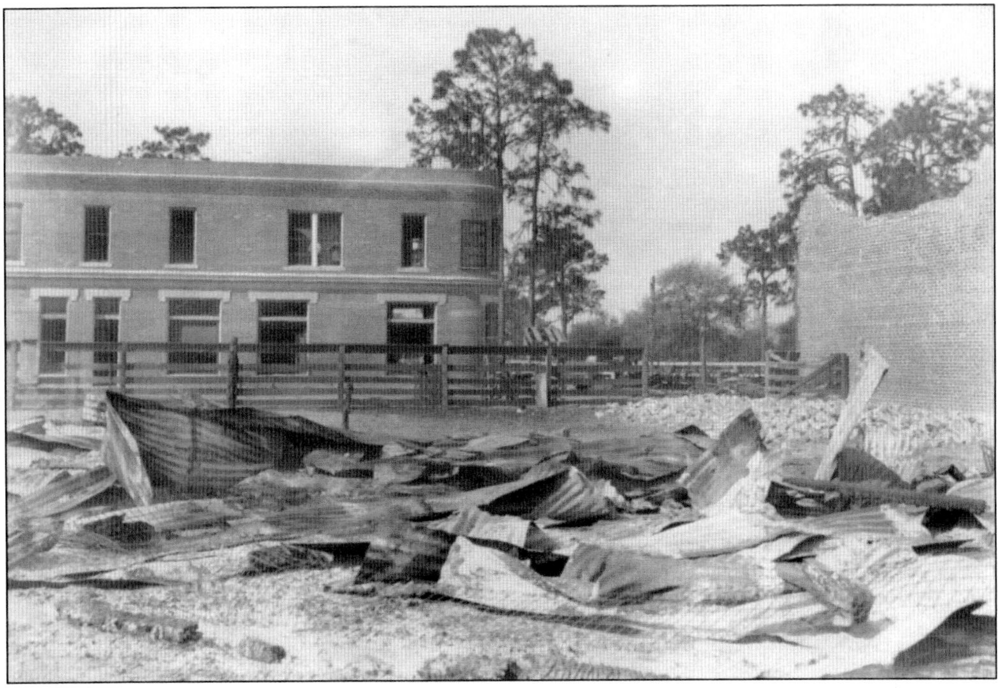

The inhabitants of Auburndale turned out the morning after the fire in 1913 to watch as Main Street smoldered. No one was hurt—even the horses in the livery stable were saved—but mail, merchandise, medicine, cash, and town records were lost. By 1915, the stores were rebuilt and open for business. These stores still stand on Main Street today.

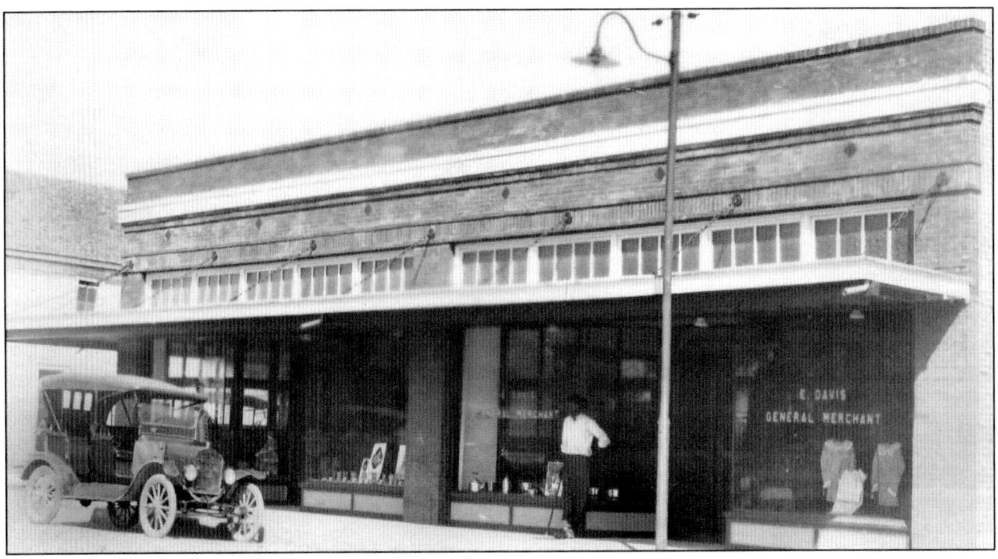

In 1931, Mel "Doc" Taylor bought the Auburndale Pharmacy and renamed it Taylor's Drug Store. It was an Auburndale landmark for 57 years. Everyone agreed Taylor's served the best hamburgers in town. Most of the adult population dropped into Taylor's in the morning for a cup of coffee and to catch up on local news. In the afternoon, it was an after-school teen hangout. Doc retired in 1988 and closed the drugstore.

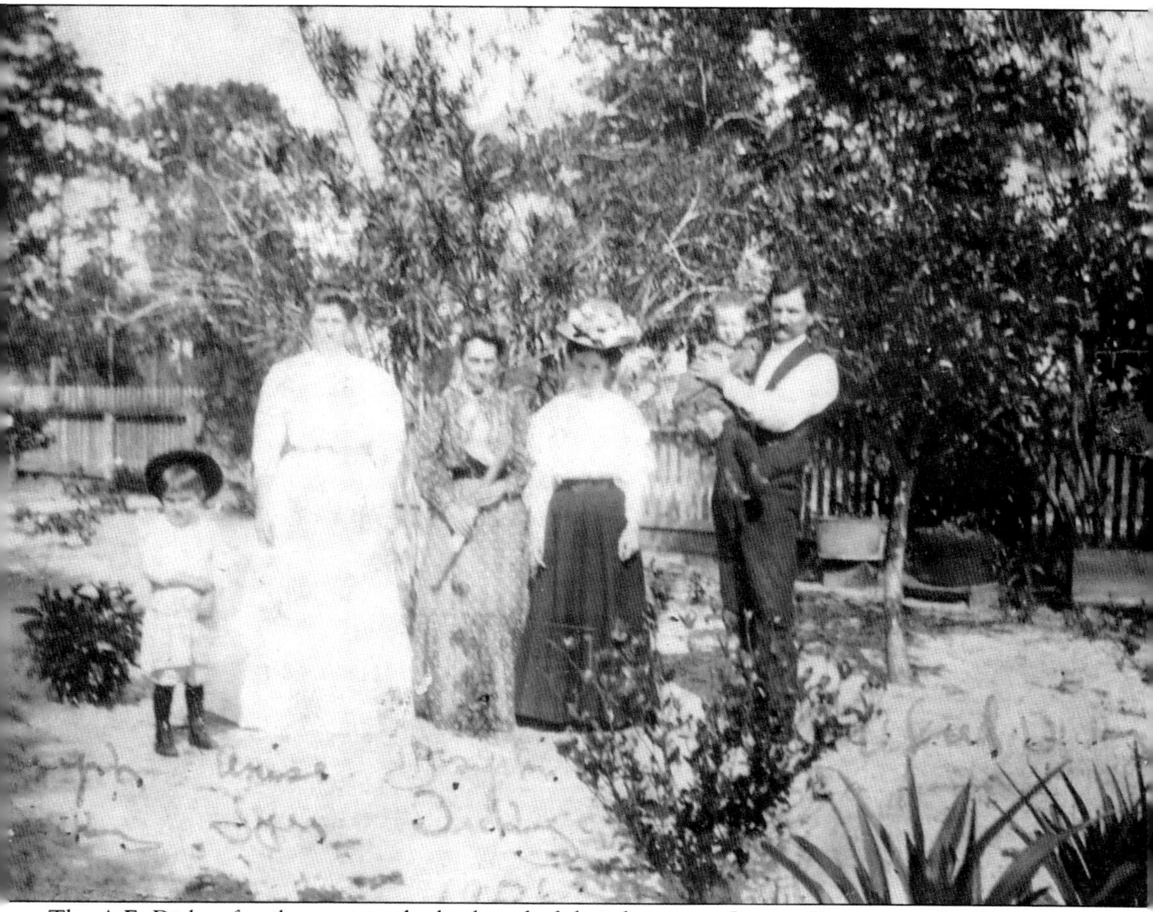

The A.E. Dickey family poses in the backyard of their home on Orange Street near the Citrus Exchange. Alfred was a business owner and active in early Auburndale city government. His first wife, Josephine, was Mike Baynard's sister. They adopted one son, Edmund. After the death of his wife, Alfred married Anise Tyre. Pictured here from left to right are an unidentified child, Anise Tyre, Josephine Baynard Dickey, an unidentified woman, and Alfred holding Edmund.

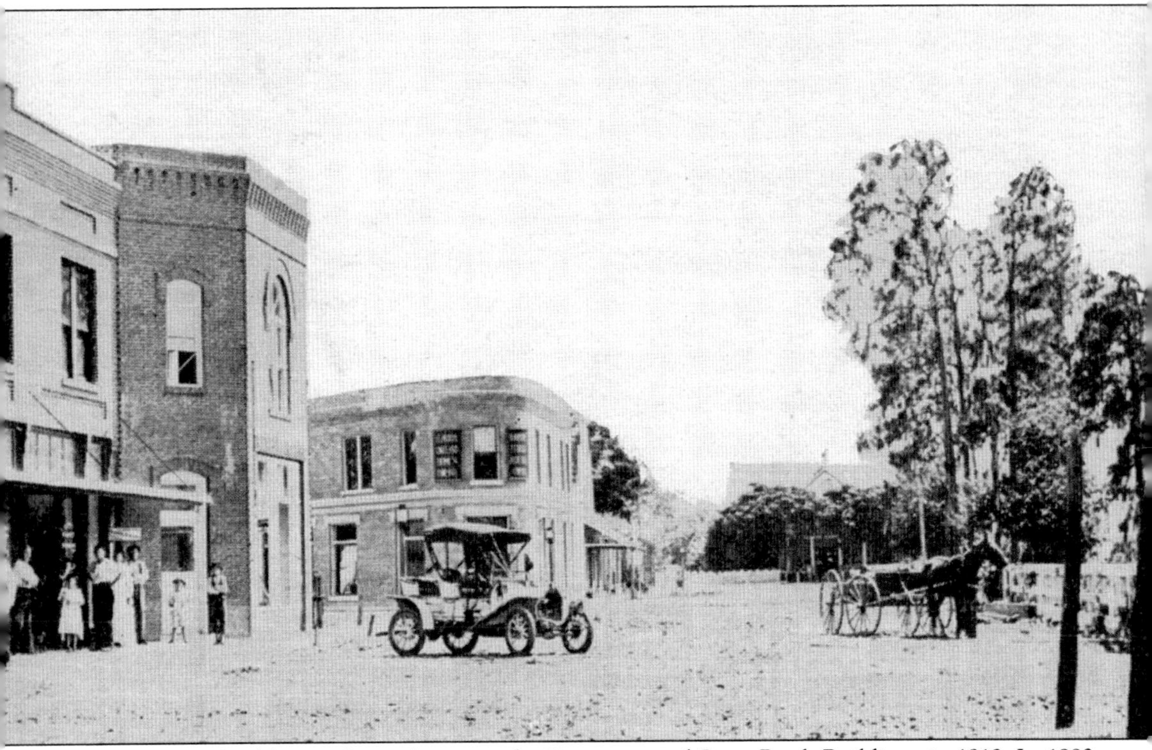

The Jones Building is shown between the Patterson and State Bank Buildings in 1912. In 1893, Werner Jones walked from Tennessee to Auburndale and bought a store on Main Street. He had a livery stable and undertaking parlor. He became discouraged after the second fire, sold his property, and moved to Bartow. He was elected county treasurer in 1914 and tax assessor in 1920, a position he held for 12 years.

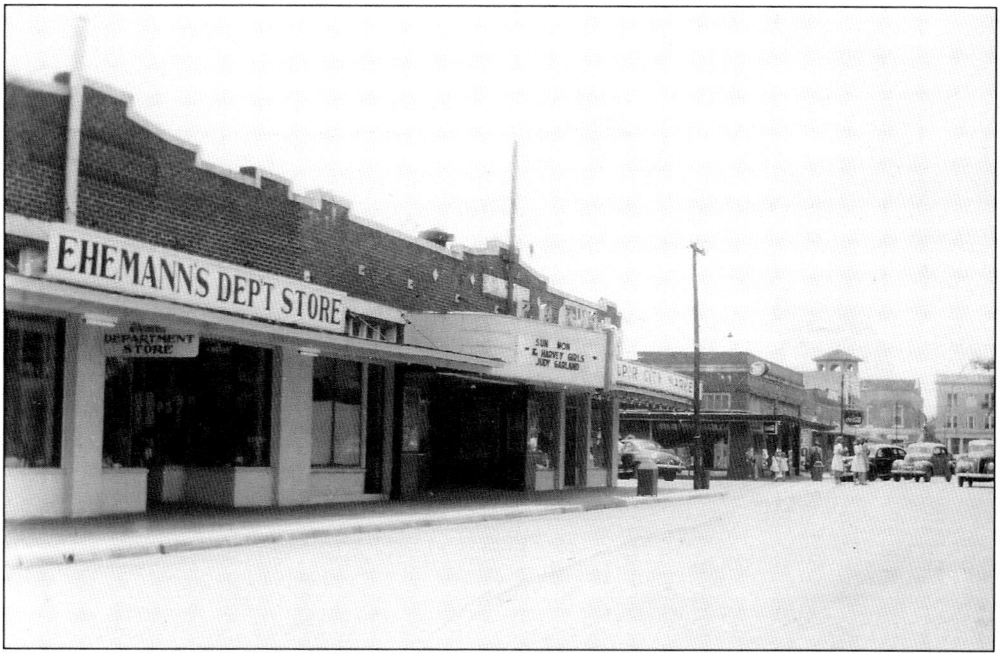

The Baynard Building was constructed in 1927 on the corner of Main Street and Lake Avenue. It contained room for four shops and a movie theater. The Park Theater, formally the Princess Ariana, opened in 1935 and closed in 1948 when the new, modern Auburn Theater opened. The Auburn closed during the movie-business slump of the 1970s.

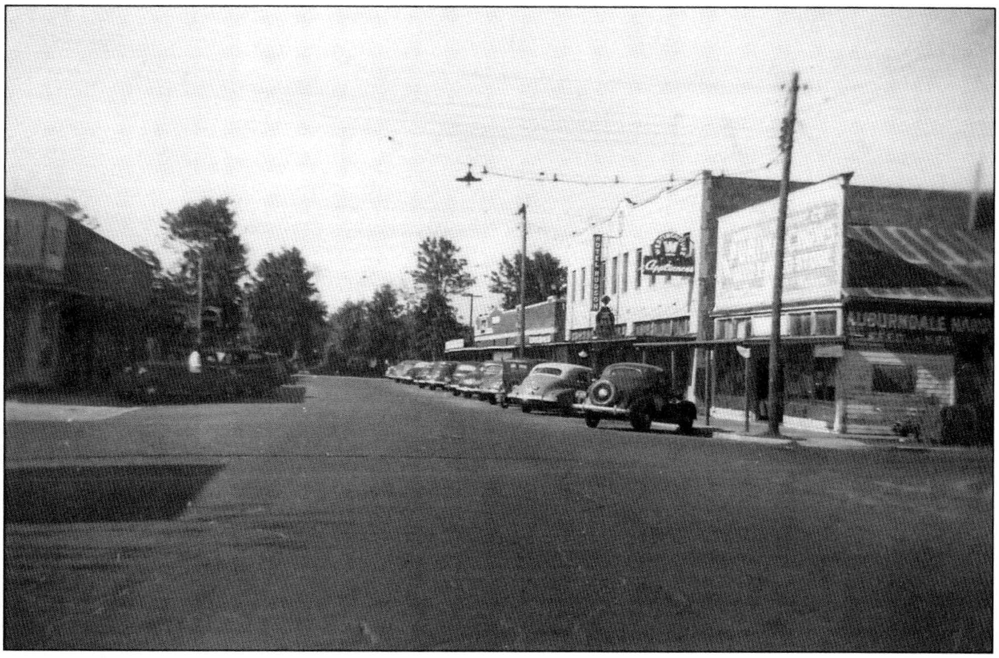

In 1925, the Princess Ariana Theater on Lake Street, the tall building with the false front pictured here, presented silent movies every weekend. Patrons sat in the dark room as a hand-operated projector cranked out the jerky movements of such greats as Rudolph Valentino and Lillian Gish. A player piano accented the drama.

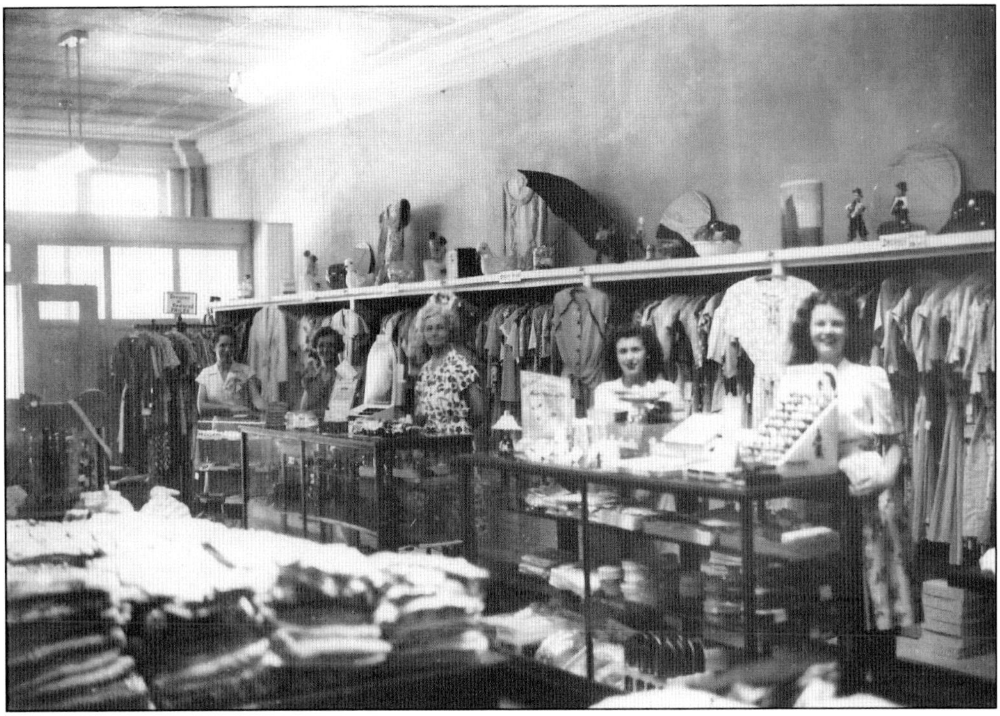

In this c. 1940 image, Laura Richie (third from the left) stands behind glass display cases in her store located at 117 East Lake Avenue on the first floor of the Hudson Hotel Building. Miss Richie sold a variety of dry goods, including men and women's clothing, notions, fabrics, and shoes.

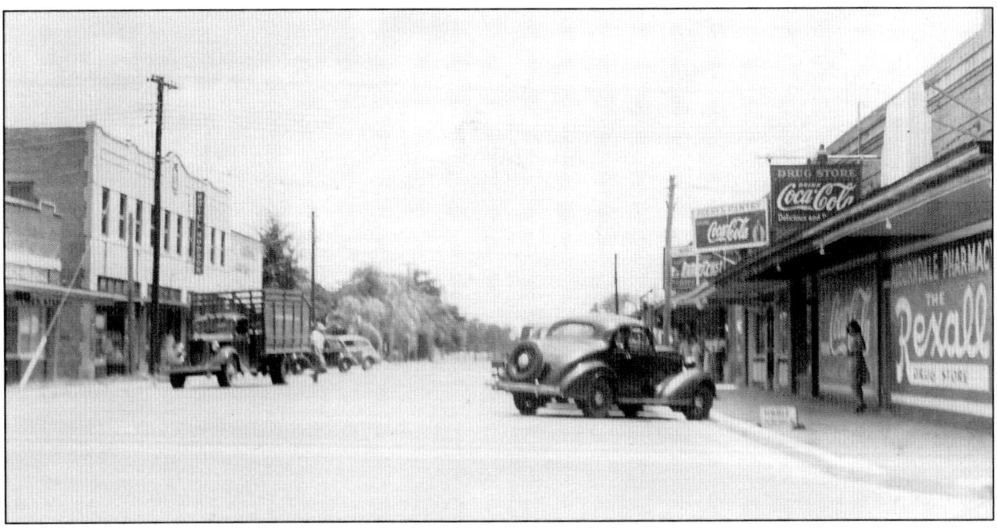

The Hudson Hotel (on the left) was on the top floor of the Baynard Building on East Lake Avenue. In 1925, Martin and Ida Hudson offered a full-course Thanksgiving dinner for $1 in their restaurant downstairs. In 1926, few people in Auburndale had radios. Martin placed his radio in the door of the hotel, and the townspeople sat on the ground outside to listen to the Jack Dempsey–Gene Tunney championship prizefight.

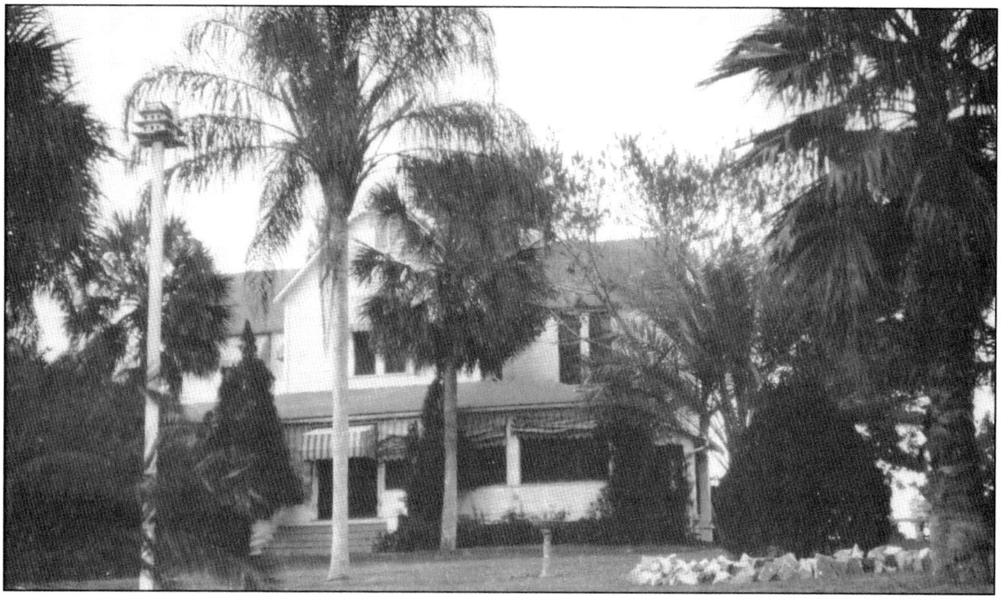

In 1903, Roland Nichols left Massachusetts in a blizzard. He said that when he stepped off the train in Auburndale, he knew he had lost his heart to the "land of sunshine." Roland bought a strip of land along the north shore of Lake Ariana that he named Winona Park. Rev. B.Q. Denham owned the first house, which was built in 1910. It was later owned by the Gerald Work family and then the Dr. Paul Tanner family.

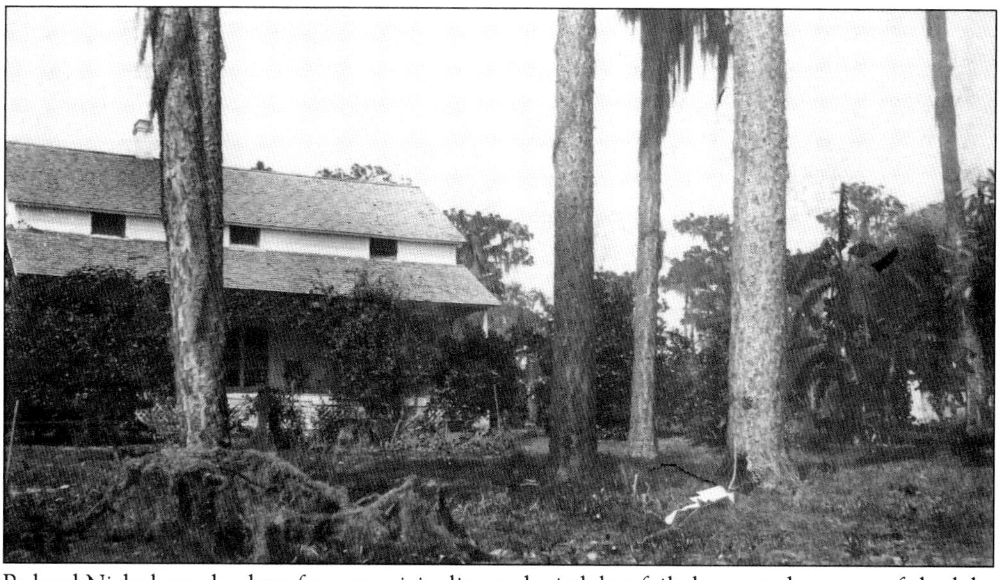

Roland Nichols made plans for a municipality and tried, but failed, to get the name of the lake changed to Winona. He planned a large hotel, and a water tower was erected for running water. This 1910 image shows the Winona Park Club House. A boat dock and recreation area was to have been in the lake here. The Harry McCollum family converted this building into a two-story, Southern-style home.

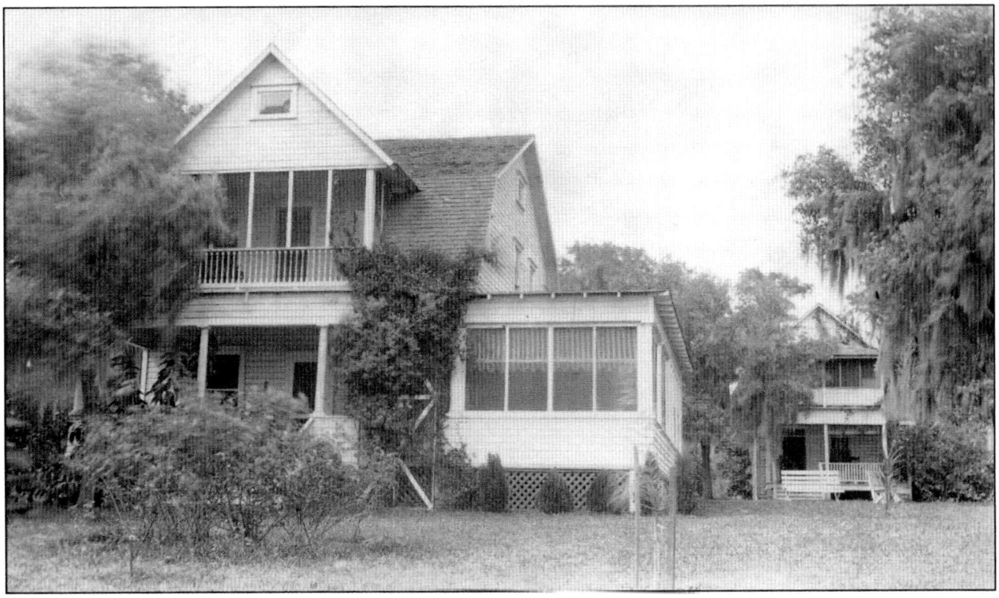

The Dr. William Rabe family home and guesthouse were completed in 1907. Dr. Rabe believed the Florida air would cure lung conditions and treated his patients in tents on the lawn. The houses passed to his daughters: Dorothy Dougan, owner of the Auburndale Red Rock Bottling Company, and husband William Dougan; and Mary Stambaugh and husband Jere Stambaugh. The main house was torn down. The guesthouse was enlarged and still stands.

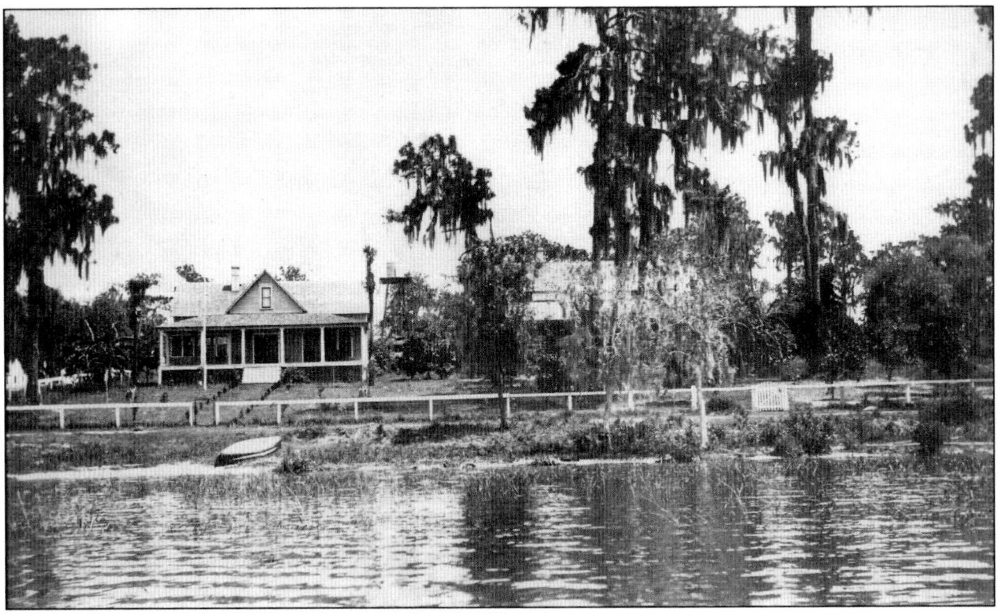

The Commodore Charles Barr family home was completed in 1908. A second floor was later added to this house. It was then owned by the Wynn James family. James was treasurer of Adams Packing Company. His wife, Helen, gave dance lessons and staged special events. The clubhouse can be seen through the trees on the right.

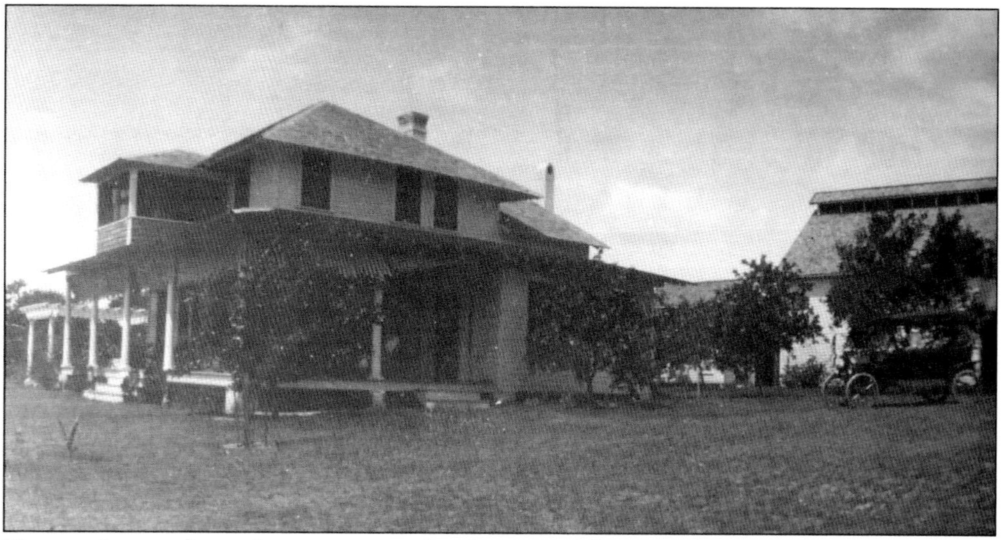

The two homes shown here were completed in 1890 (above) and 1920 (below). Three homes were completed during the land boom of the 1920s. Due to increased home building, it became harder to get supplies, and construction slowed down. Equipment ordered from Atlanta took two months to arrive. The Winona Realty and Fruit Company dissolved. Of the 40 lots, 39 had been sold, including 4 lots Roland Nichols had reserved for himself, when Winona Park, like the rest of the country, entered the Great Depression. Roland said he lost everything in what he called the "boomerang." Through the efforts of realtor Dean Hickman, Winona Park was annexed into Auburndale.

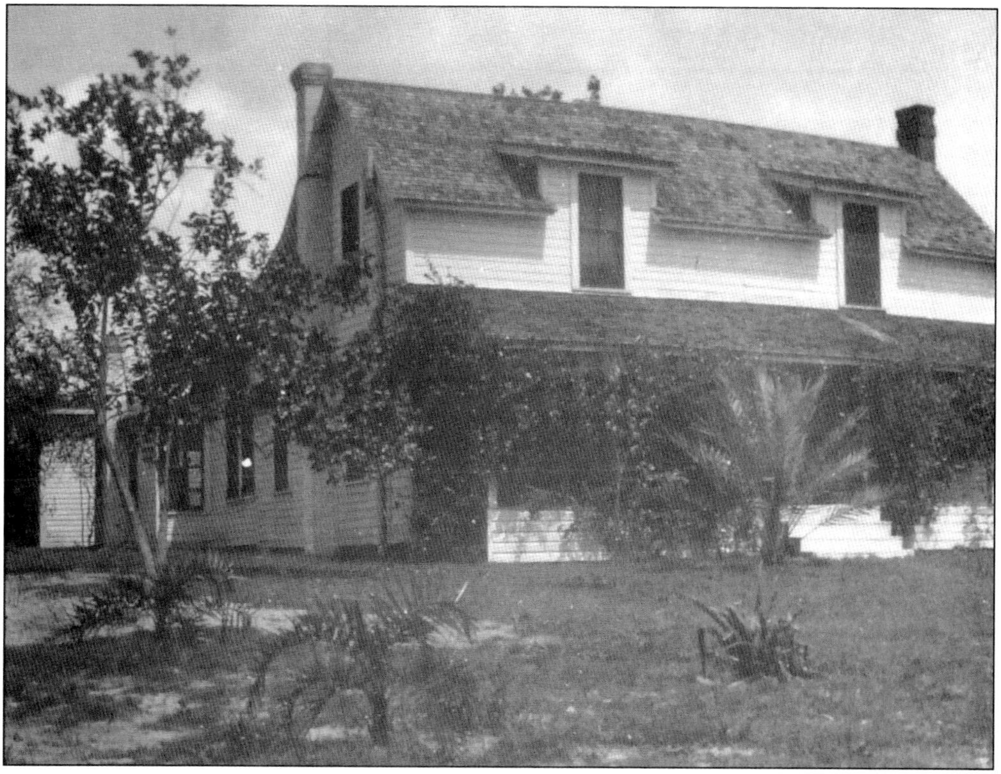

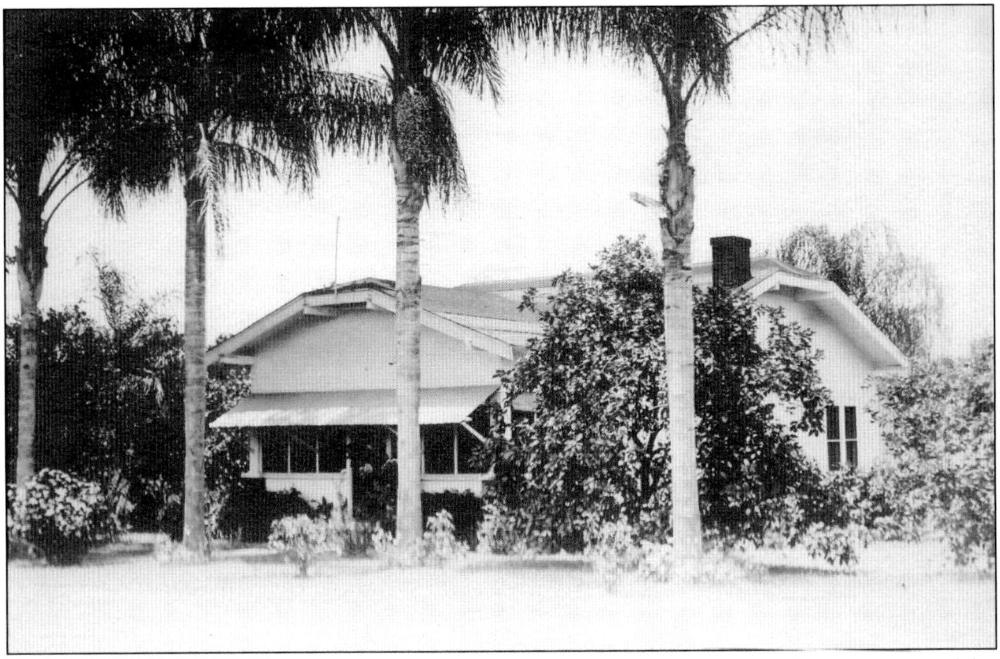

Built in 1890, the Edmiston home (shown here) was already in Winona Park. This was part of the original Edmiston homestead. Laird Boyd and his son William arrived by covered wagon in 1883 to file for their homestead. Romance bloomed, and Mattie Boyd married William Edmiston.

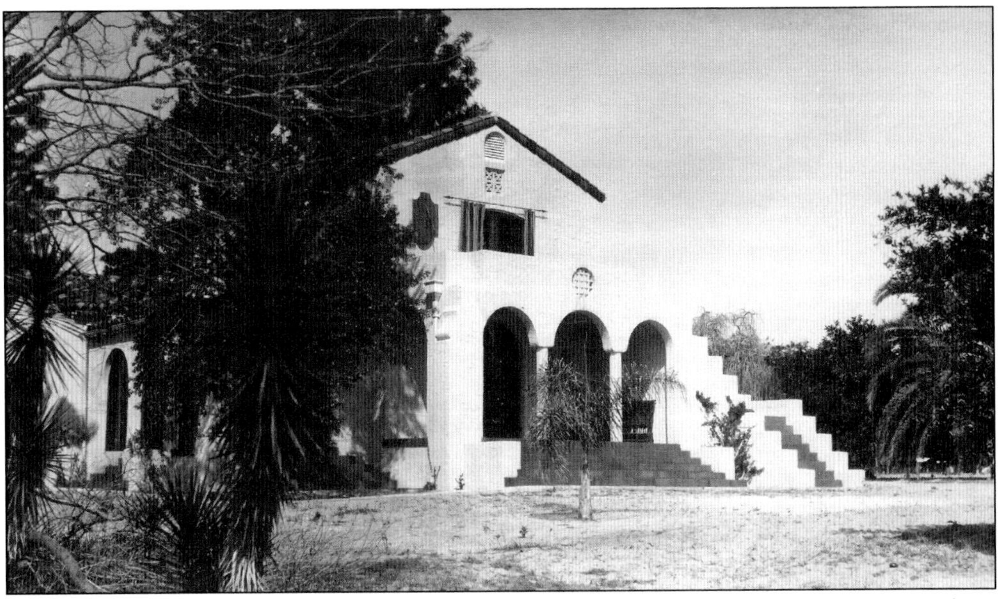

The Holland Jenks house, built in 1925, was on the east shore of Lake Juliana. Jenks came from Washington, DC. This was the largest home in the area. After Jenks's death, his son Stuart lived in the home. The house is in the National Register of Historic Places. The land around the house is now a housing community.

Four

LIVING AND LEARNING

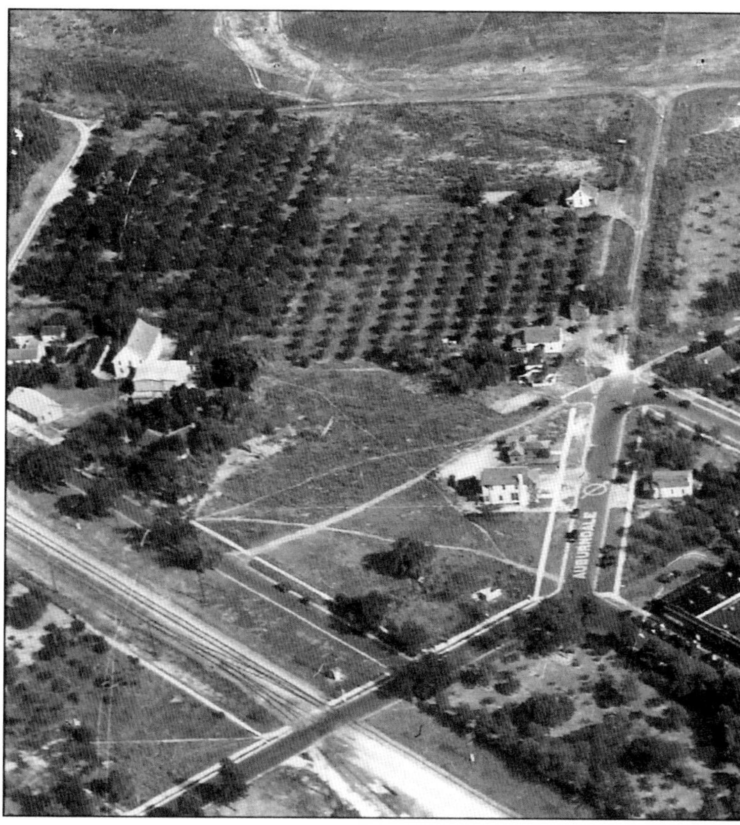

In 1883, the Patterson, Newman, and Edmiston families met at the Patterson home on Lake Ariana to organize the Sanitaria Presbyterian Church. Because Auburndale had attracted some undesirables, it was suggested that a church was needed. The Auburndale Presbyterian Church was built on a lot east of town, the large white building on the left. This served the congregation for 35 years. It was then made into apartments but was later torn down.

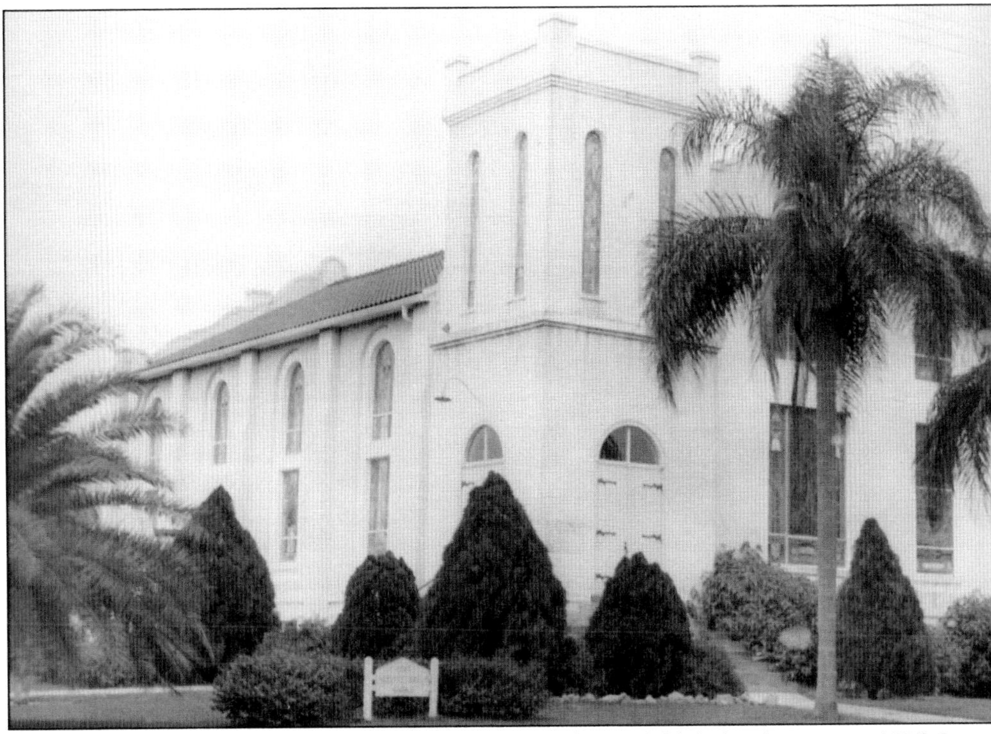

The stately new Presbyterian church was constructed on Pilaklakaha Avenue in 1925. Large wooden beams supported the ceiling of the sanctuary. One set of stairs climbed to a balcony, and another set descended to the social hall in the basement. A majestic stained-glass window, dedicated to Dr. John Patterson and his son, dominated the front wall. The bell tower was later removed due to persistence leaks.

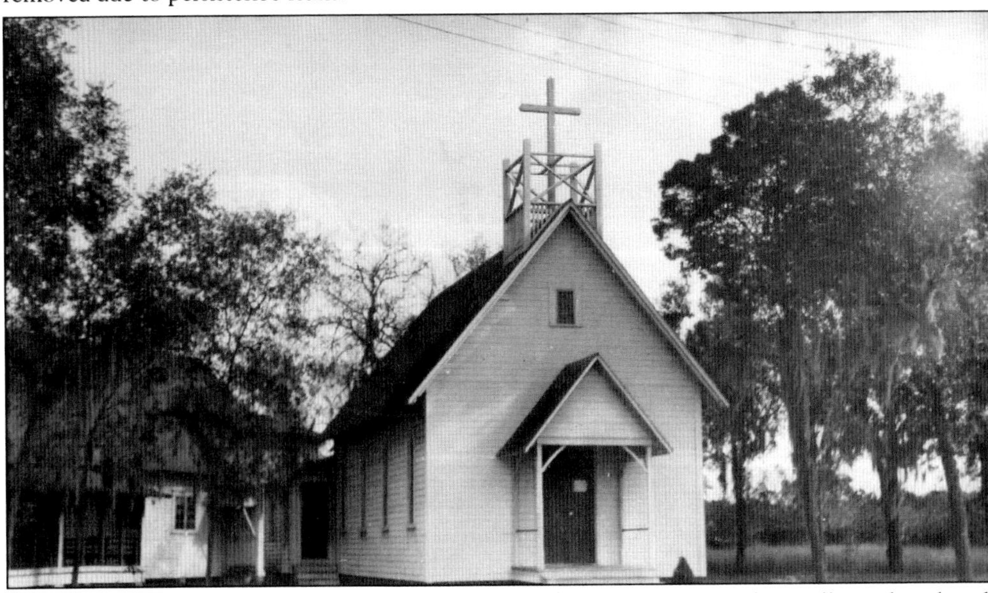

In 1897, the Episcopalians purchased a plot of land for $75 and constructed a small wooden church just off Main Street. The church was consecrated on June 25, 1939, and named St. Alban. A parish house was added later. The Episcopal church is the oldest standing church in Auburndale.

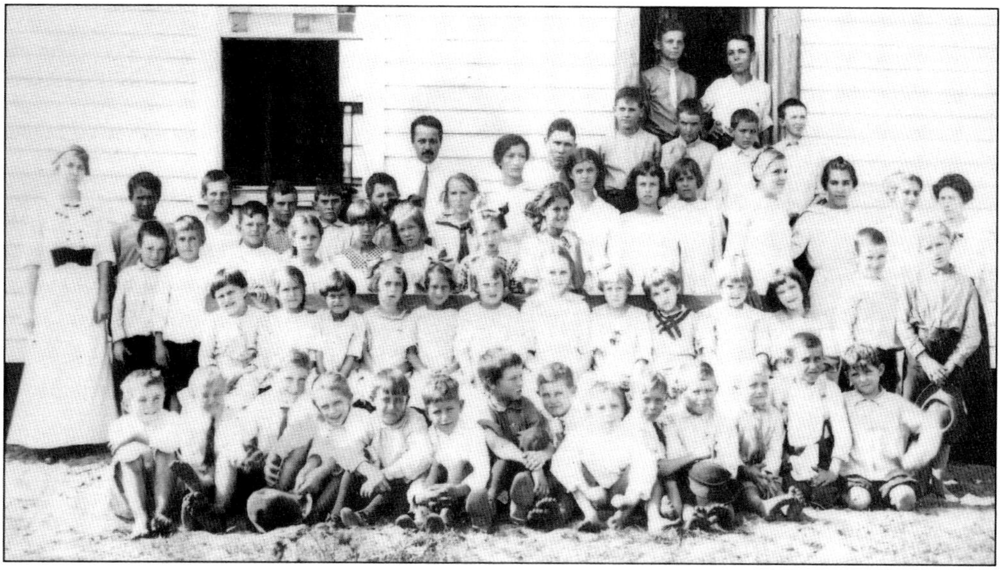

The entire student body, the principal, and the teacher stand outside an abandoned church that served as Auburndale's second school from 1911 to 1915. The first official school was in an unstable building that swayed when the wind blew. It was constructed on high pillars, and Auburndale's free-roaming hogs took advantage of this to scratch their backs on the exposed floor joists underneath. Classes came to a halt until the building stopped shaking. In 1898, James A. Cox was the teacher, and there was an enrollment of 23 students. Cox had just returned from serving in the state legislature for Polk County. Classes from the first to the eighth grades were held in the same room. Students who wanted a higher education had to travel to Lakeland or Orlando; very few students could to do this. This first school was destroyed by a hurricane in 1911, and classes had to be held in the church for the next four years until the new school was completed. The church building was moved and became a home in a neighboring town.

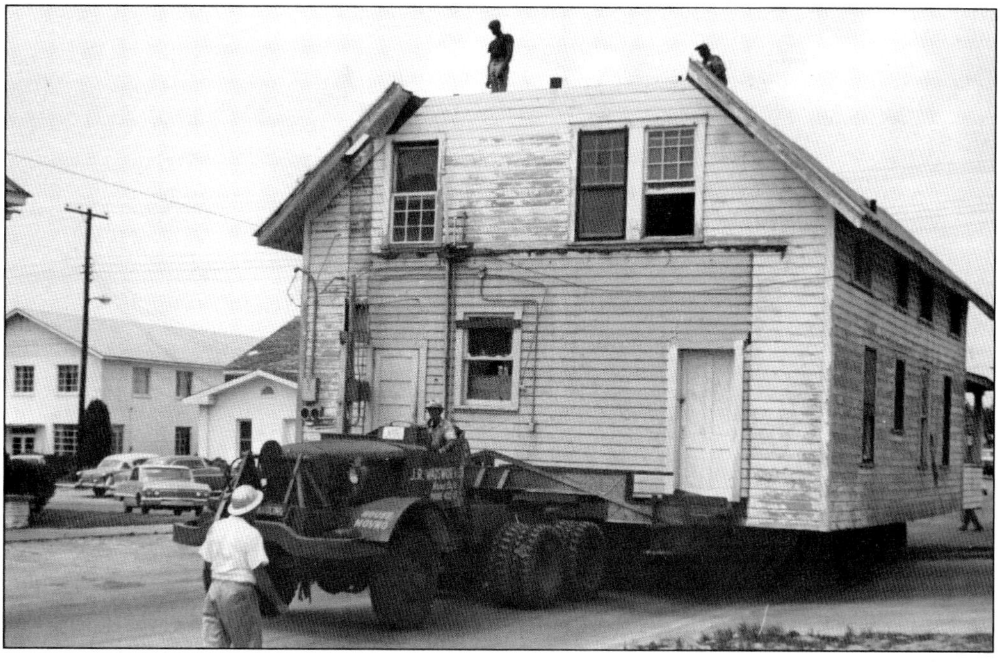

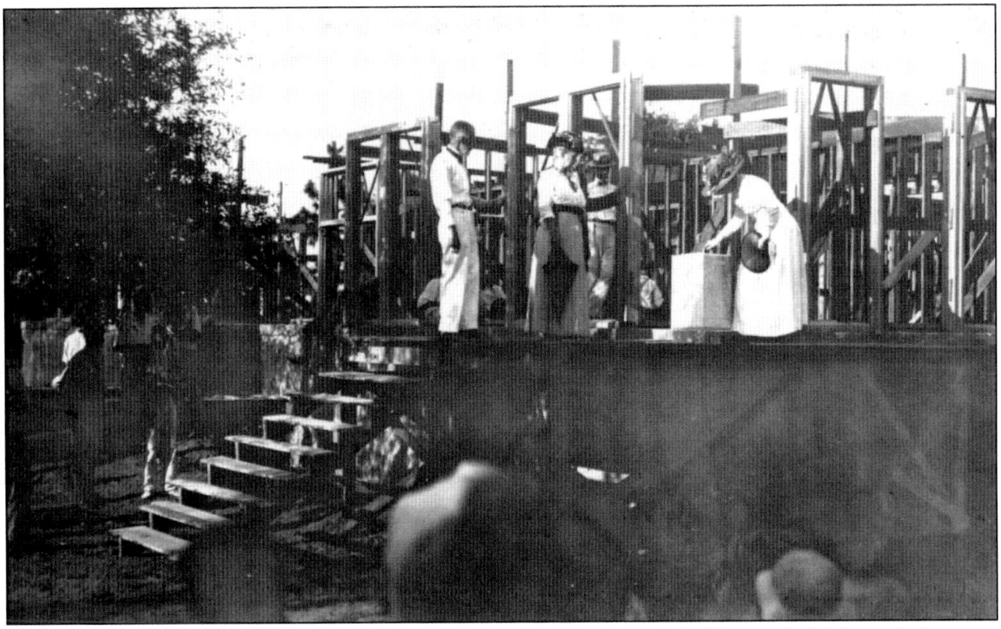

On September 8, 1915, Mrs. F.I. Stone, president of the Auburndale Women's Club, sealed a time capsule in the cornerstone for the new red-brick school. The Women's Club was largely responsible for the building of the school. Some residents were upset because they thought the school was too large and that it would take 50 years before the town would have enough children to fill it. They were wrong.

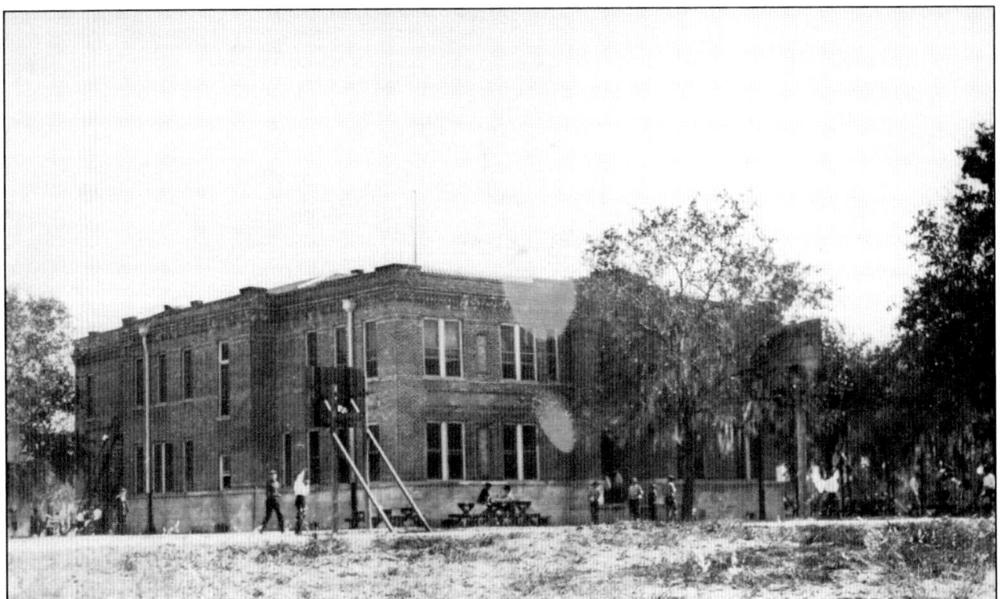

The new school opened for classes in 1916. There were six classrooms and two restrooms on the first floor. Two wide staircases led to six classrooms and an auditorium on the second floor. When the high school and auditorium opened in 1925, this auditorium was closed in and made into two additional classrooms. The stage was enclosed and became the principal's office.

In 1925, a two-story red-brick high school was added next to the elementary school, and for the first time Auburndale students could complete their education at home. The building contained eight classrooms, a library, an office, a chemistry lab, and a large auditorium for school and community events. The 1921 class picture below shows Mattie Van Fleet Dickey's eighth-grade class. The teacher and principal, Miss Mattie, as everyone called her, is standing in the back row. She was the daughter of William Van Fleet and the sister of General Van Fleet. Others pictured are, from left to right, (first row) Herman McLain, Don Schieble, Everette Allen, and Vernon Ryals; (second row) Enoch Thomas, Laird Anderson, Laura Hobbs, Christine Hamlin, Troupye Allen, and Edith Edmiston; (third row) Alton Dobson, unidentified, Marvin Cooley, Albert Hines, Marie Brown, Clair Burdette, and Ruth White. This would be the first class to graduate from the new high school.

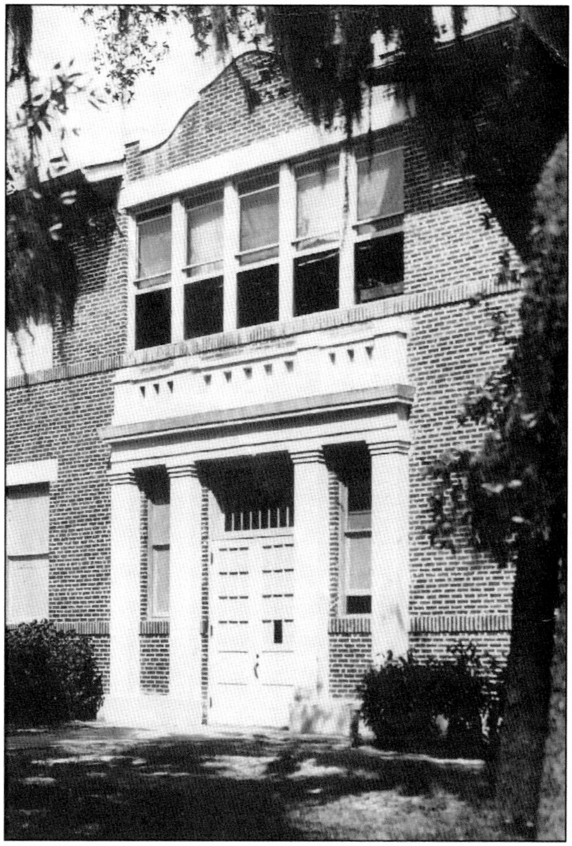

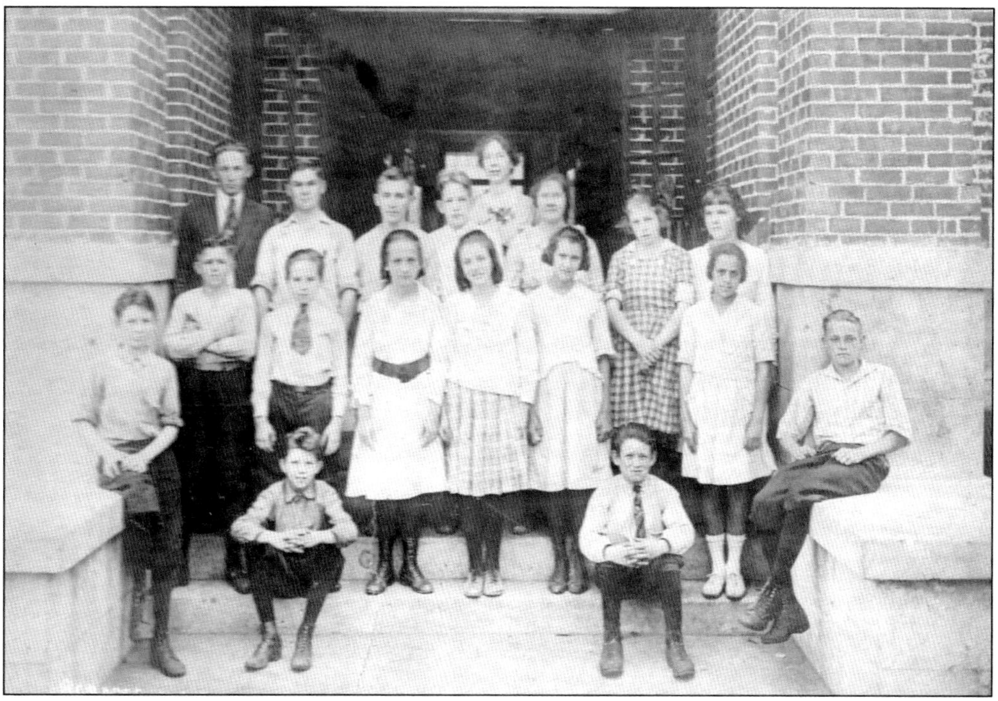

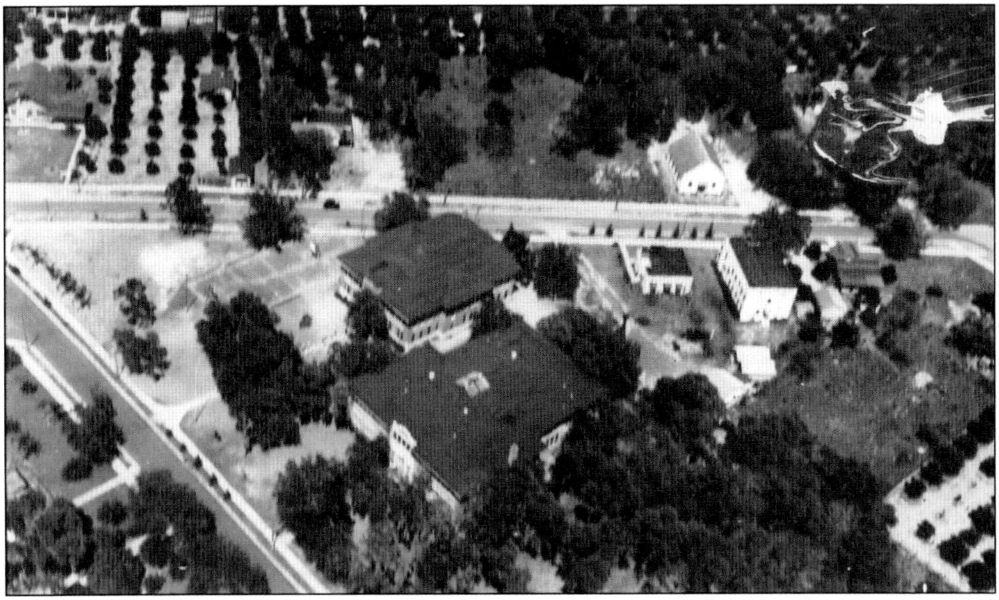

In this image, the school is seen from an airplane around 1940. Looking north, the 1915 school is above, and the high school is in the center. The two-story white building on the left was the teachers' dormitory. Teachers were required to live in Auburndale, so housing was provided. The church across the street was later used as classrooms. Within five years, the school was at capacity, and another elementary was opened on South Main Street.

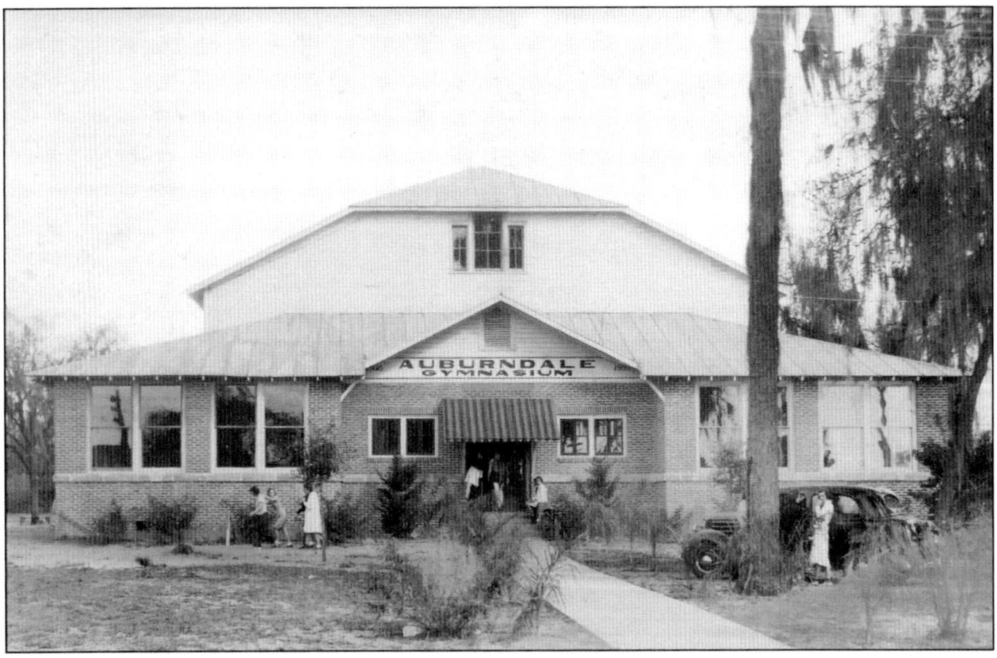

During the Depression, Auburndale received a new gym with Roosevelt's WPA money and labor. In his final report, the inspector noted concern that the first big snowfall would cave the roof in. The gym survived several hurricanes and the 1979 tornado that destroyed the elementary and high schools. The roof leaked, but the building stood firm. The roof has never been tested with a big snowstorm.

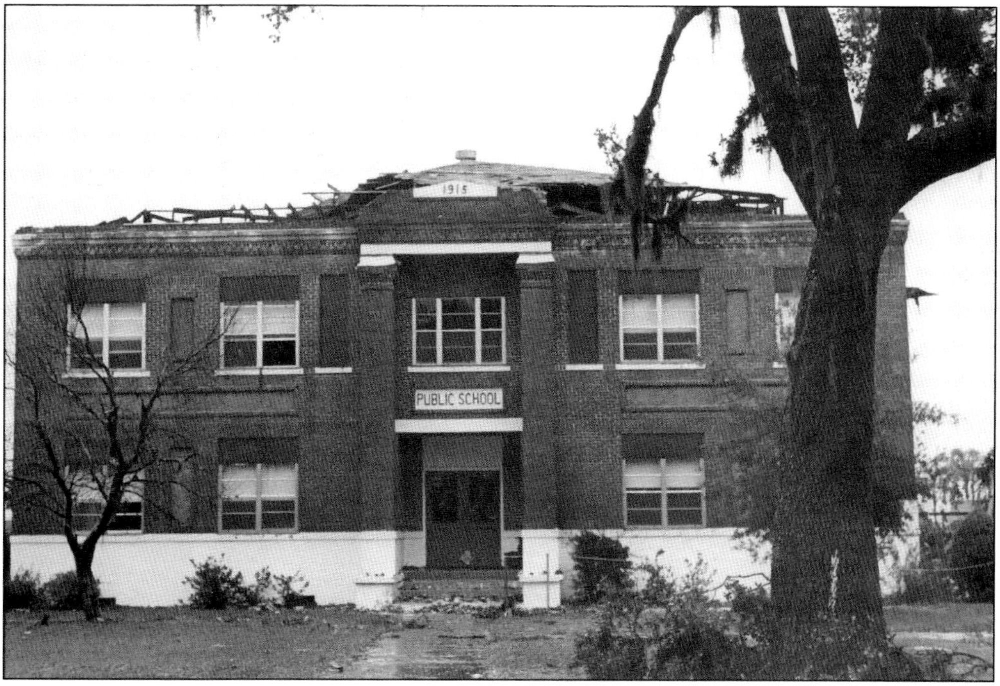

In these photographs, the 1915 elementary school (above) and the 1925 high school (below) stand in ruins after a tornado touched down on May 8, 1979. Classes were in session at the time. Due to previous training and drills, no one was seriously injured. Students recalled many heroic acts by teachers. After inspections, both buildings were deemed unsafe and had to be torn down. The Jere Stambaugh Middle School was constructed on the site. Several homes in the area were destroyed in the storm. (Both courtesy of the *Auburndale Star* archives.)

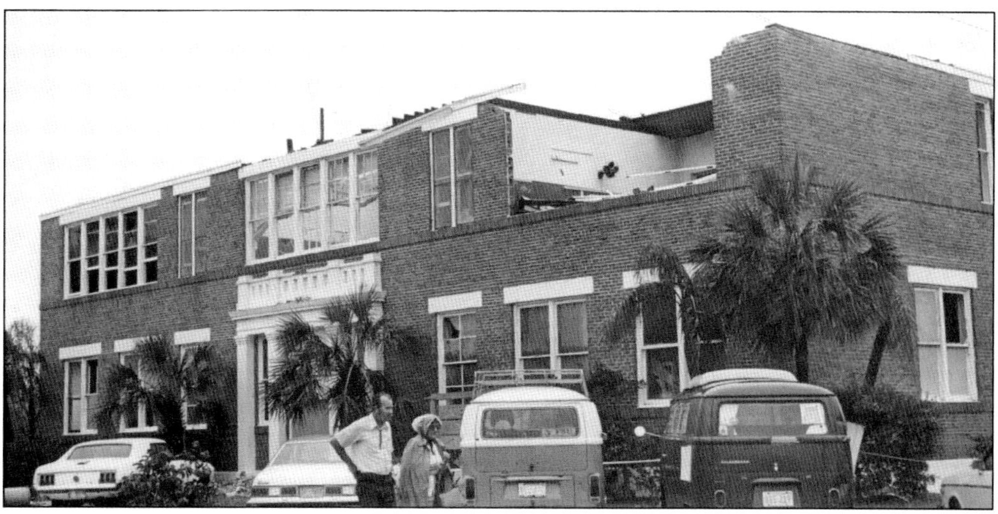

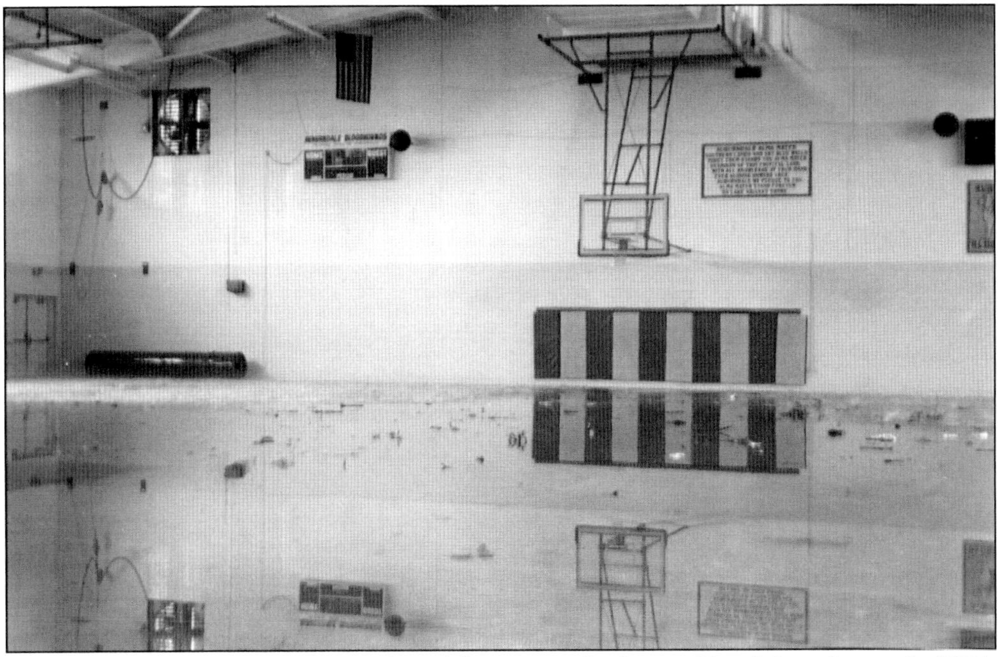

The tornado that touched down in Auburndale in May 1979 damaged but did not destroy the WPA gym. In this image, a foot of water can be seen covering the floor of the high school gym. The roof and the floor were repaired, and the gym saw many more basketball games. A lunchroom, added to the rear of the gym in 1938, was undamaged. (Courtesy of the *Auburndale Star* archives.)

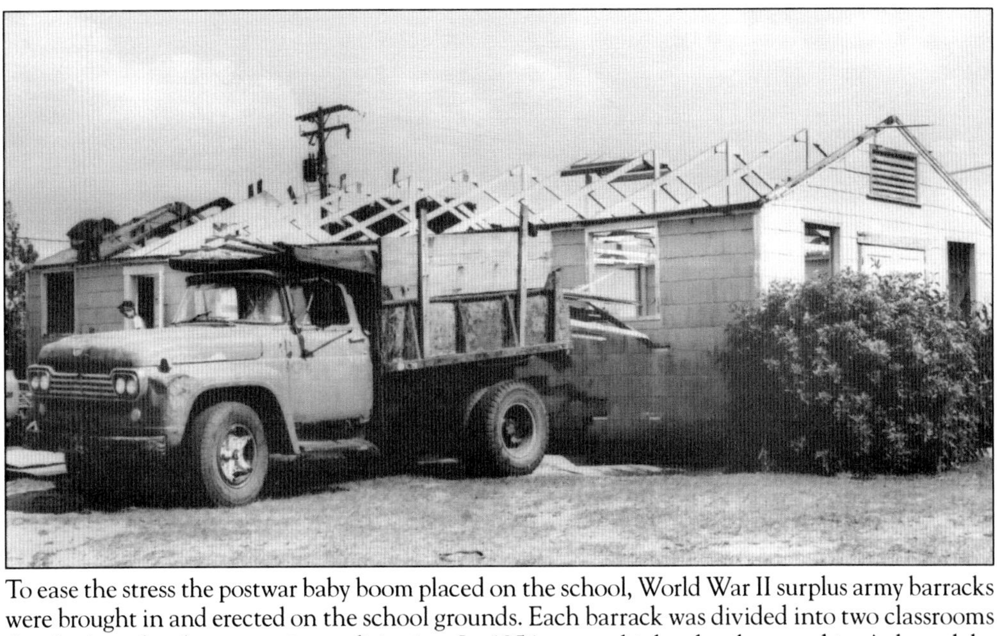

To ease the stress the postwar baby boom placed on the school, World War II surplus army barracks were brought in and erected on the school grounds. Each barrack was divided into two classrooms that had neither heat nor air-conditioning. In 1954, a new high school opened in Auburndale, and the barracks were torn down. (Courtesy of the *Auburndale Star* archives.)

Commencement
Auburndale High School

TUESDAY, MAY 28, 1929

Eight O'Clock

HIGH SCHOOL AUDITORIUM

Processional .... *Orchestra*

Invocation .... *Rev. A. B. Cannady*

Salutatory .... *Lucille Braddock*

Valedictory .... *Clara Mae Brewer*

Venetian Summer Night—Moszkowiski .... *Glee Club*

Address—*Dr. Ludd M. Spivey, Pres. Southern College*

Violin Solo—Schumann .... *Betty White*

Awarding D. A. R. Prize .... *Mrs. Markley*

Presentation of Diplomas .... *Mr. T. T. Hatton*

Benediction .... *Rev. W. J. Jones*

GRADUATES

Lucile Braddock	Helen Forsythe
Clara Mae Brewer	Joseph D. Jeffords
Leland Hugh DeGraaf, Jr.	James Luther Phelps
Elsie Driver	Ruth Sharrett
Wilford Driver	Lillie Spivey

Elaine D. Thompson

As shown in this 1929 commencement program, Lucile Braddock, Clara Mae Brewer, Leland DeGraaf Jr., Elsie Driver, Wilford Driver, Helen Forsythe, Joseph Jeffords, James Luther Phelps, Ruth Sharrett, Lilly Spivey, and Elaine Thompson were part of the graduating class. Dr. Ludd Spivey, president of Florida Southern College, was the guest speaker.

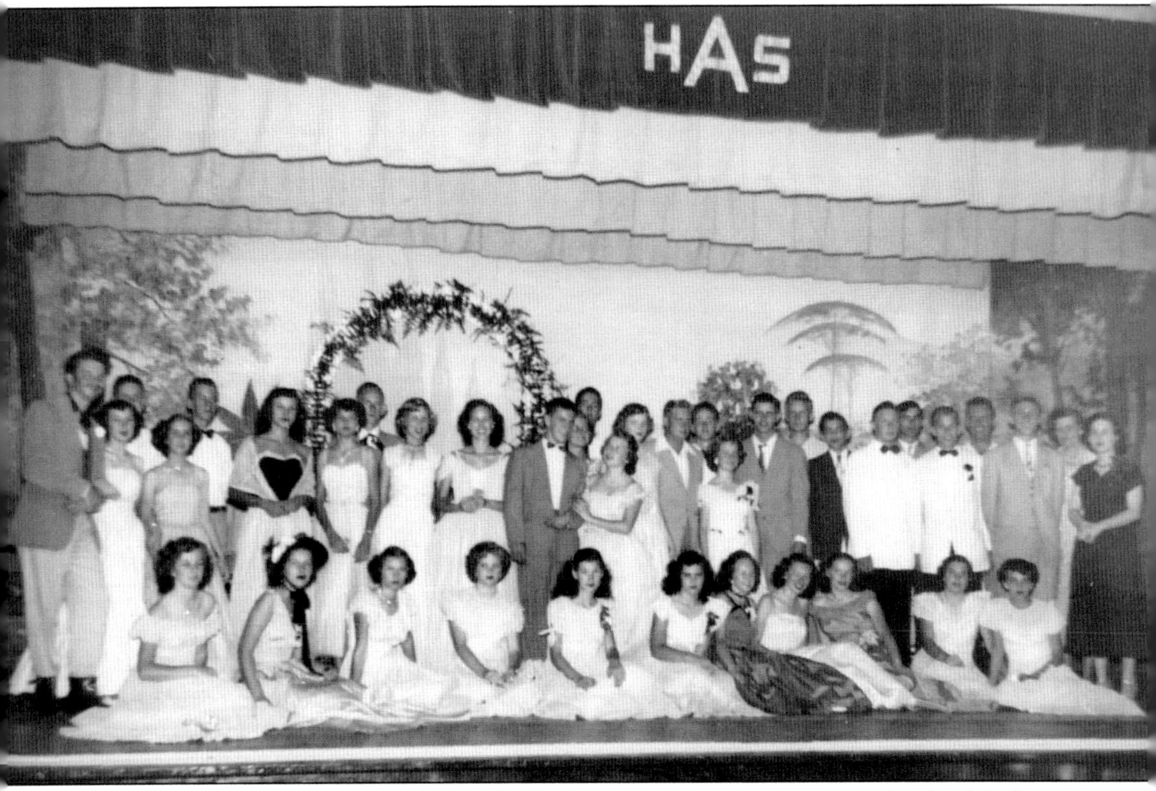

This 1953 photograph shows the annual student "Stunt Night" in the high school auditorium. King Joel Mercer and Queen Mary Kate Griffin were elected, and various skits were performed for the entertainment of students, parents, and guests. It was a big night for the students, and the whole town tuned out for the festivities. This auditorium was destroyed in the 1979 tornado.

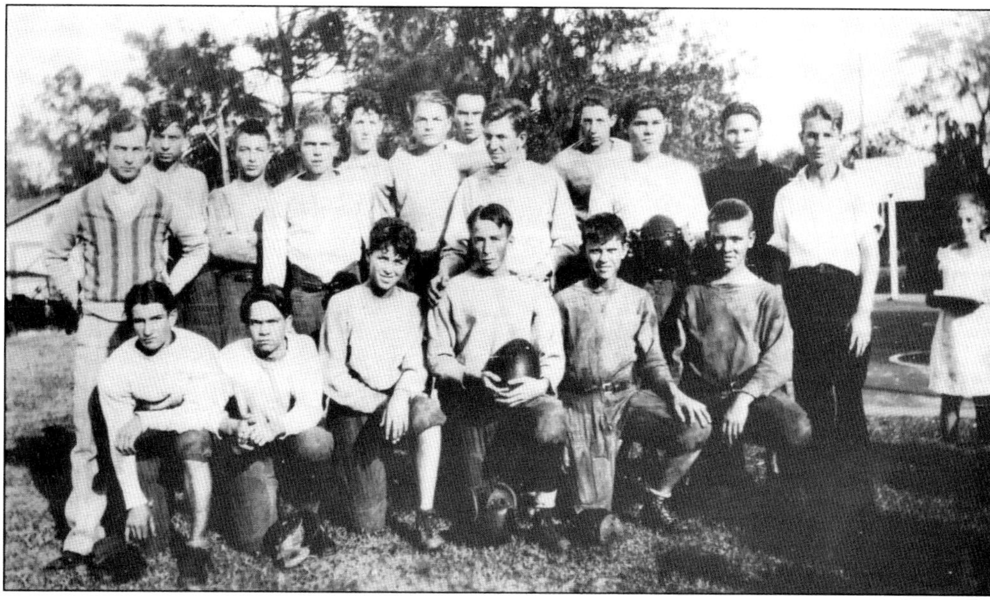

In 1927, Auburndale had its first football team. Sixteen boys took to the field to play neighboring towns; they usually lost. Some games had to be forfeited because transportation could not be arranged or not enough boys could play. Uniforms were mismatched, and equipment was scarce. Headgear came in the form of World War I army surplus helmets. The boys on the team referred to themselves as the Bloodhounds. Their coach was R.C. "Doc" Brunson.

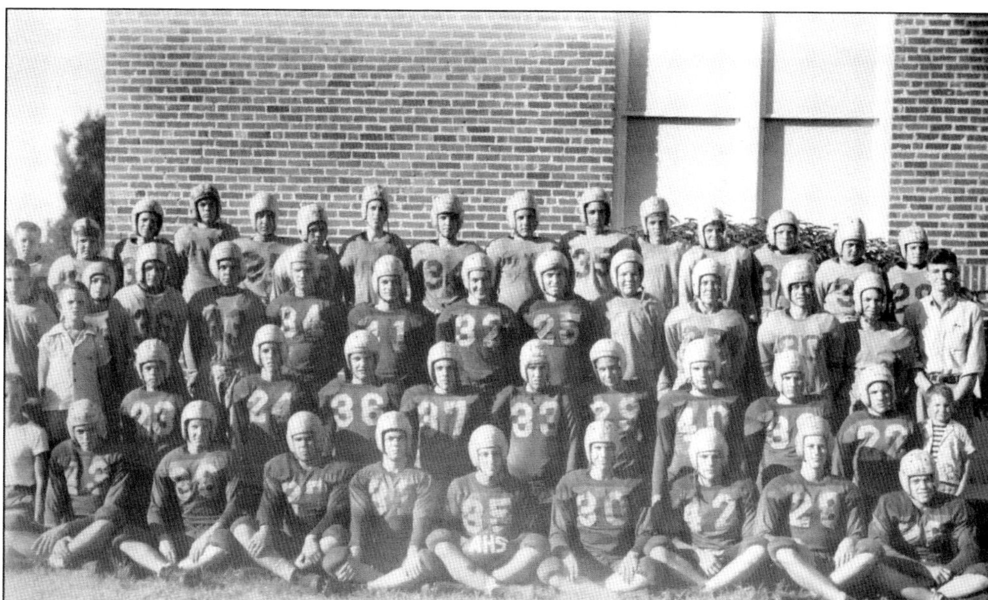

The 1948 Bloodhound football team had 42 players. The coach was C.R. Gutteridge. Bobby Williamson and Billy Turner were the managers. Games were played on a field on the east side of Lake Ariana. This property had been bought by the school board for unpaid taxes after it was abandoned by a development company. While the high school was being built here, games were played on a field on West Bridgers Avenue.

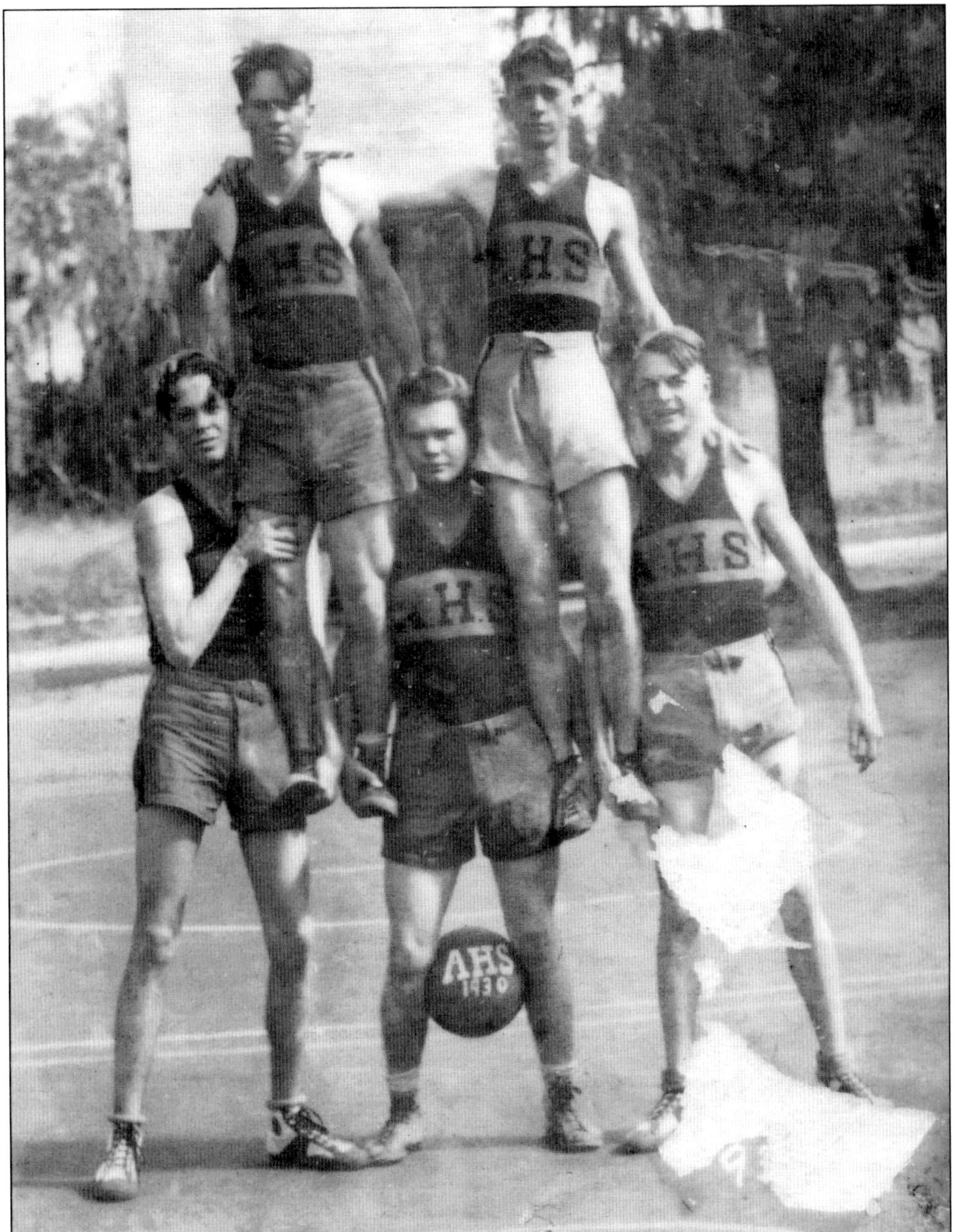

The 1930 boys' basketball team stands in formation. Until the gym was completed in 1935, games were played on outdoor asphalt courts on the school grounds. Pictured from left to right are (standing) Paisley Jones, Otto Moore, and "Bogas" Owens; (on shoulders) Scott "Sub" Jordan and Harold "Bud" Deal. Other players were recruited on a game-by-game basis. It was not uncommon for a game to be forfeited for not enough players.

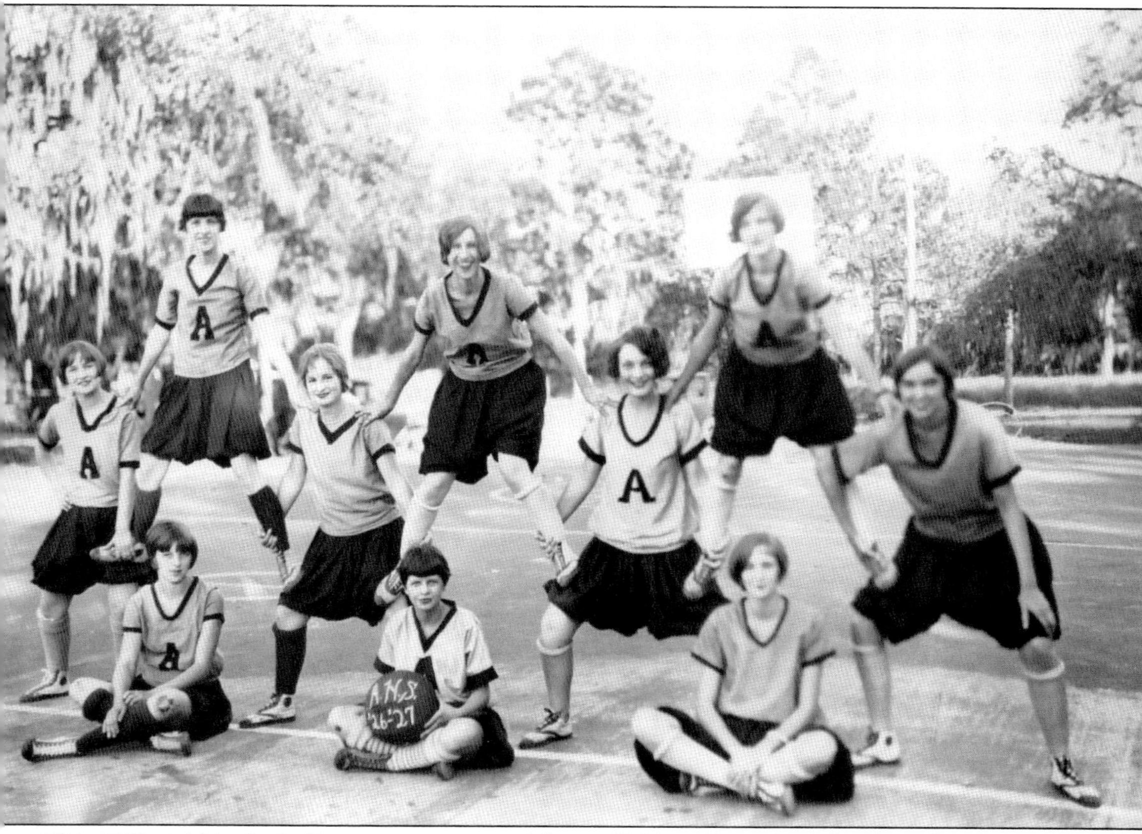

This 1927 girls' basketball team, consisting of Emmy Balcom, Dorothy Schieble, Lilly Spivey, Pearl Deal, Fannie Thompkins, Betty Cowan, Helen Clary, Blanch McLean, Mildred Kimbrough, and Hazel Kimbrough, was county champions. The team's coach was Nancy Poole. Probably due to the athletic training she received as a member of this championship team, Cowan drove her Cadillac in an amateur race on Daytona Beach. Elizabeth won with speeds of over 100 miles per hour. Judges wanted to disqualify her because they could not believe she was not a professional.

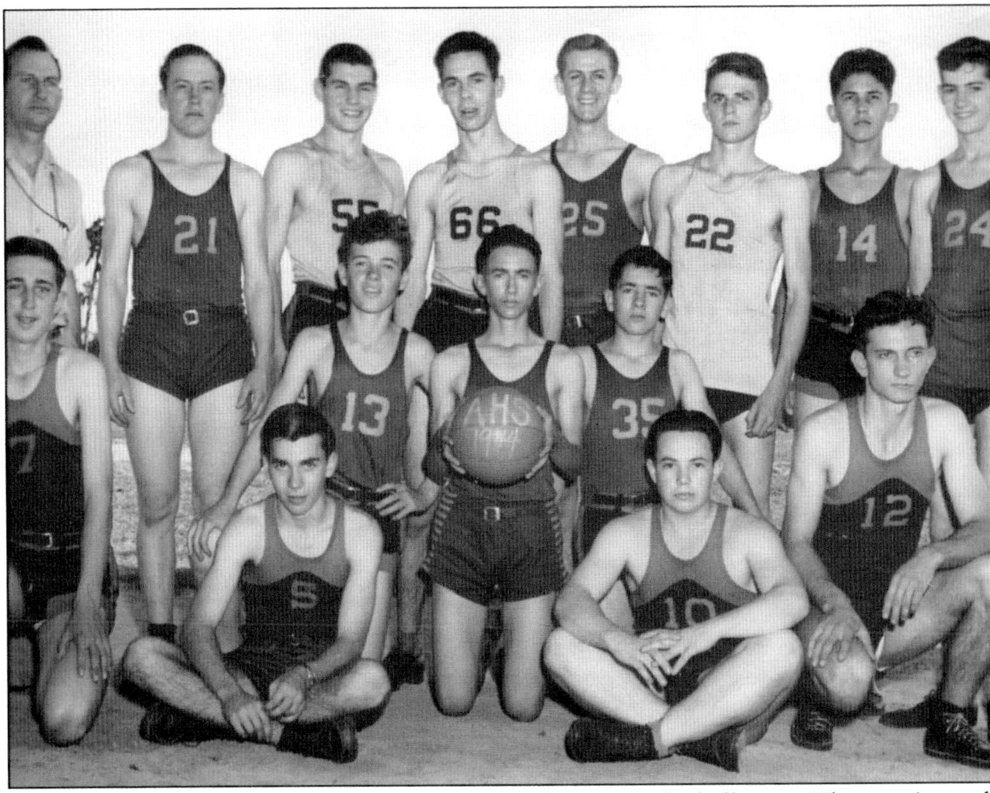

Pictured here is the lineup for the 1944 Auburndale boys' basketball team. The team's coach was C.R. Gutteridge. Most of the boys in this group would soon be enlisted in the military. Steve Hensler (no. 13) was killed in 1954 when his airplane went down in Korea. He is buried in Arlington National Cemetery. David Clements (no. 14) enlisted in the air corps. He died in 1953 when his airplane crashed off the coast of Japan.

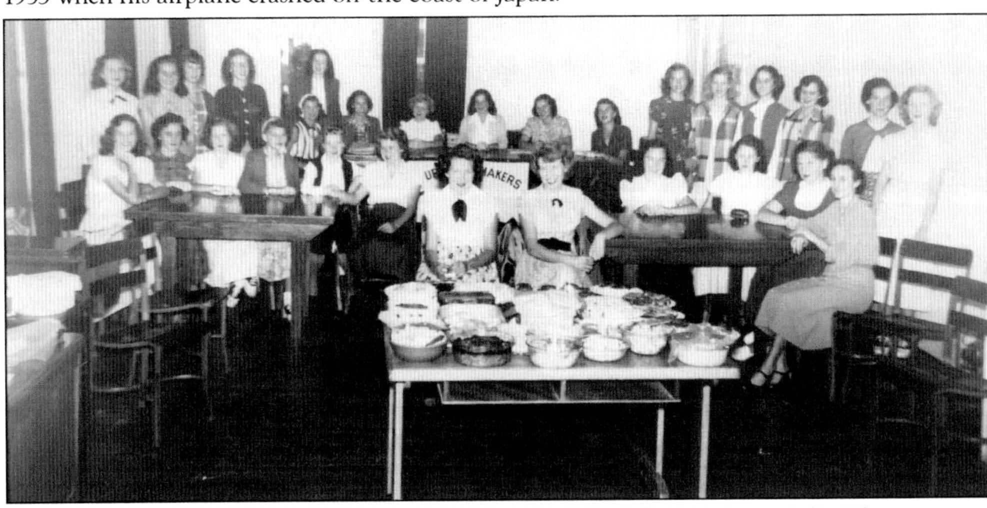

In 1952, the AHS Future Homemakers of America displayed their cooking skills. The group was supervised by teacher Nell Dendinger. This photograph was taken in a building that had been added to the rear of the gym. The lunchroom was on the first floor, and the home economics class was on the second floor.

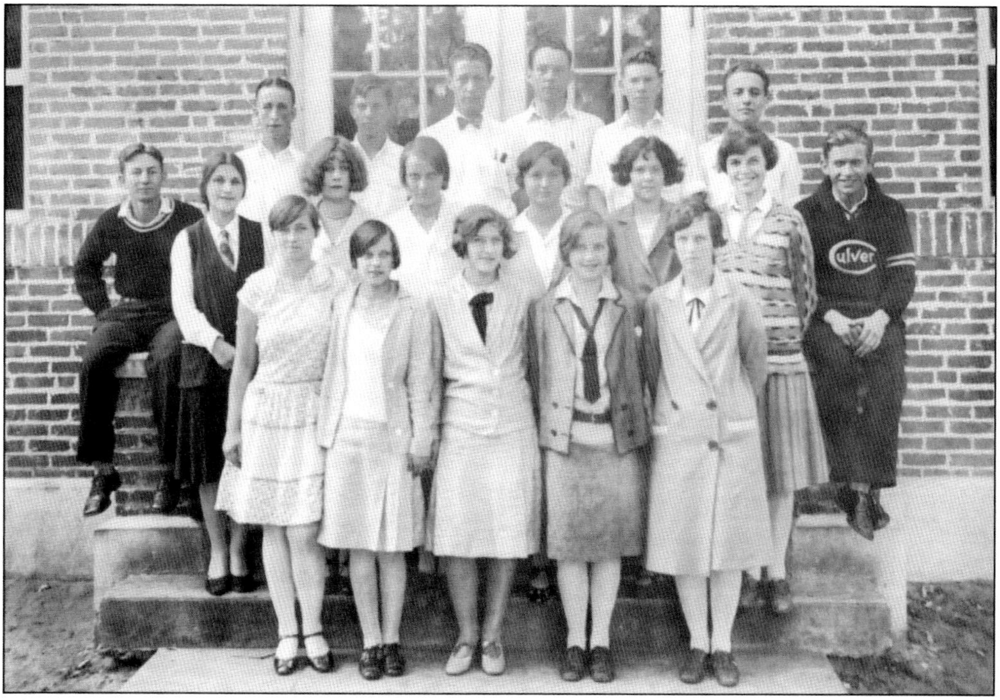

This image is of the class of 1928. From left to right are (first row) Pearl Deal, Hallie Kimbrough, Hazel Kimbrough, Thelma Baber, and Lenora Weeks; (second row) Larry Vander Hulse, Ruth DeGraaf, Annie Gladden, Vivian Hancock, Marguerite Haney, Lillian Linder, Dorothy Christ, and Wallace Mize; (third row) Lucian Thornbrough, Bruce Jones, Tom Agerton, William Gladden, James Pierce, and Kenneth Vander Hulse.

Members of the class of 1930 pose for a class portrait. In no particular order are Jack Agerton, Ruth Allen, Lucile Colton, Virginia DeGaaf, Marion Driver, Thelma Edmiston, Herbert Forsythe, Frances Hodge, Harriet Hodge, Eva Hughes, Edna Langley, Arthur Linder, Otto Moore, Vera Perry, Harold Smith, Mary Stevenson, Louise Turner, Betty White, and Patricia Wynn. The teacher is unidentified.

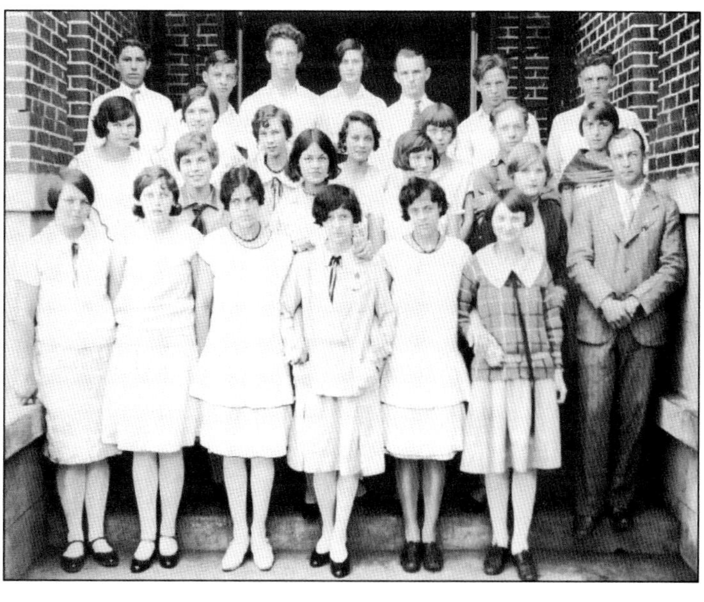

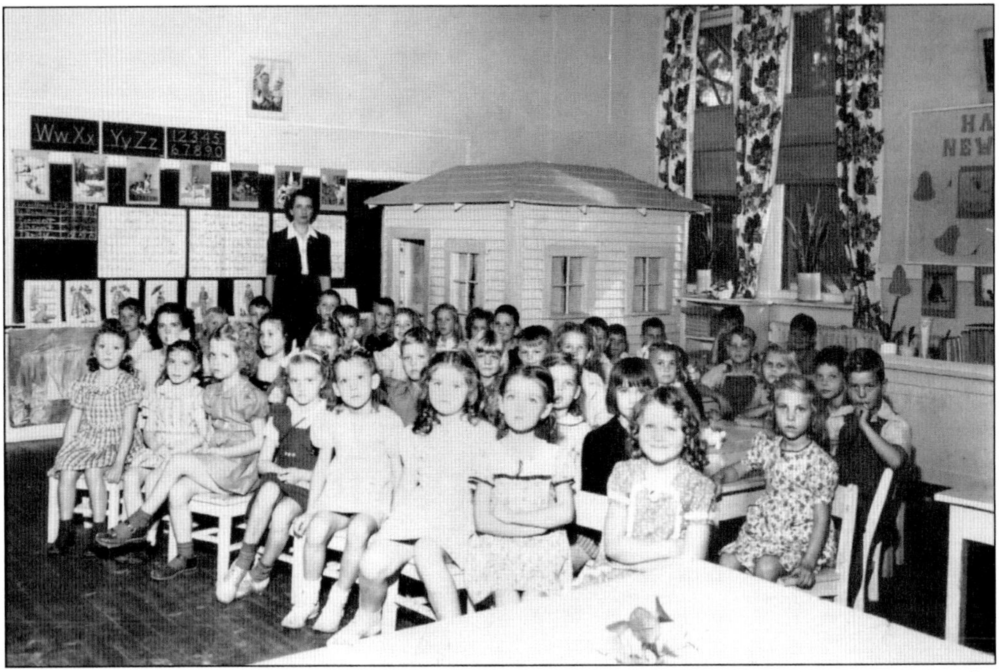

This image, from around 1942, is of Edna Driver Adams's first-grade class. The classroom was in the 1915 school building. Each child sat at a table, and for reading, the chairs were placed in a circle. The playhouse included in the photograph was made by Percy Watts as a treat for the children.

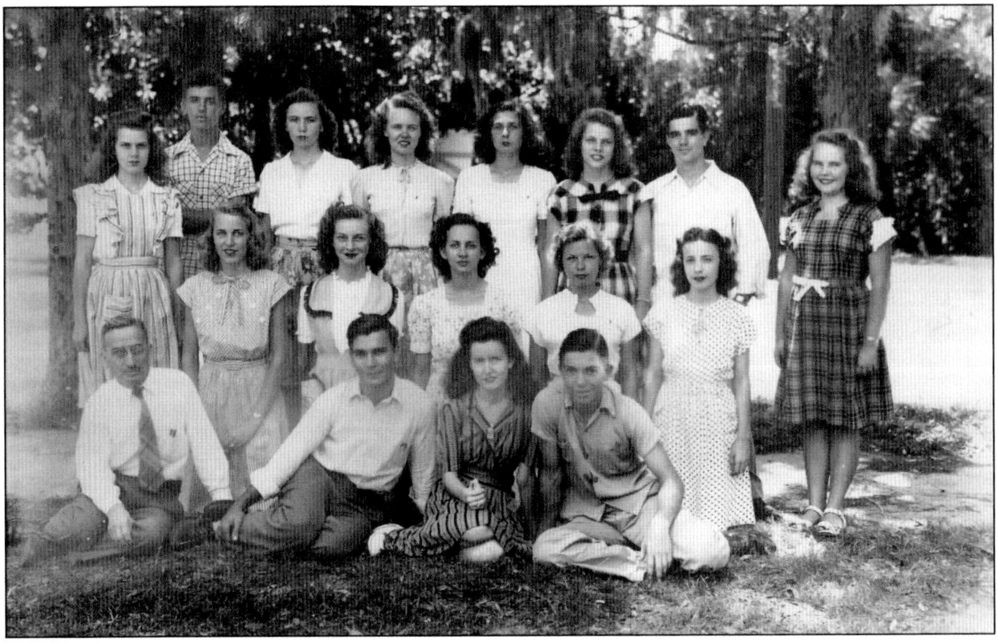

This high school group picture was taken about 1947 outside the 1925 high school. Harold McGrath, the principal, is sitting on the ground in the front left. Glenn Anna Thorp Lewis is in the center of the second row. Glenn Anna's father and grandfather built the Baynard house, as well as many of Auburndale's early homes. Betty Lou McDowell Gutteridge is on the far right. Betty Lou's parents owned Macs Beach.

Five

AUBURNDALE WORKS

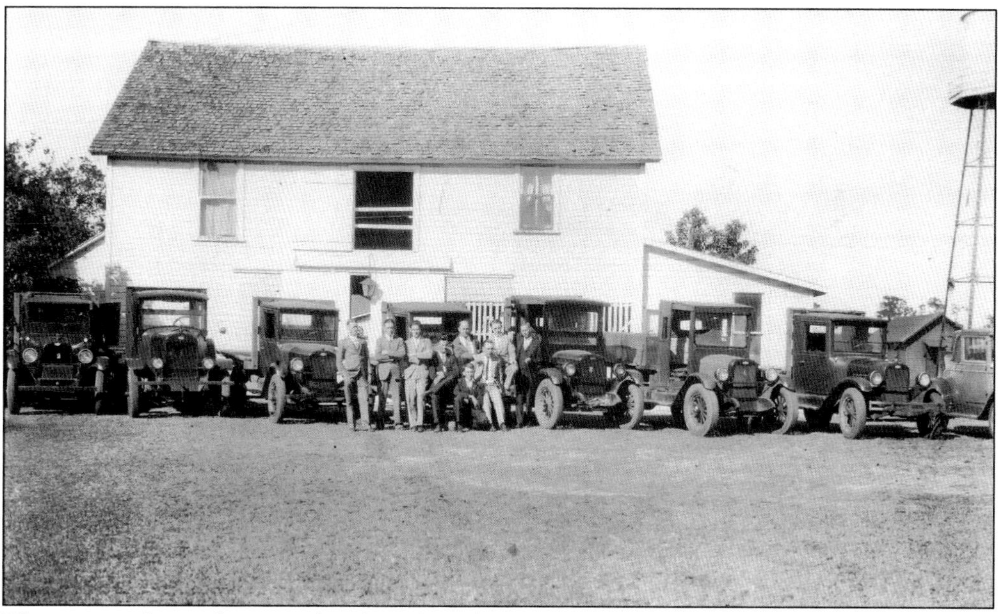

The citrus industry dominated early Auburndale. Almost everyone had at least a small grove, if only in the backyard. Support services were vital. Jere Stambaugh came to Auburndale in 1922 from Akron. He maintained a fleet of trucks, shown here, that was used in the growing, gathering, production, and distribution of his groves, as well as those of others. The new middle school was named in his honor for his many contributions to the community.

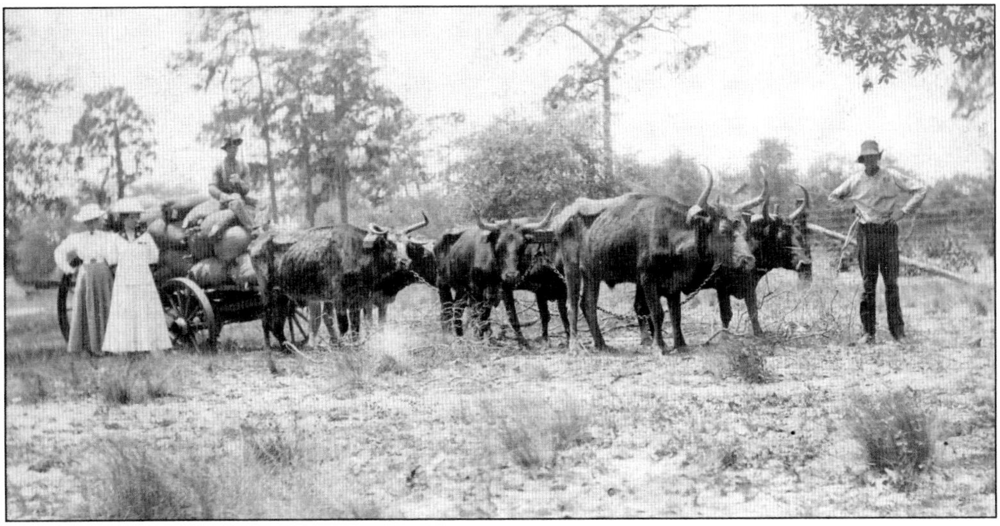

Alice and Mary Kaszer pose above with two unidentified men beside an ox-drawn wagon loaded with citrus fertilizer in 1911. By this time, the trees killed in the major freeze in 1894 had been replanted and were producing. Each tree was planted, fertilized, and set by hand. Irrigation was dependent on rainwater. Spraying was done with one person on a wagon working a hand pump while another activated the spray head. In the image below, two unidentified men spray citrus trees. When the oranges were ready to be harvested, a picker carried his ladder to reach the top of the tree. Each orange was placed in a large sack that the worker carried around his or her neck. When full, the sack was emptied into wooden boxes to go to the processing plant. It was a hot, dirty, and dangerous job with frequent injuries.

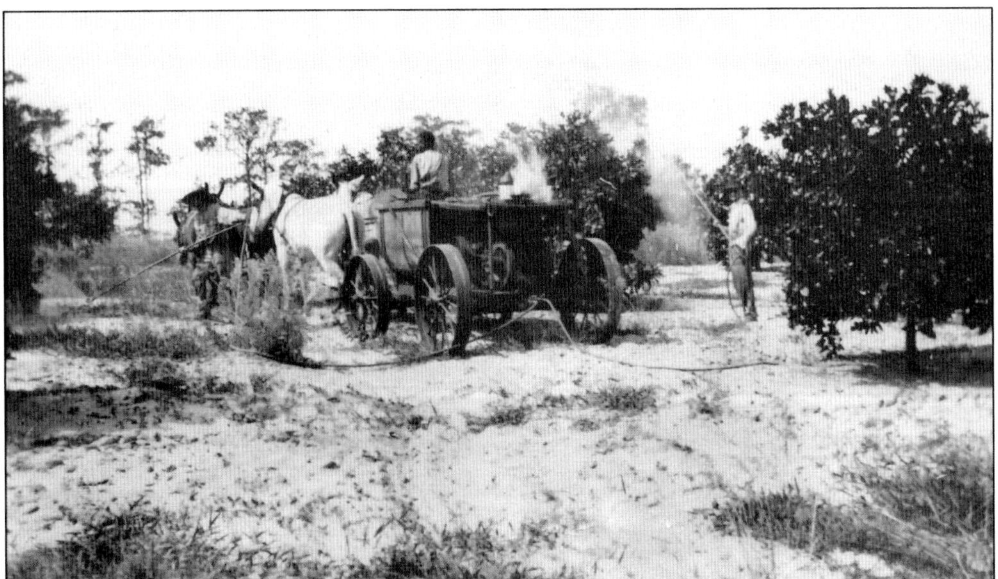

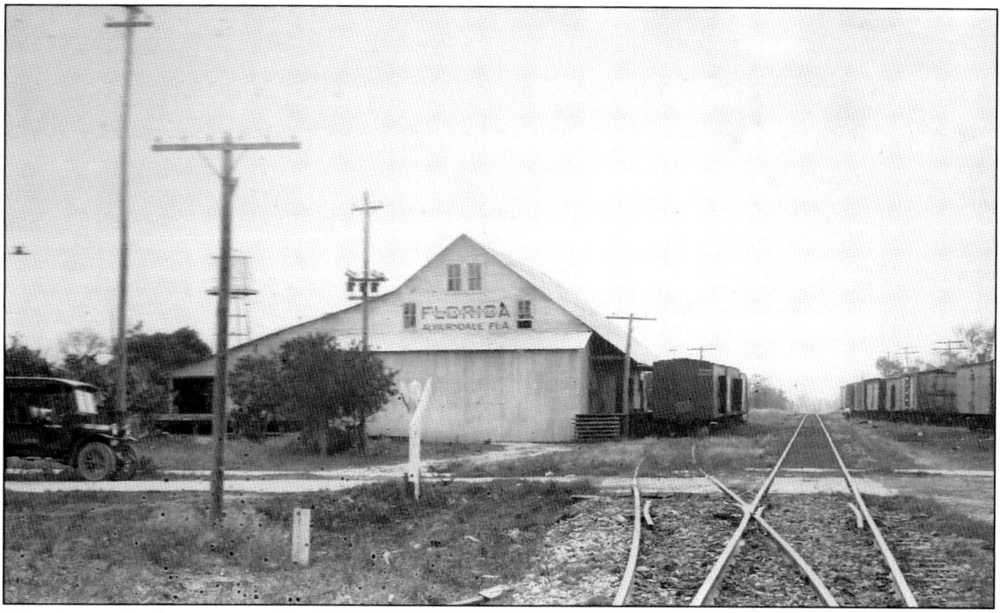

The Citrus Exchange was formed in 1901. It was a co-op composed of local growers. The exchange building was constructed in the middle of a grove on Orange Street along the railroad. Fruit was brought in by wagon and sorted by hand. Each orange was wrapped in protective paper and packed for shipment. Fresh fruit could go from the tree to a table in the North in a few days.

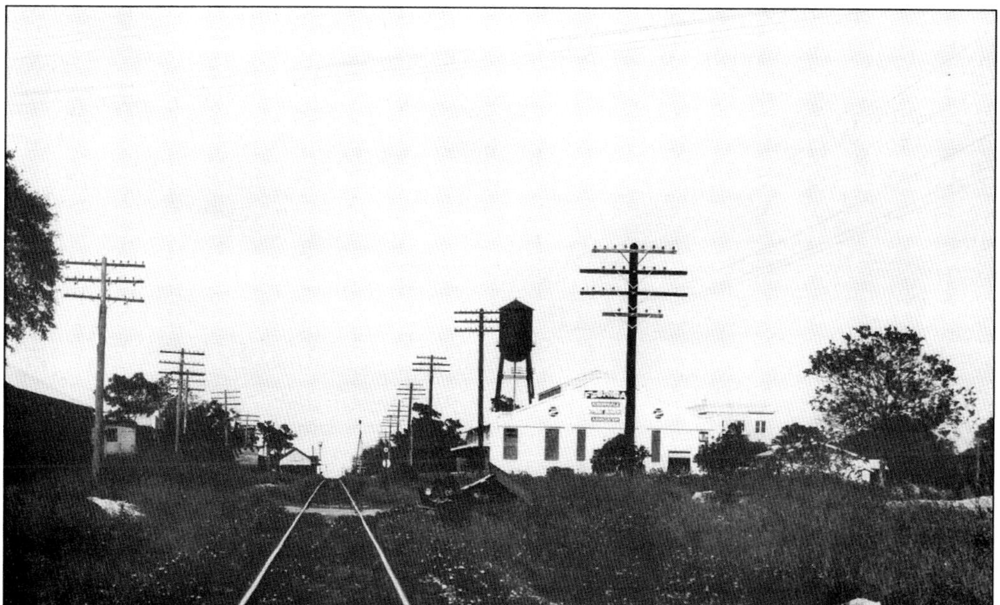

A new, larger Citrus Exchange building was constructed in 1925 near the location of the first one. Fruit was processed here until 1960, when the exchange was sold to Adams Packing Company and used for storage. After being vacant for many years, the exchange was restored. It is listed in the National Register of Historic Places.

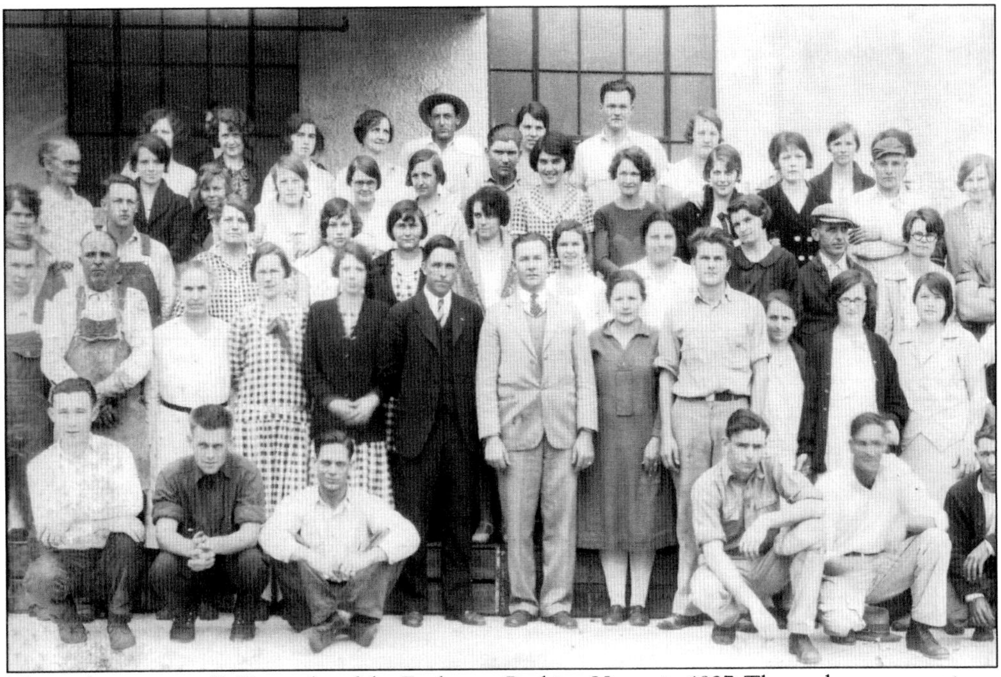

This is the entire staff, 56 people, of the Exchange Packing House in 1927. The exchange sometimes employed whole families, including teenagers, for the many jobs, including sorting, packing, and loading the fruit. Some workers specialized in making the boxes the fruit were shipped in. Many Auburndale families were supported during the Great Depression by this plant.

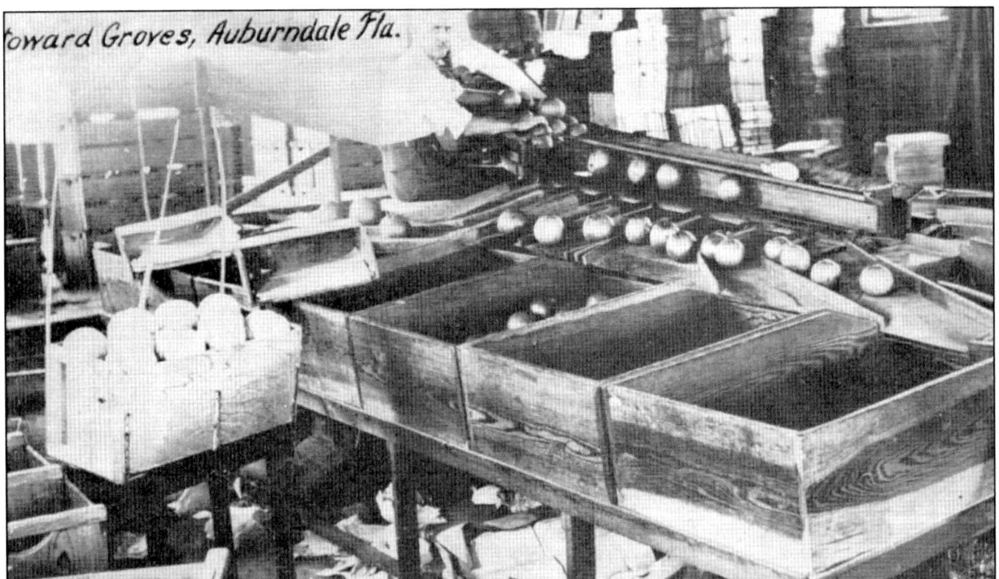

In the Howard citrus-processing plant, a man sits while he sorts oranges by size. The fruit rolled down a trough and into slots that varied in size. The fruit then rolled into boxes and were loaded onto the train. This plant was owned by Edwin Howard, whose father donated part of their homestead for the depot, park, and Auburndale's first school.

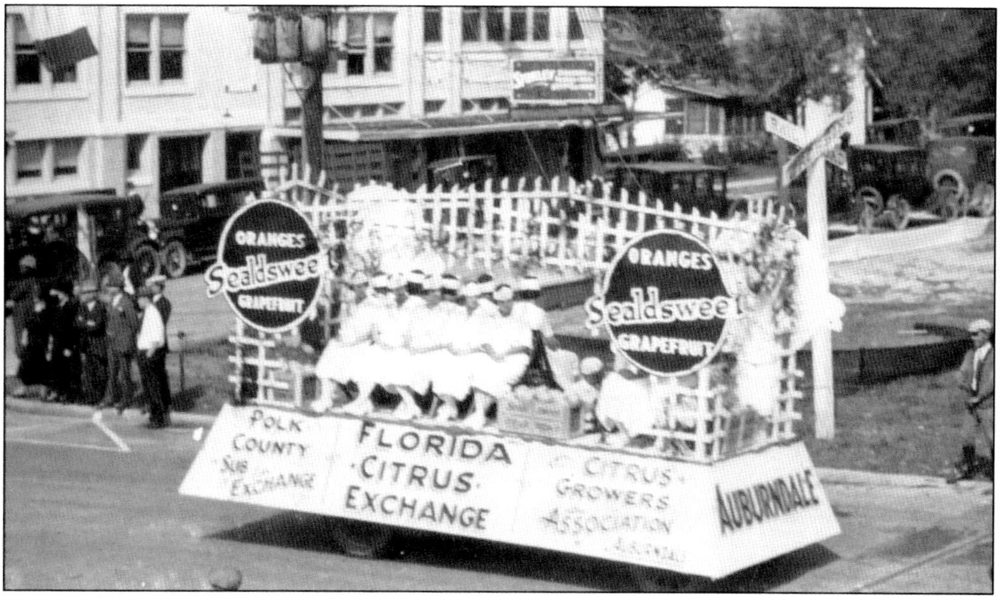

In 1923, the Orange Festival was created to provide exposure to the trade. This Citrus Exchange float was entered into the annual Orange Festival parade in Winter Haven. Seated from left to right, Auburndale beauties Lessie Smith, Montene Canon, Burma Dobson, Thelma Edministon, and Grace Hebb ride the float. Dewey Jolley is driving the truck. The festival, later called the Citrus Exposition, was held for over 75 years, except during World War II, when it could not open due to shortages.

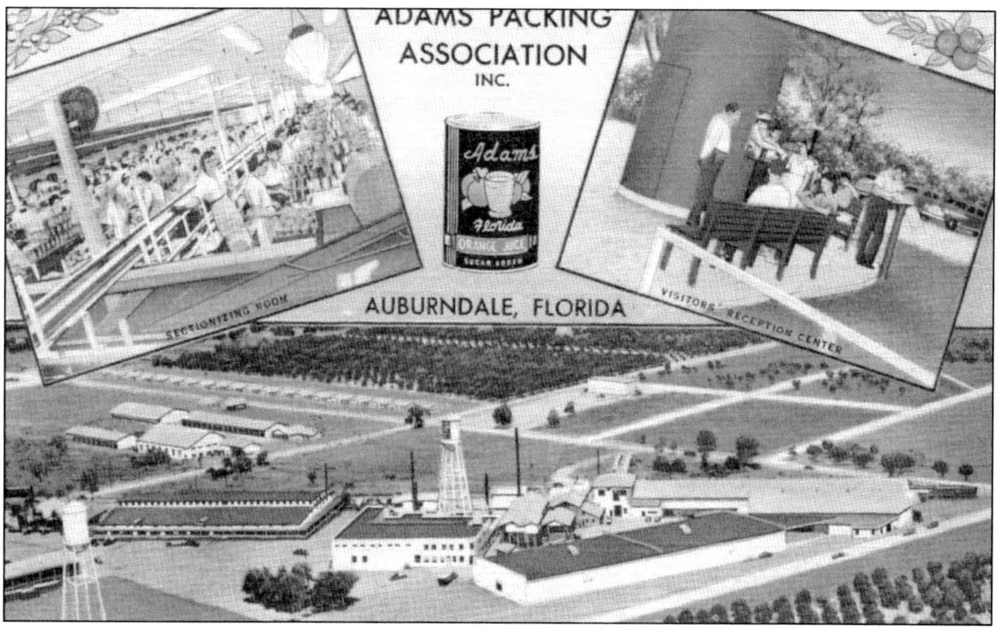

In 1925, Dr. Charles Adams, a dentist from Chicago, opened Adams Packing Company. This vintage postcard was distributed about 1940, the same year a new canning section was added to the plant. In 1948, the University of Florida Citrus Research Center in Lake Alfred developed a way to concentrate juice, and Adams installed a large frozen operation. By 1962, Adams was the largest, most modern citrus packing plant in the world.

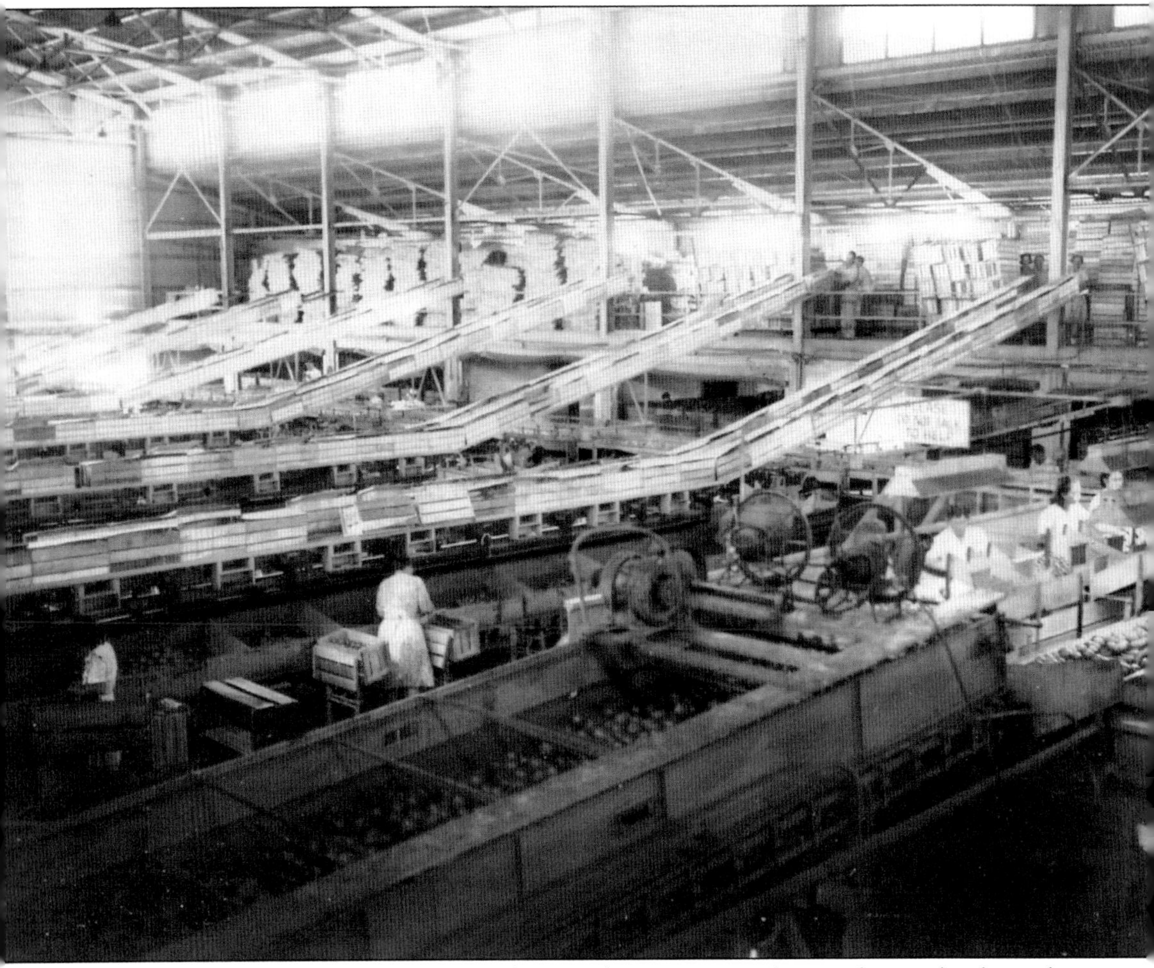

This photograph shows workers at Adams Packing Company boxing fruit to be shipped out. After the trucks brought the freshly picked oranges in from the grove, the oranges were placed on conveyor belts. Inside the plant, oranges were sorted into crates and again moved by conveyor belt to the loading dock.

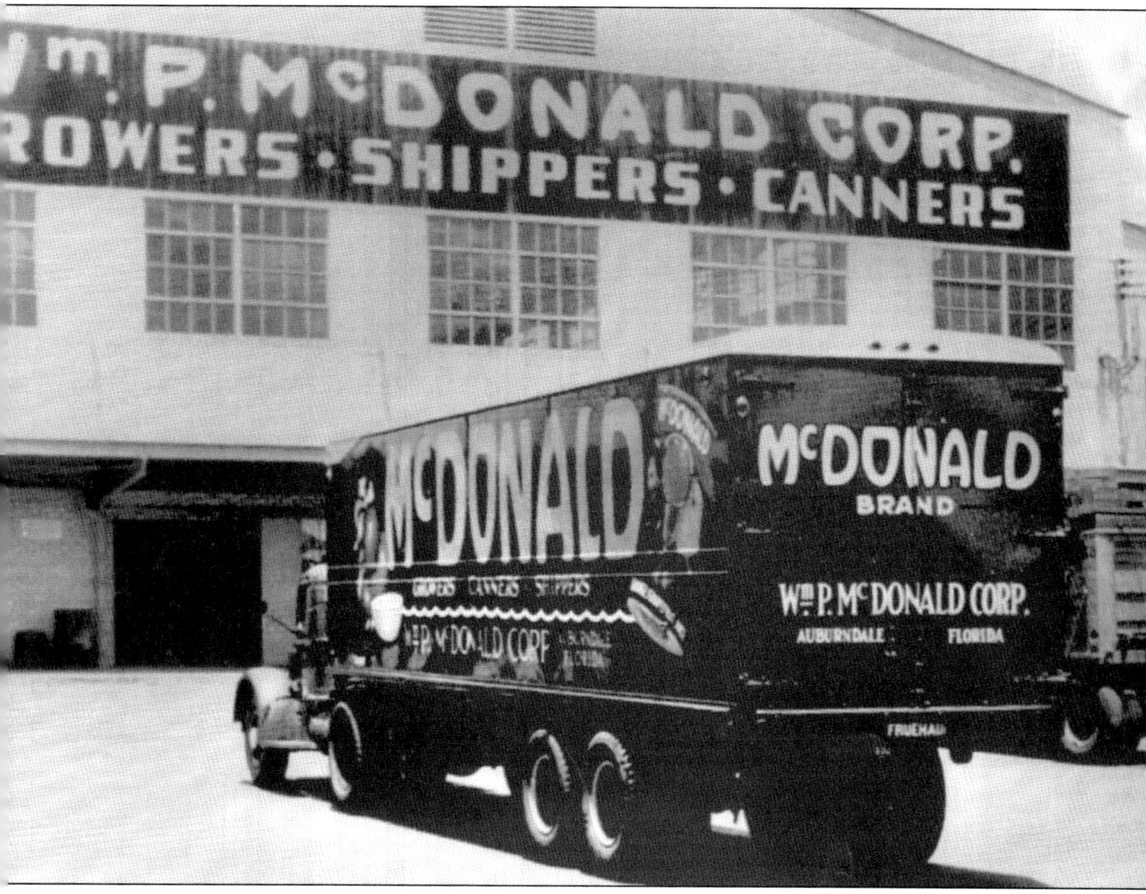

In 1925, the citrus industry was strong. The Auburndale Citrus Growers Association and the Lake Ariana Citrus Growers Association were active at the time, and Adams Packing Company, Howard's, Baynard's, McDonald, Chase, and Stewart packinghouses were in operation. In 1929, a new threat emerged in the citrus industry. The Mediterranean fruit fly was found in Orlando and quickly spread. This little fly was capable of wiping out entire groves.

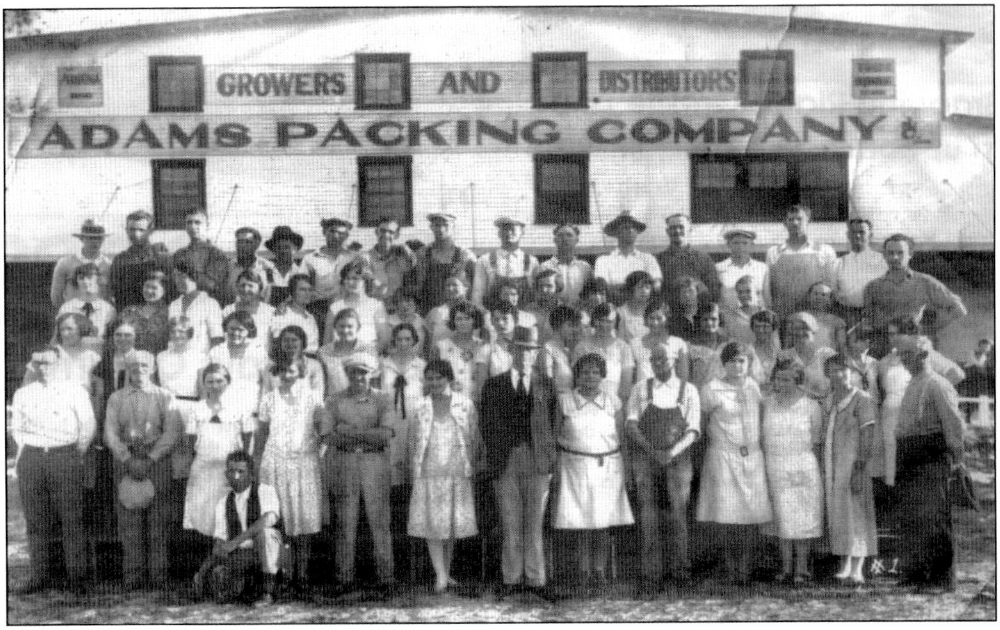

In 1950, the citrus workers of Adams took time from their duties to have a picture taken. Adams Packing Company was the largest employer in Auburndale. There were few families who did not have at least one member employed by Adams. By 1960, a series of devastating freezes had taken their toll on the industry, and groves were being planted farther south. It was the start of the end of an era for Auburndale.

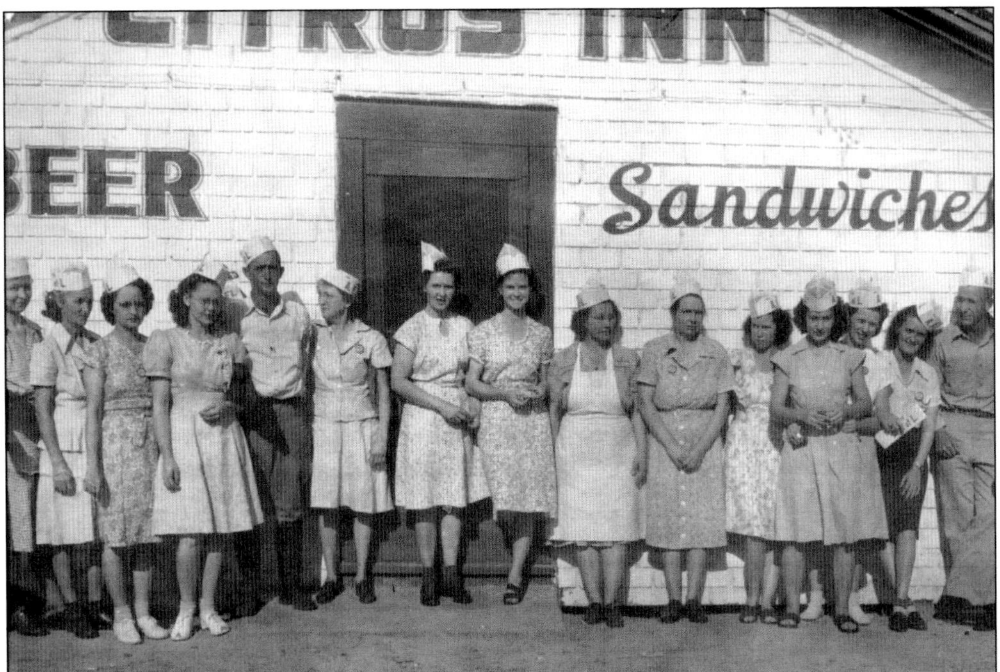

During the 1940s, the Citrus Inn was located across the street from Adams Packing House. It was a gathering place for some of the Adams workforce to relax, unwind, and grab a quick sandwich or a cool drink to help the long workday go by.

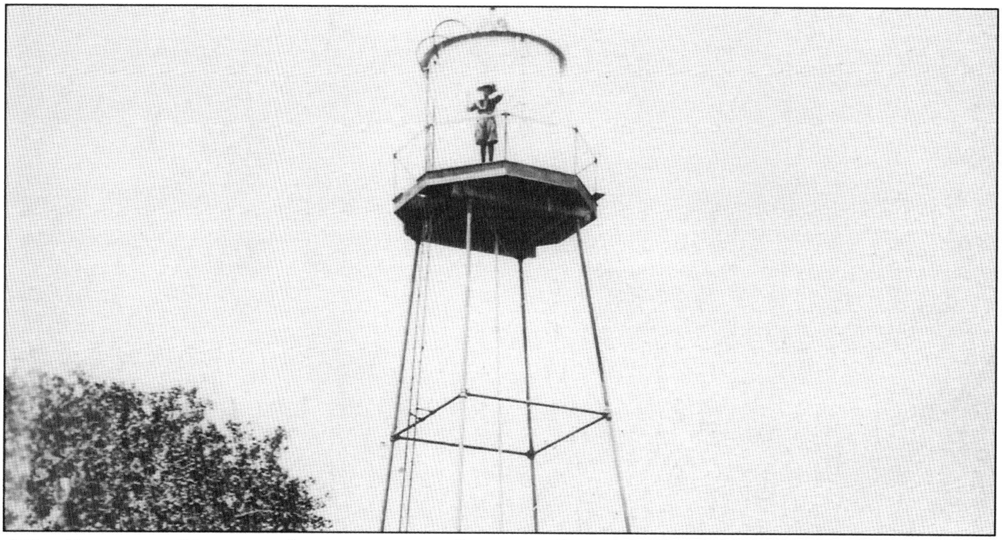

Alice Kaszer would go anywhere to capture the scene she wanted. Nothing was too high, too low, or too far for her. On this day, she climbed the water tower to get an aerial view of the surrounding territory. Nothing seemed to faze Alice. She would go anywhere or do just about anything to get a photograph.

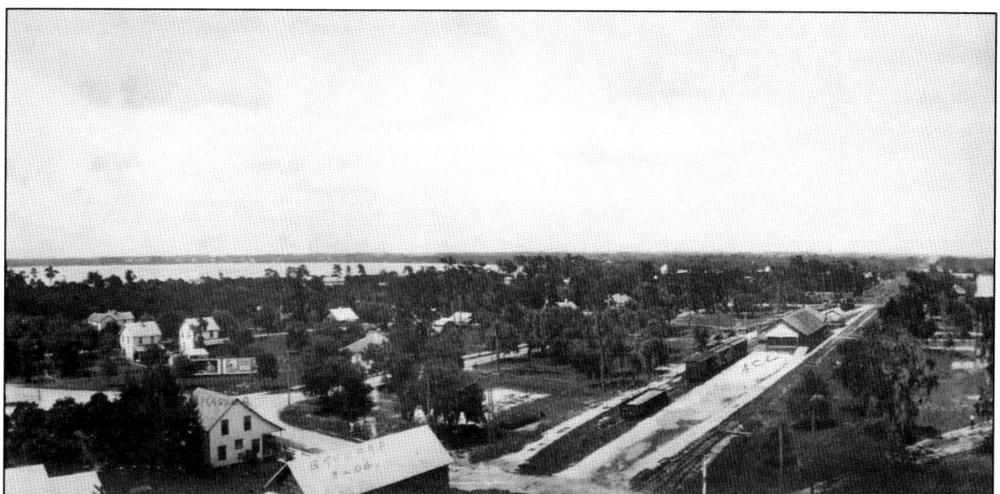

In this aerial view from the water tower, the roof of the Kaszer house and the Baynard Packing House are seen on the left. The packinghouse burned in 1944. The depot is in the center right, and the park is on the far right. Along the railroad track to the left (not in view) are the Furniture Company, the Howard Packing Plant, and the Chase Packing House.

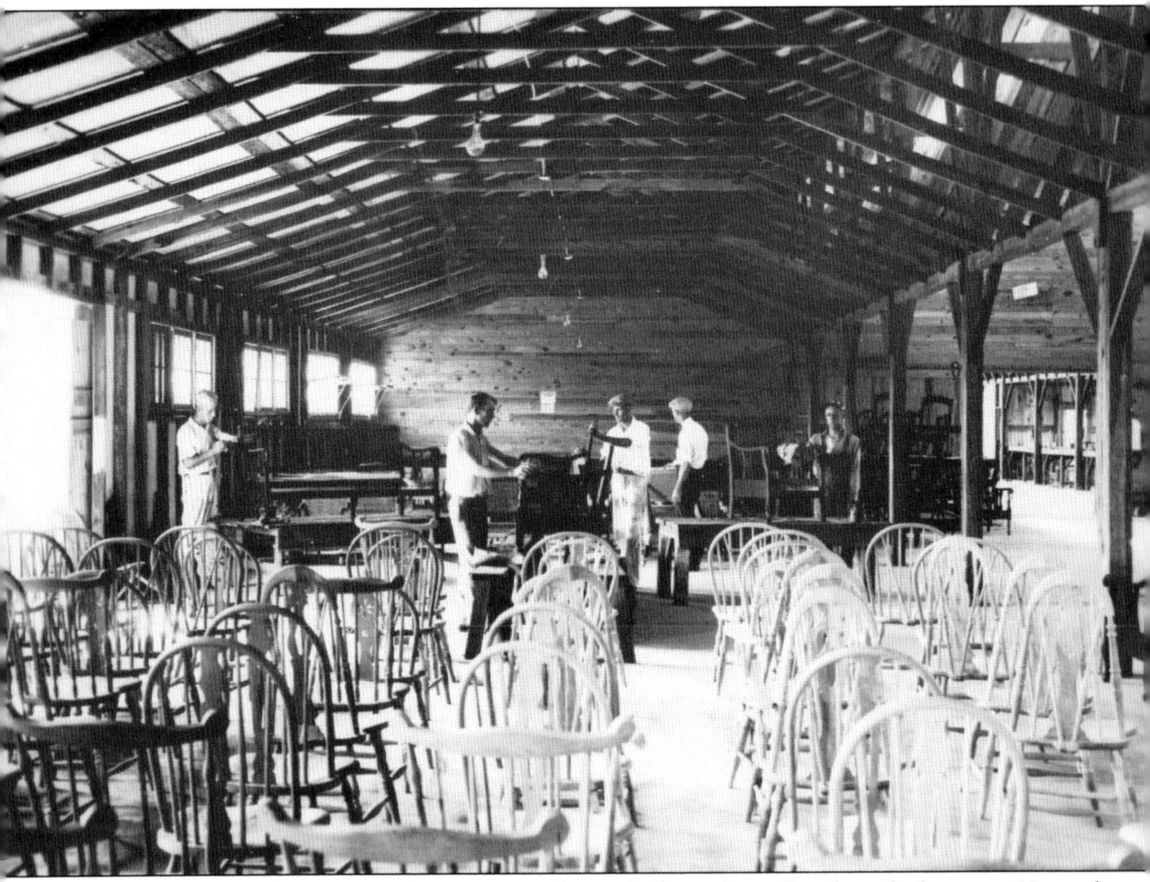

The Auburndale Furniture Company was located along the railroad tracks between Howard Street and Ariana Avenue. It was known throughout the South for its well-made sofas, chairs, and tables. Each piece was hand cut and assembled, and the wood was cut from local trees. The chairs in this photograph are all one of a kind.

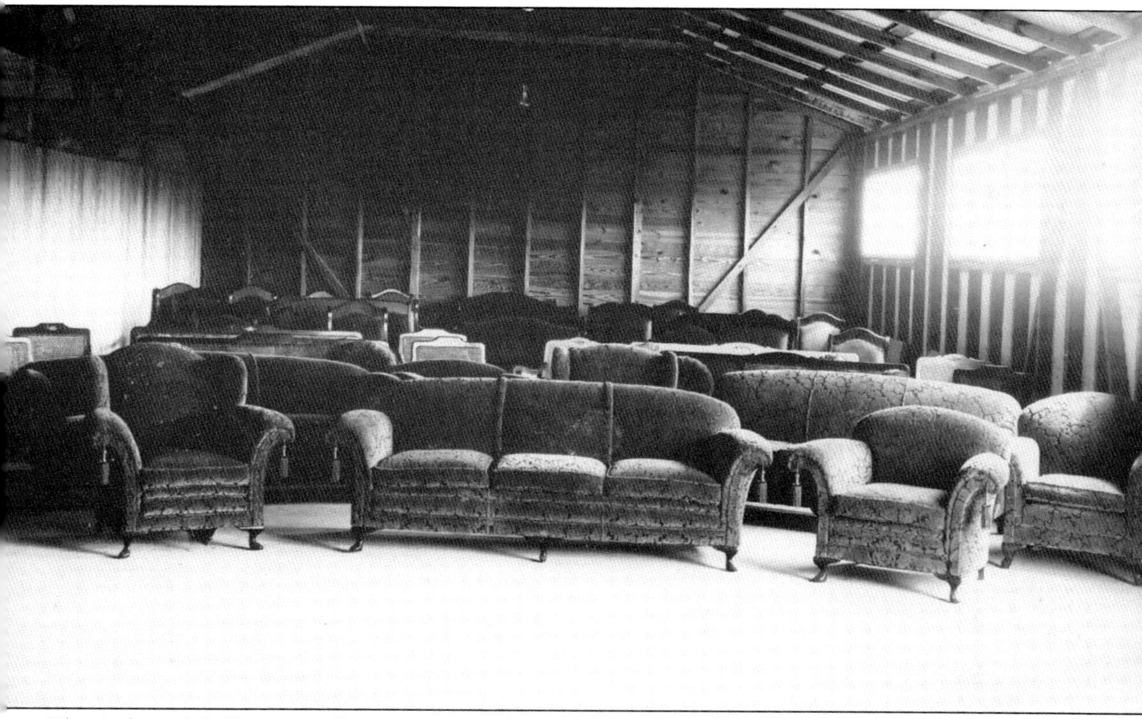

The Auburndale Furniture Company not only made wooden furniture but also stuffed sofas and chairs, as shown here. All furniture was made by hand. The furniture company was in business from 1925 until 1931, when it caught fire and burned. It was not replaced.

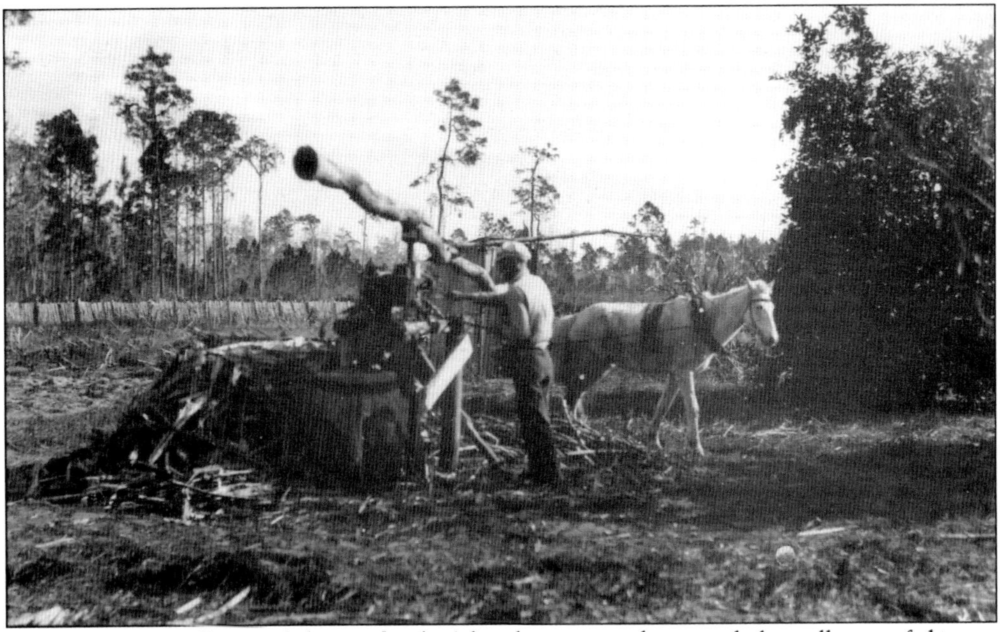

Sugar cane grew well in sandy bottomlands. After the cane was harvested, the stalks were fed into a stone grinder to squeeze the juice out. A horse walked in a circle around the grinder to turn it, and the cane juice came out via a spout. It was then cooked in large kettles until it became syrup.

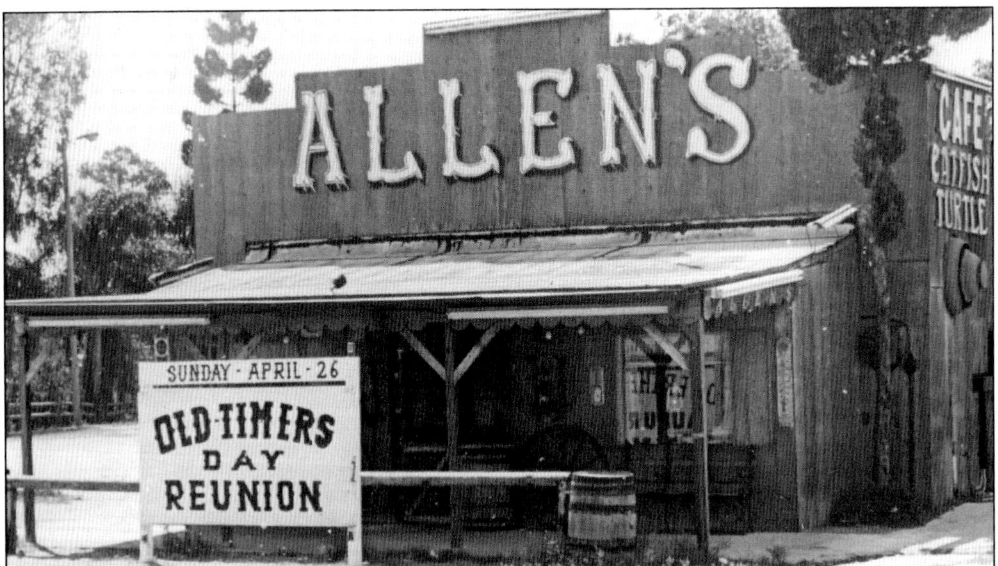

Carl Allen's Catfish Café was well known for Southern food. Catfish was the specialty, but people could also order fried rattlesnake, if it was in season of course. The café walls were covered with pieces of Auburndale history. Carl was an Auburndale native, a writer, a yarn-spinner, and an avid local historian. The once-a-week bluegrass jam sessions and once-a-year Old-timer's Day at the café were always well attended. The café closed after Carl's death in 1996 and has been torn down.

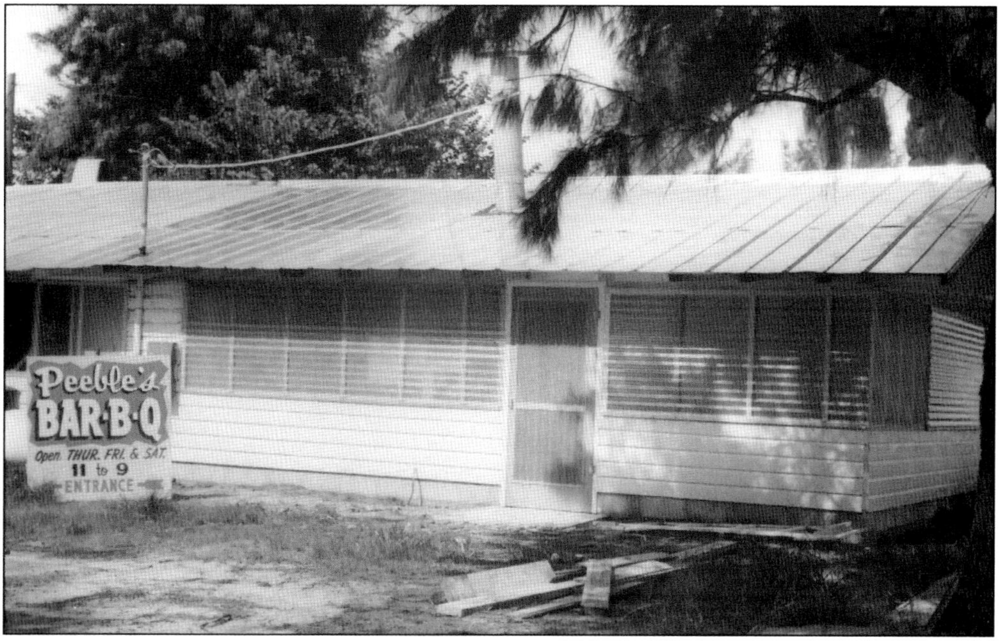

Peebles Bar-B-Q, located on Old Dixie Highway, has been an Auburndale landmark for more than 70 years. Owners Ellie and Gladys Peebles opened their rustic barbecue restaurant in 1947. The building, fixtures, menu, and recipes have all remained unchanged since then. The parking lot is unpaved, there is no air-conditioning, and the windows are screened with shutters—only the people have changed. The family continues the tradition.

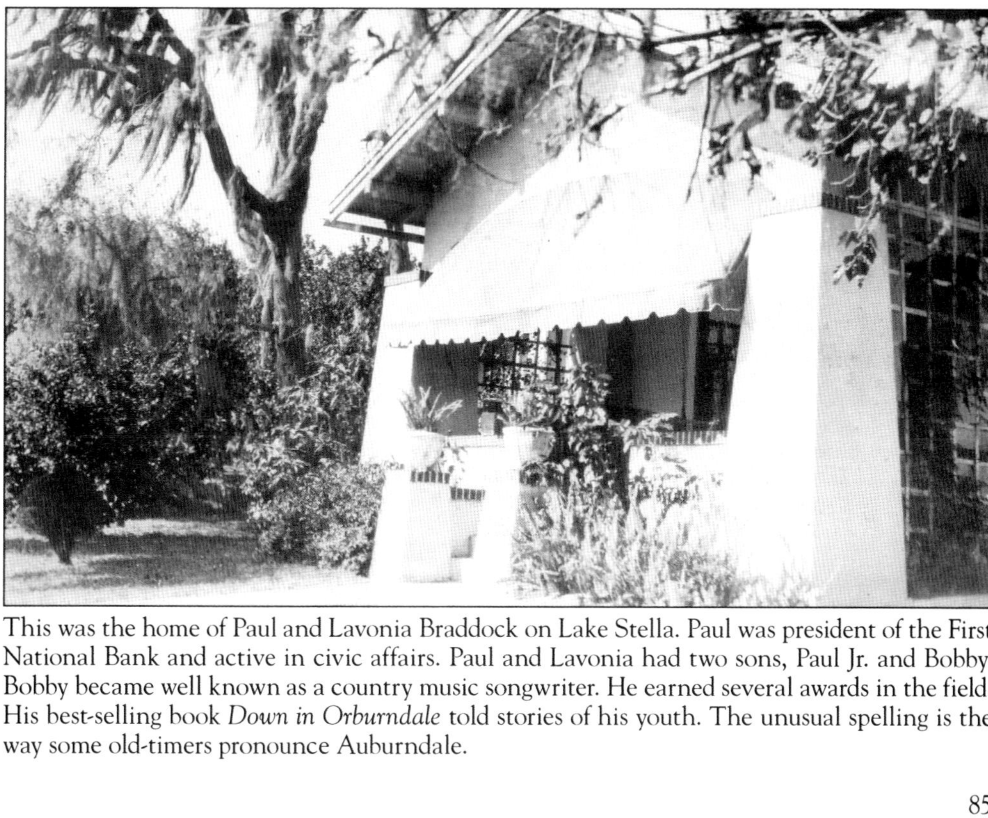

This was the home of Paul and Lavonia Braddock on Lake Stella. Paul was president of the First National Bank and active in civic affairs. Paul and Lavonia had two sons, Paul Jr. and Bobby. Bobby became well known as a country music songwriter. He earned several awards in the field. His best-selling book *Down in Orburndale* told stories of his youth. The unusual spelling is the way some old-timers pronounce Auburndale.

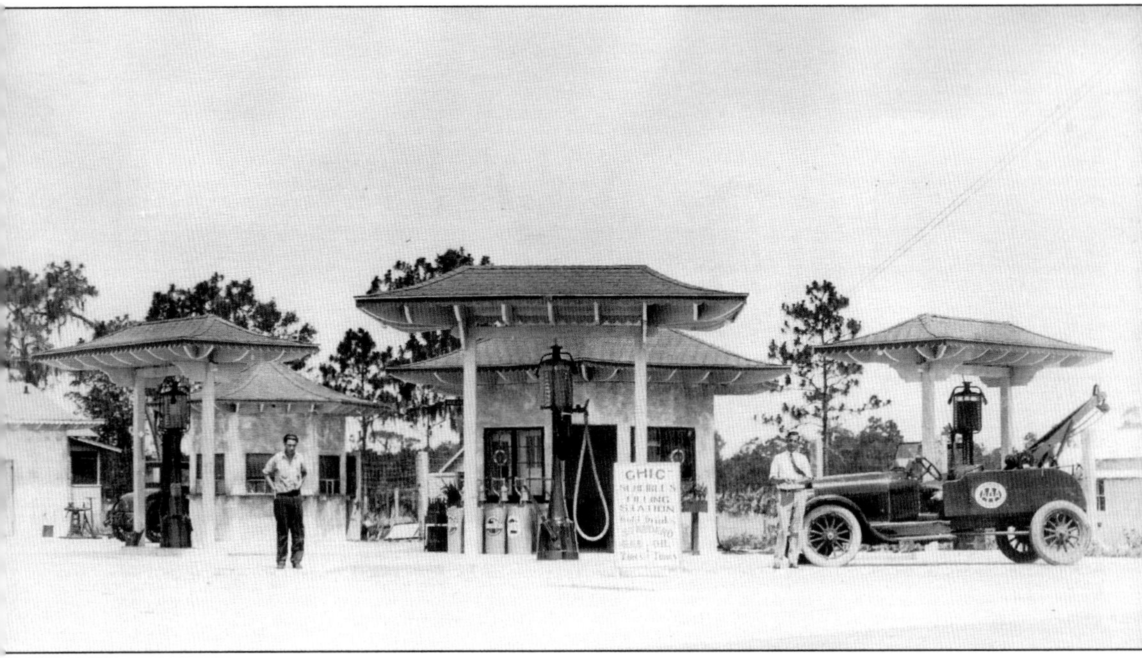

Jay T. Fallin's Service Station was on the corner of Pontotoc Street and Bartow Avenue, shown here around 1945. Fallin sold gas and automobile supplies and offered wrecker service. He often bragged that the tires he replaced on Auburndale's first fire truck, a LaFrance, served the city for many years. Jay's home at 212 Howard Street is now the Magnolia Tearoom.

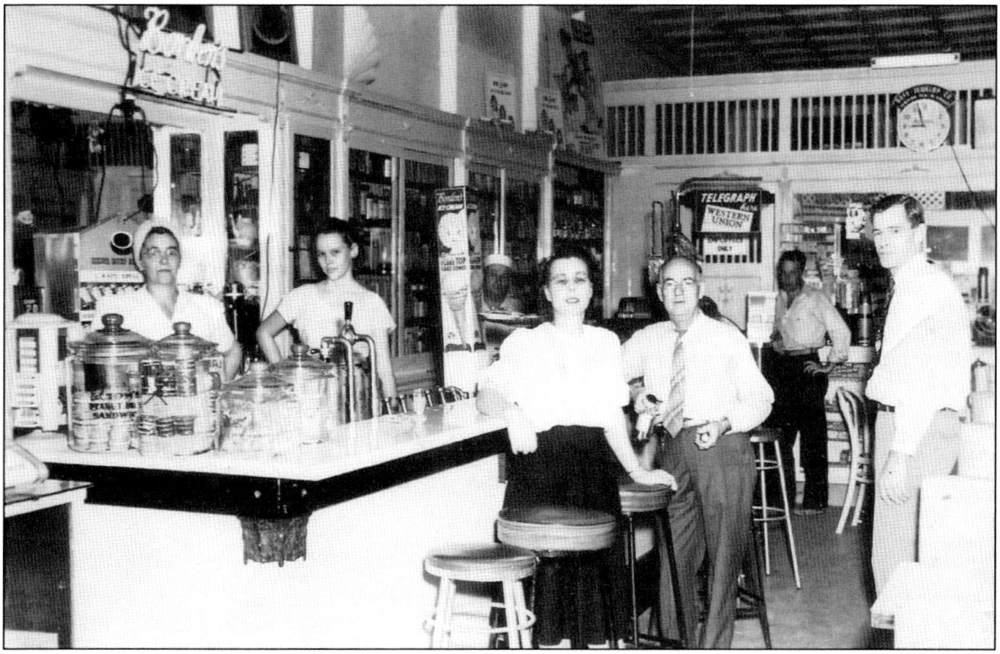

William and Ola Hobby's Drug Store, located in the Patterson Building, opened in 1925. In addition to medication and soda fountain goods, Dr. Hobby stocked the shelves in his small shop with some household items. After he retired, this building housed a clothing store. Later, it was an insurance office.

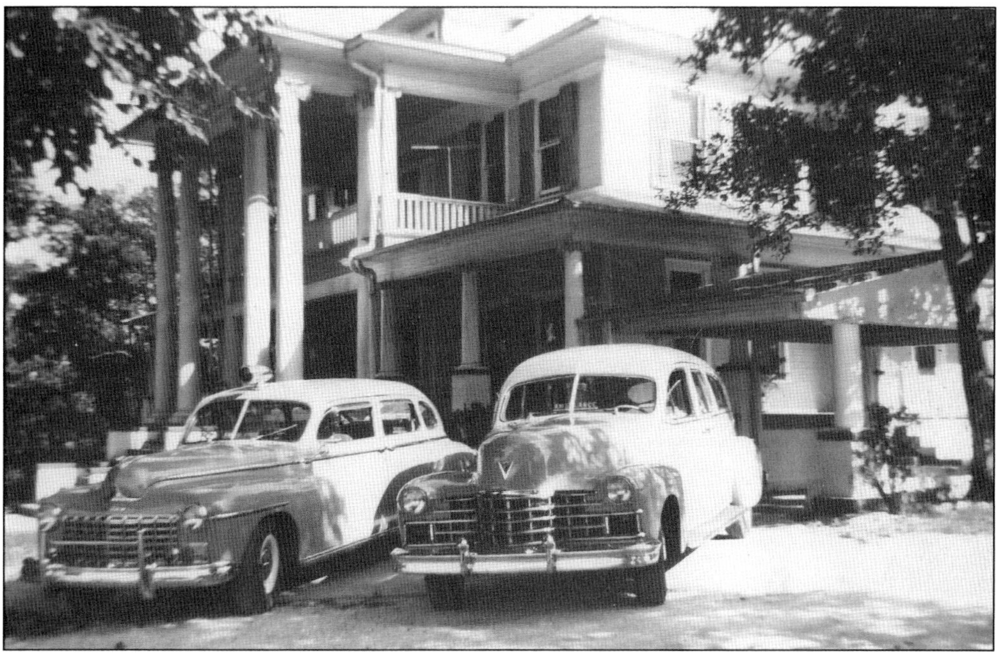
This was the Kersey Funeral Home shortly after Walter Kersey purchased the building from Ruth Penn, Mile Baynard's daughter, in 1951. This had been the Baynard's second home. In the days before the county had emergency medical transport, Mr. Kersey had personnel on call for 24-hour ambulance service.

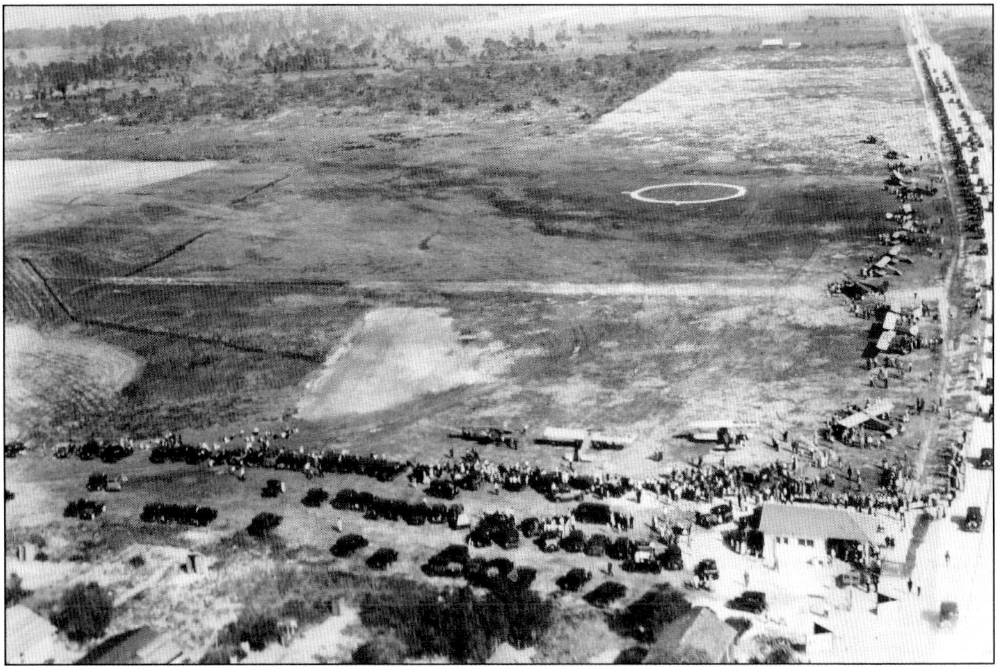

The Auburndale Airport was located east of Bennett Street, along Bridgers Avenue. In this c. 1940 image, the planes are lined up for an air show. Harrison Fraser was a local mechanic and pilot who offered flying lessons and airplane rides. In 1942, he was shot and killed by an irate customer who did not want to pay for the repairs of his plane. This photograph was taken by Alice Kaszer from an airplane.

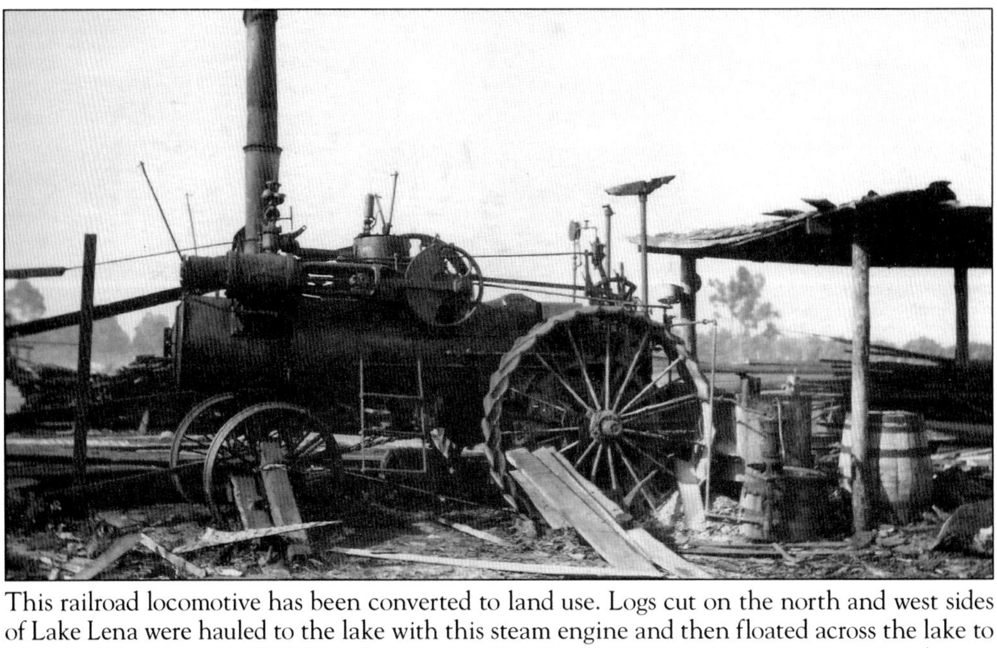

This railroad locomotive has been converted to land use. Logs cut on the north and west sides of Lake Lena were hauled to the lake with this steam engine and then floated across the lake to the sawmill at the end of Pilaklakaha Avenue. Shortly after Werner Jones came to town, he was injured when the steam engine in the locomotive blew up. Elmer Cline repaired the engine and the sawmill, and they were back in business.

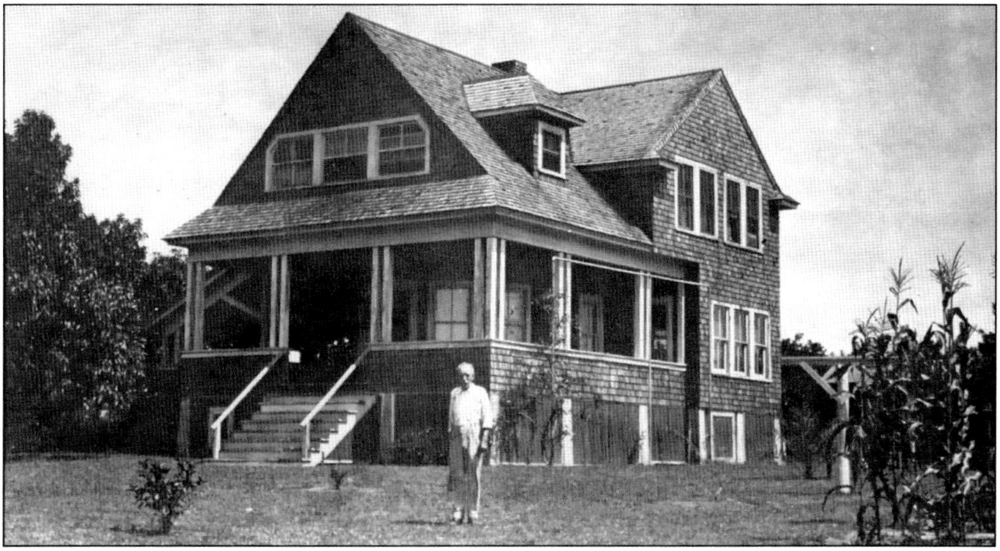

This house on Lake Ariania belonged to James and Mary Morrow. James was a citrus producer. In their will, the Morrows left this house, the property, and money for a hospital. The house was moved across the street and used as a home for unwed mothers and then torn down. The Morrow Hospital existed for 20 years, and then it became a rehab center and then a hospice.

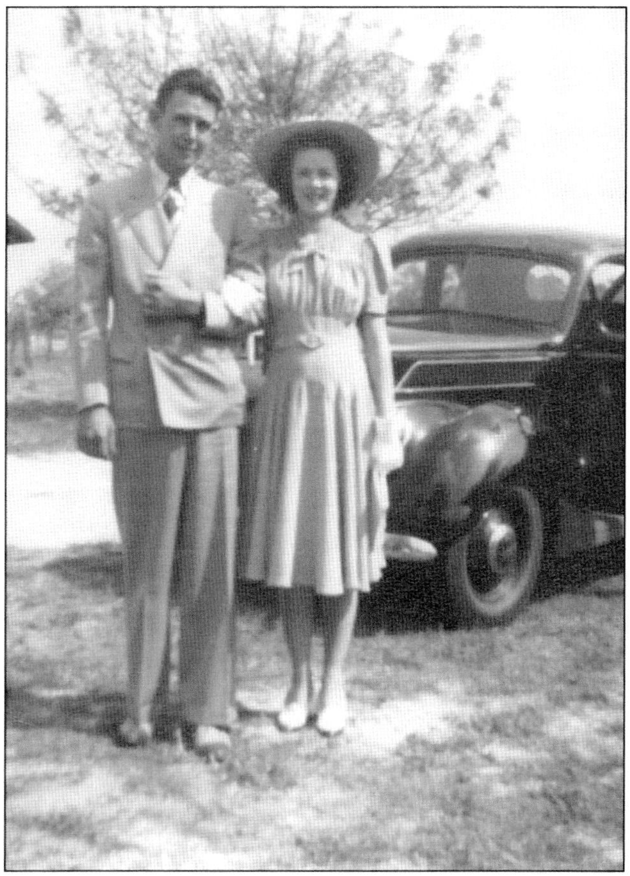

Barbara and Samuel Killebrew owned a company on Thornhill Road that built equipment for citrus production. Samuel was inducted into the Citrus Hall of Fame for inventing a machine in 1952 that greatly reduced the labor needed for spreading fertilizer. He also improved the wind machines used to protect the groves from freezes.

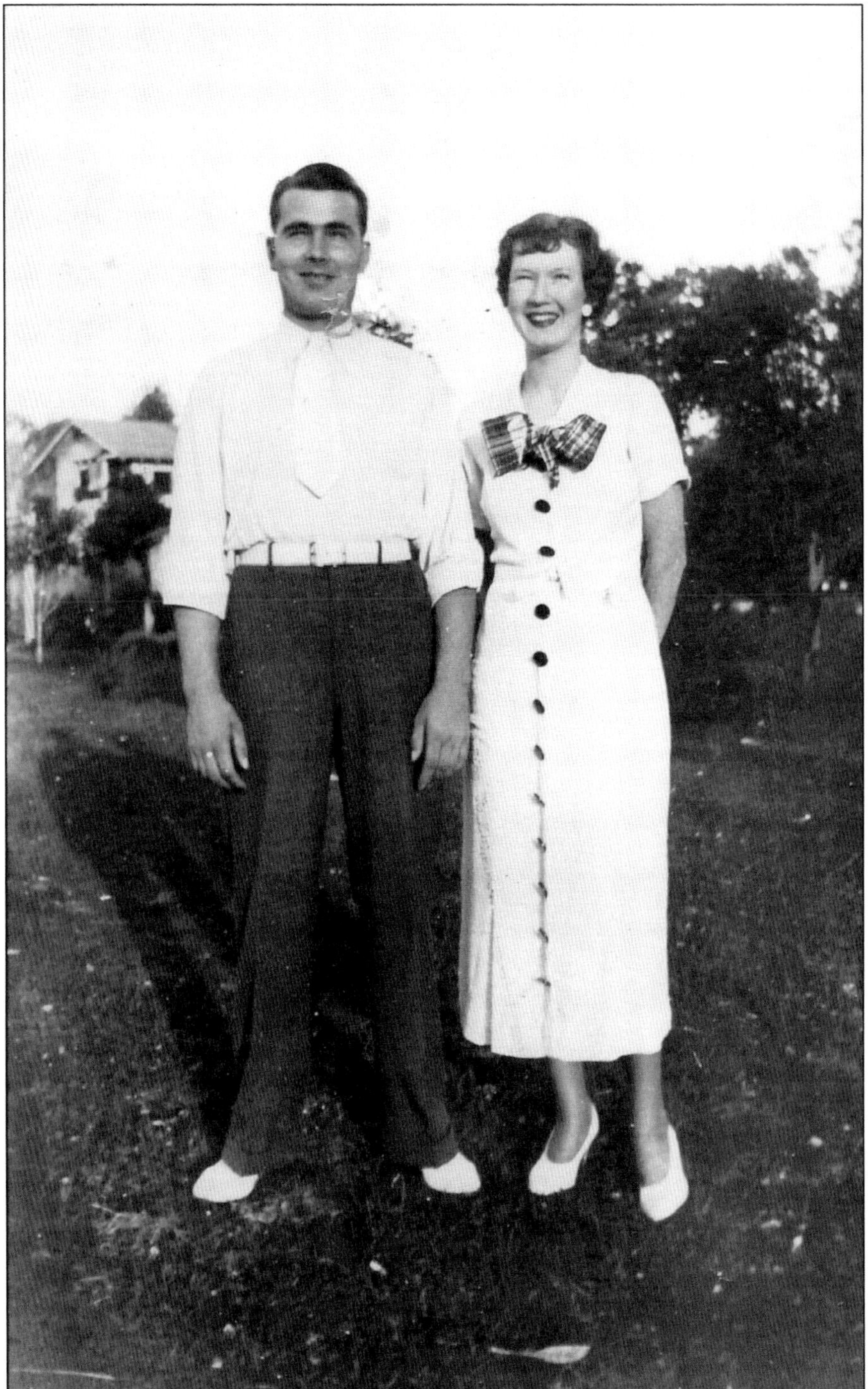

In 1951, Fred and Vivian Cline Bowen's Drug Store was located in the Jones Building on Main Street. In addition to the pharmacy, the store had a soda fountain and sold sandwiches and toiletries. Young people frequented this store for the enormous banana splits. The All American Store had previously occupied this site.

Six

The Boom Heard All Over Florida

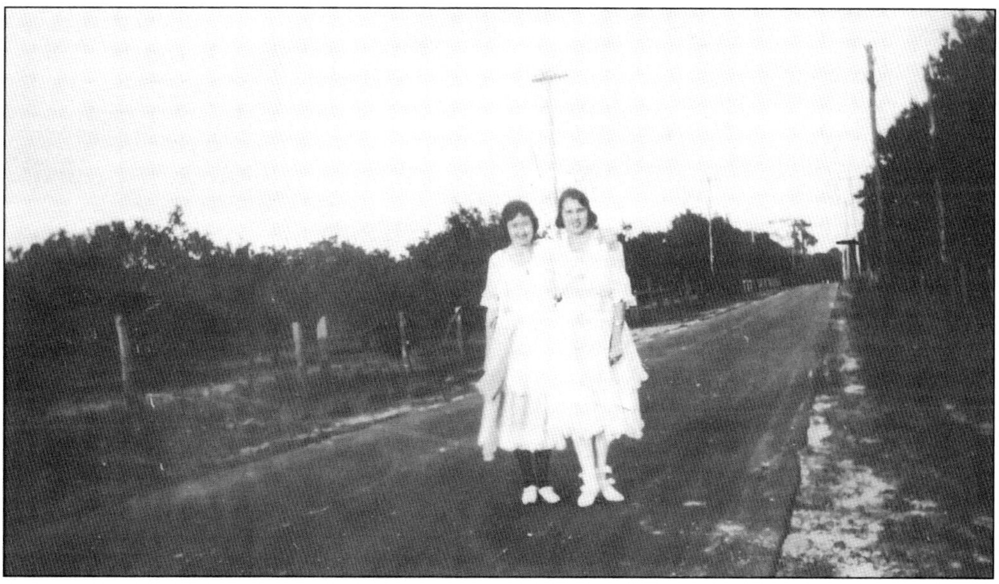

Marion Hines (left) and Leta Manning stand along the Dixie Highway (Pilaklakaha Avenue) in Auburndale in 1918. In 1915, Carl Fisher, an investor from Chicago, completed the first paved highway in Florida along the east coast, with an extension across the state to Tampa. The nine-foot-wide Dixie Highway entered Auburndale on the east side of Lake Ariana, continued down West Park, wound its way through town, and continued to Lakeland.

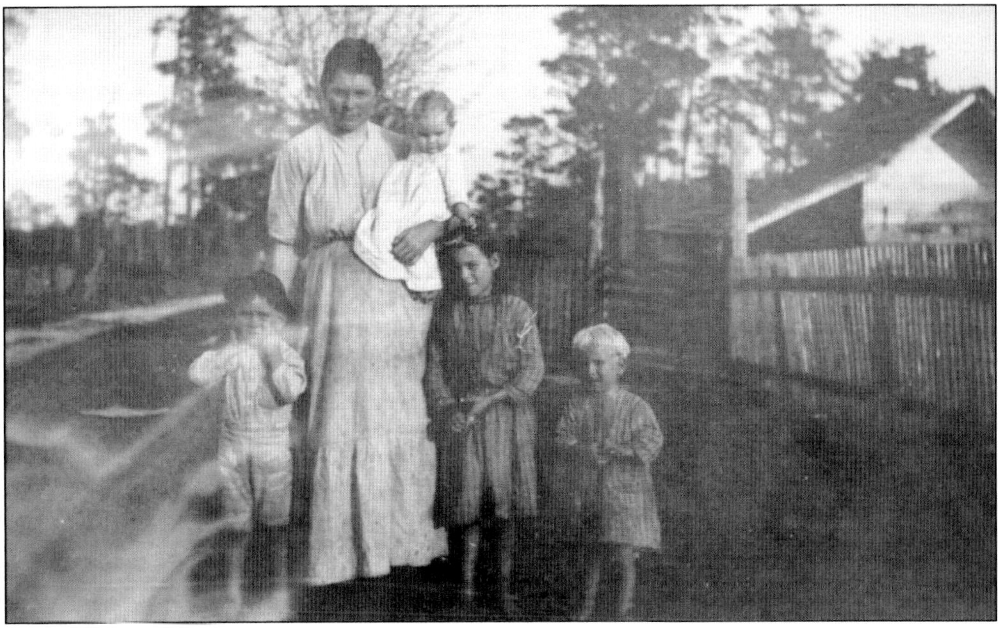

The Clark family poses at their farm along the Dixie Highway west of Auburndale. In most areas, the road followed the railroad, but after leaving Auburndale it turned northwest along the Collins, Griffin, and Fussell homesteads. For many years, every paved road in Florida was part of the Dixie Highway System. The name was retained in some areas.

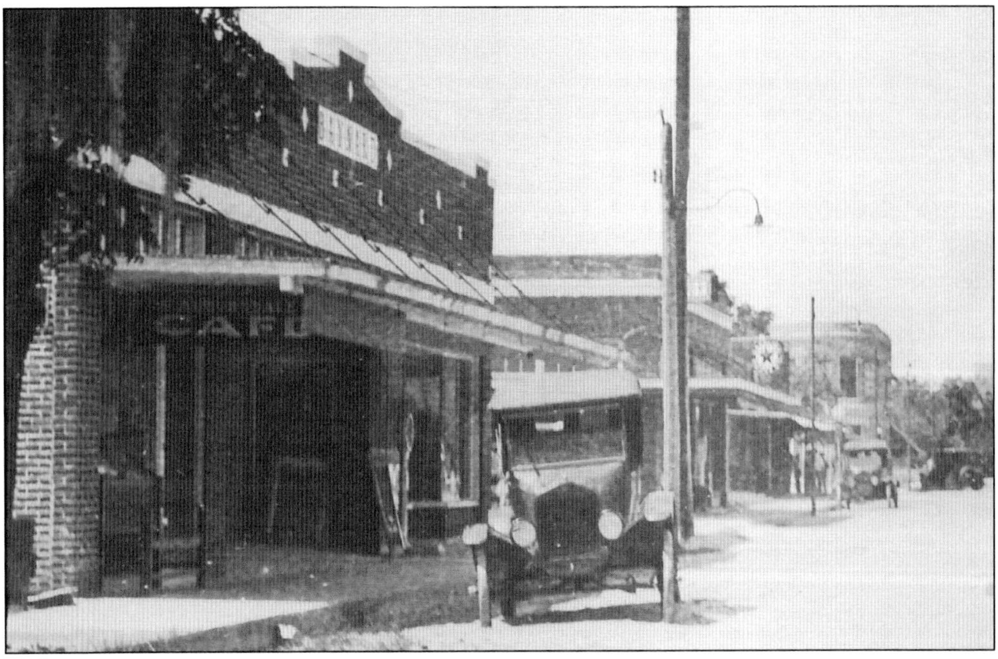

By the early 1920s, Henry Ford had improved his assembly line and was selling his Model T for $360, well within reach of the average American family—the automobile had forever lost its status as a curiosity. By this time, more people in the United States had cars than had bathtubs. With a new paved road to drive on, they headed south. Some people brought tents; others put a cover on their Fords and made a kind of camper, the forerunner of the RV.

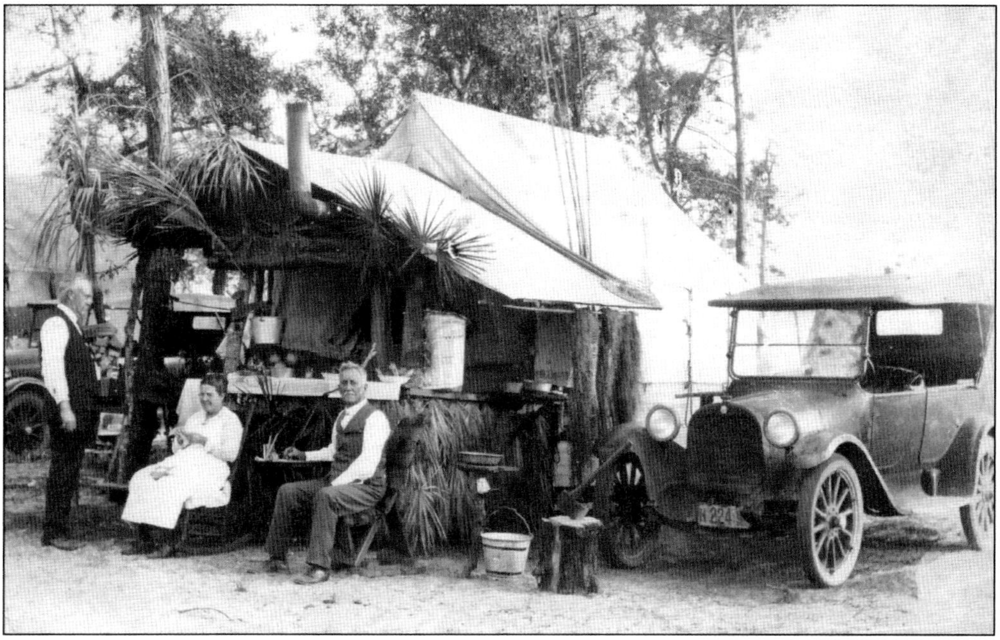

"Tin can tourists" Hugh, Retta, and Andy Waycroff pose in their tent near Auburndale. It is unknown if the term "tin can tourist" came from the Tin Lizzies they drove or the tins of food they brought with them, but the name stuck. They were the only people who ever lived in and out of a can. One local said the men came with one shirt and a $20 bill and never changed either.

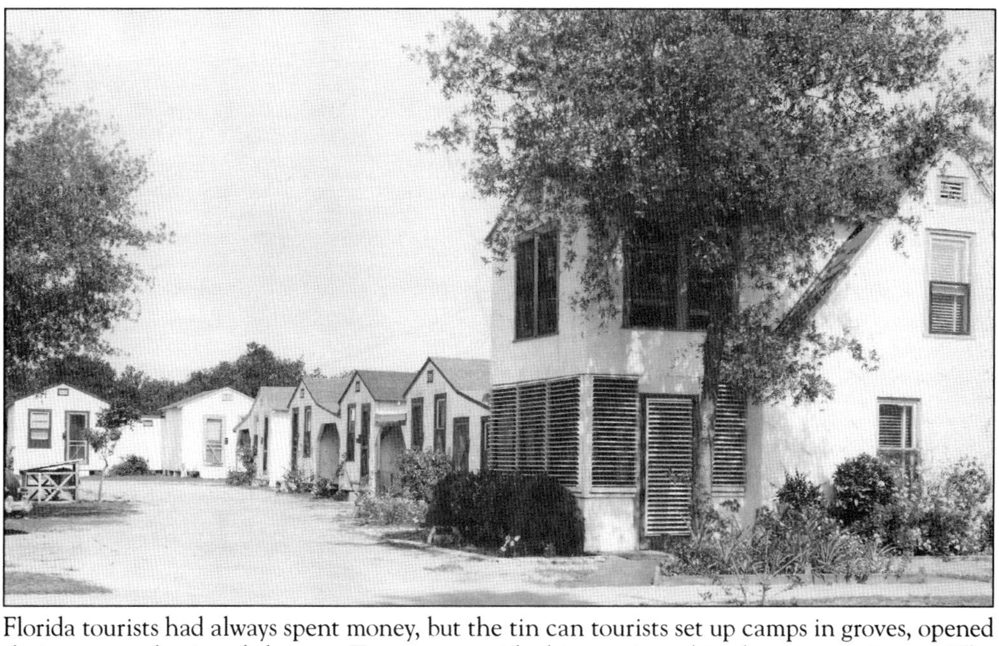

Florida tourists had always spent money, but the tin can tourists set up camps in groves, opened their cans, and enjoyed the sun. To compete with this, tourist cabins began to spring up. The Jacaranda Cabins on Pine Street offered a place to park the car, a room to sleep in, and a one-for-all toilet, but not much more.

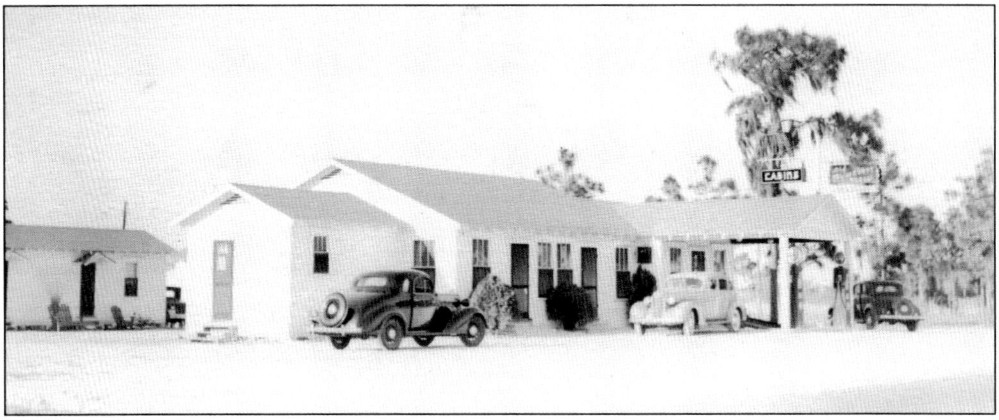

Most of the Nelson's Cabins on Lake Lena on Magnolia Avenue were one room with outdoor washstands and no running water. But they appealed to the less-than-rich visitors. The establishment also rented out campsites for those who wanted to stay in their makeshift RVs. Visitors could get gas and basic supplies from the one-room store located in the main building.

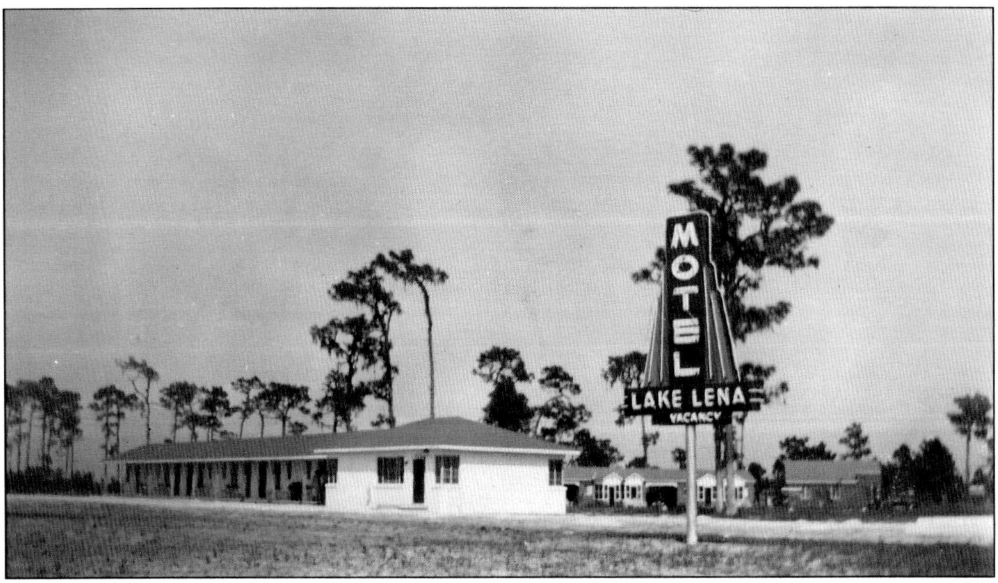

Tourist cabins eventually evolved onto the more modern motel. Lake Lena Motel was located next door to Nelson's Cabins. For the first time, short-stay visitors to Auburndale could relax in a comfortable bed with sheets and towels furnished.

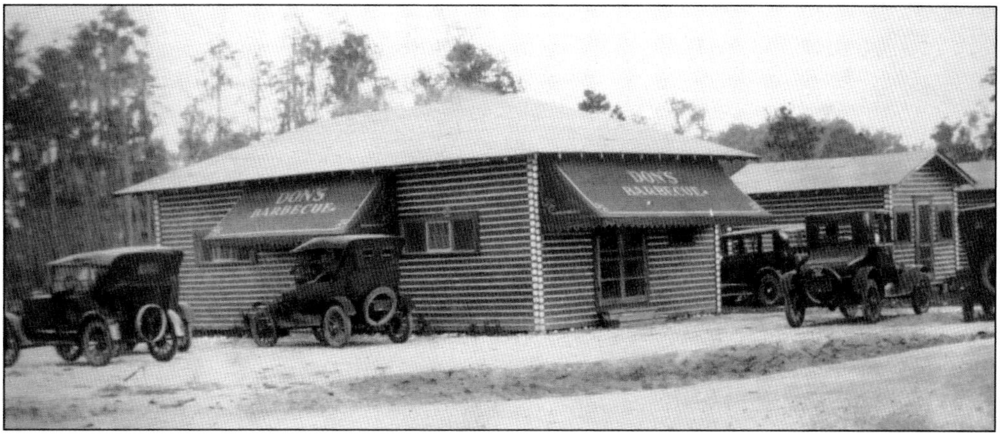

Don's not only offered cabins but also provided barbecue for locals and visitors. It was owned by Jim Nelson. On the left, out of the frame, was a single gas pump. To get fuel, one just turned the handle to pump the gas from an underground tank into a glass container. From there, it flowed by gravity into the vehicle.

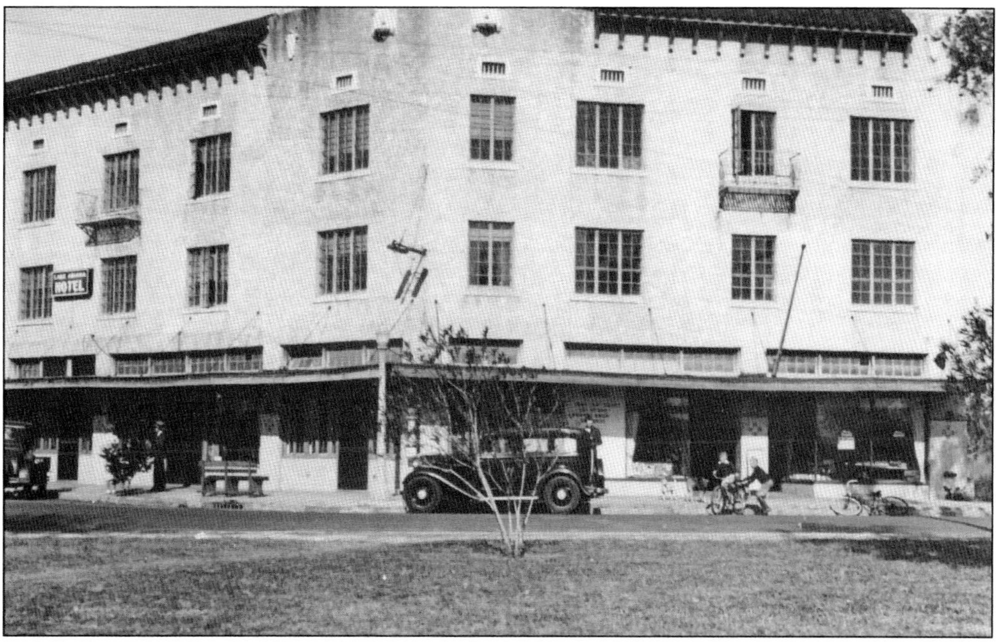

When A.E. Thorp agreed to sell property to Paul Smith to build a hotel on West Park Street, there was one stipulation: he felt Auburndale would grow faster if the hotel had three floors. Music, both local and professional, could often be heard drifting out over the town from the third-floor ballroom. Note the Western Union boys on their bicycles waiting to deliver telegrams.

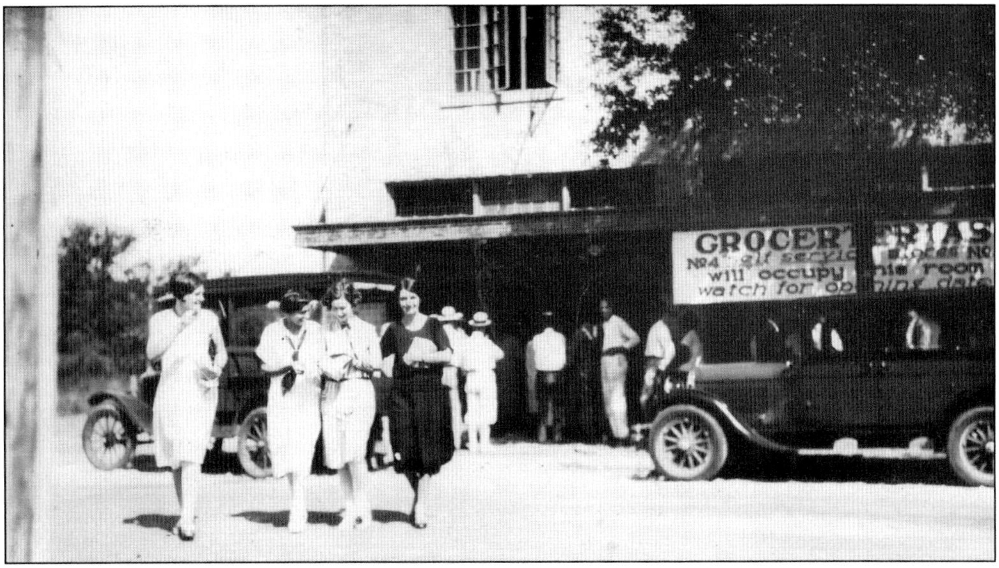

The first floor of the Paul Smith Hotel had room for six stores. Here, people wander about the Ariana Pharmacy and Grocerteria No. 4, which was having its grand opening. The Auburndale Post Office was located here from 1940 to 1954. The Paul Smith was later named Lake Ariana Hotel.

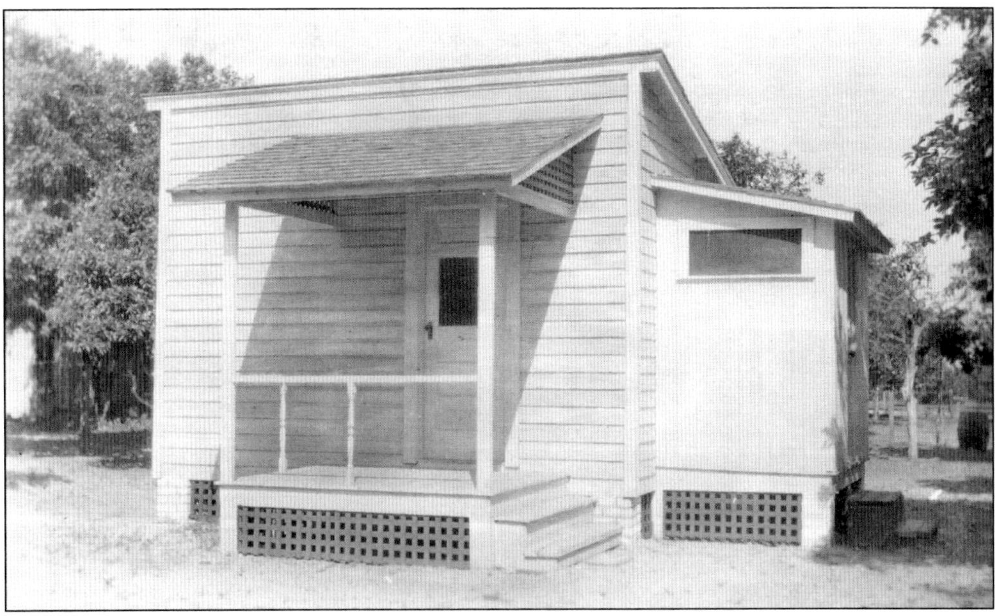

It was the Roaring Twenties, the "Big Boom," when it seemed as if everyone in the United States was headed south with one thing in mind: they wanted a piece of Florida. Land that the government had trouble giving away 50 years before was now prime real estate. There was a real estate office on every corner. Properties sometimes changed hands three times in a day. Millionaires were made overnight.

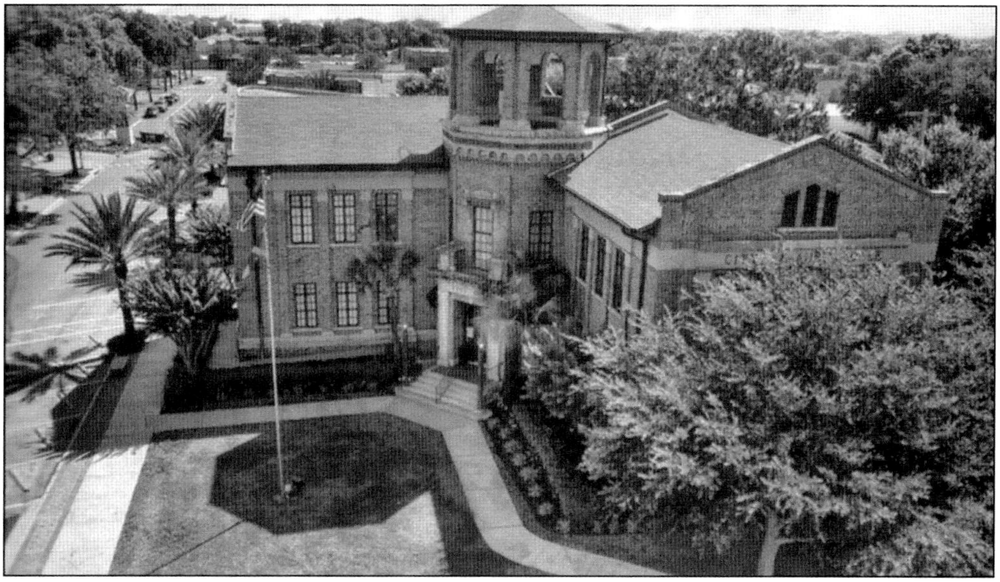

Auburndale City Hall was completed in 1927 at a cost of $60,000. Designed by Rolland Buckey and built under the direction of Paul Smith, the stately building's domed roof towered above the town. All city business was conducted inside these yellow-brick walls. The office of Auburndale's first city manager was here.

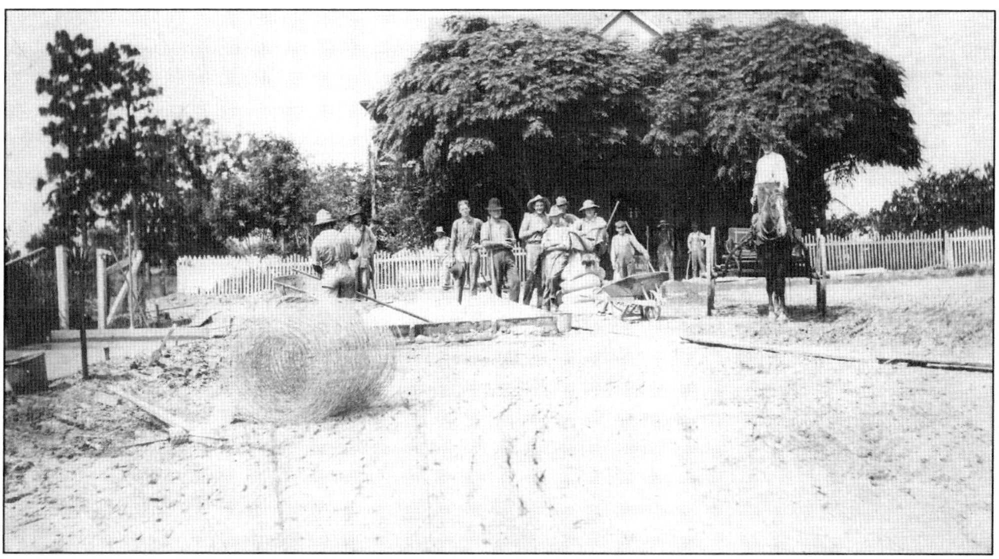

In this 1925 image, workers have just begun construction on the new city hall. East Park Street was still unpaved. The Patrick Hotel is at the end of the street behind the trees. Before the city hall was completed, the Patrick was gone; it burned down that year.

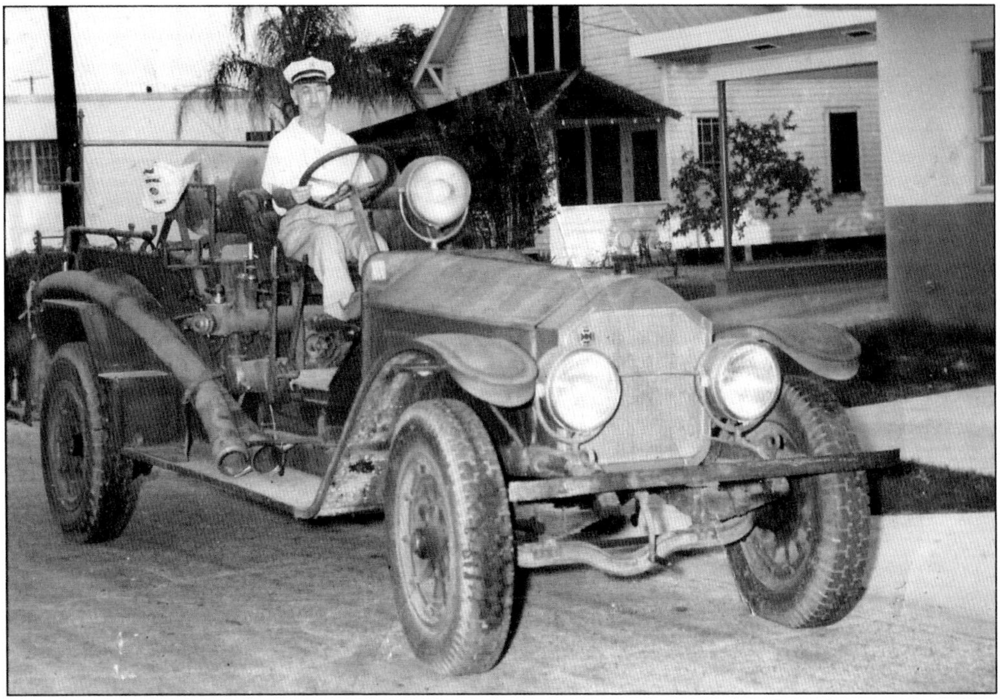

In 1927, the city purchased a LaFrance model 75 fire truck. It was housed in the garage in city hall. Firefighters could stay overnight in the room above the garage. A brass pole provided quick descent when needed. With the exception of the chief, all firefighters were volunteers. Here, Jess Periman poses aboard "Old Grand Ma." The house in the background is Auburndale's second school.

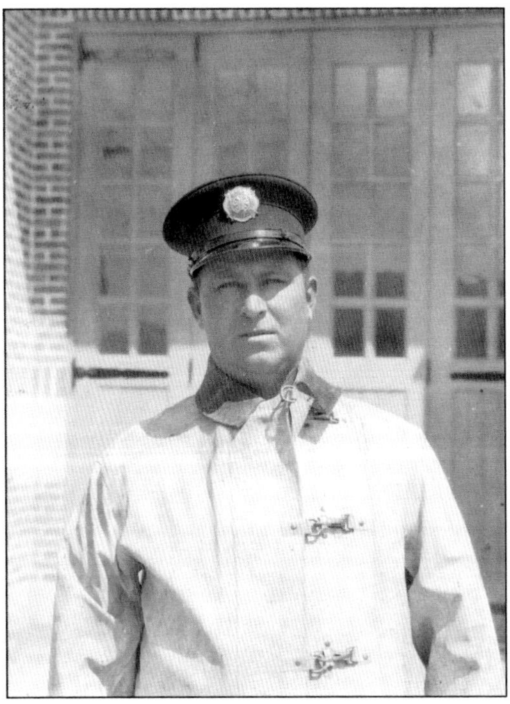

Fred Linder, pictured here, was appointed fire chief but resigned when the city stored the fire truck in a tin building on Lake Avenue and rented the firehouse to a "bunch of Republicans." Jesse Periman was then chief for more than three decades. He would activate the alarm on the water tower: three blasts for a structure, two for a field, and one at noon so all would know it was time for a break.

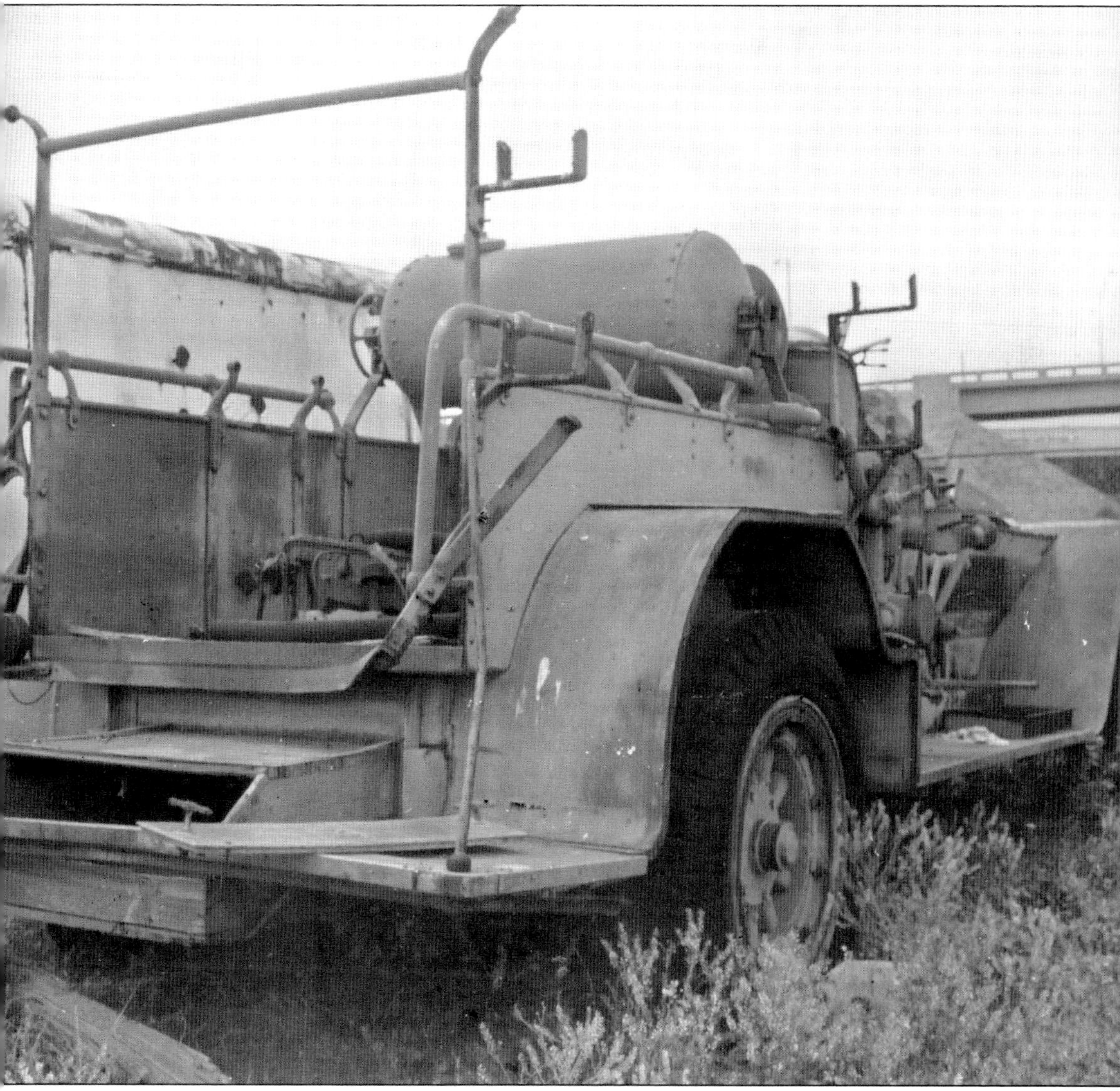

The LaFrance battled many fires but was finally retired to a field where it sat, exposed to the elements, for more than 40 years. Then, one day, the truck, rusted and covered with weeds, was towed to be restored by loving hands. Now "Old Grand Ma" is stored in its own glass room at the fire station for all to admire.

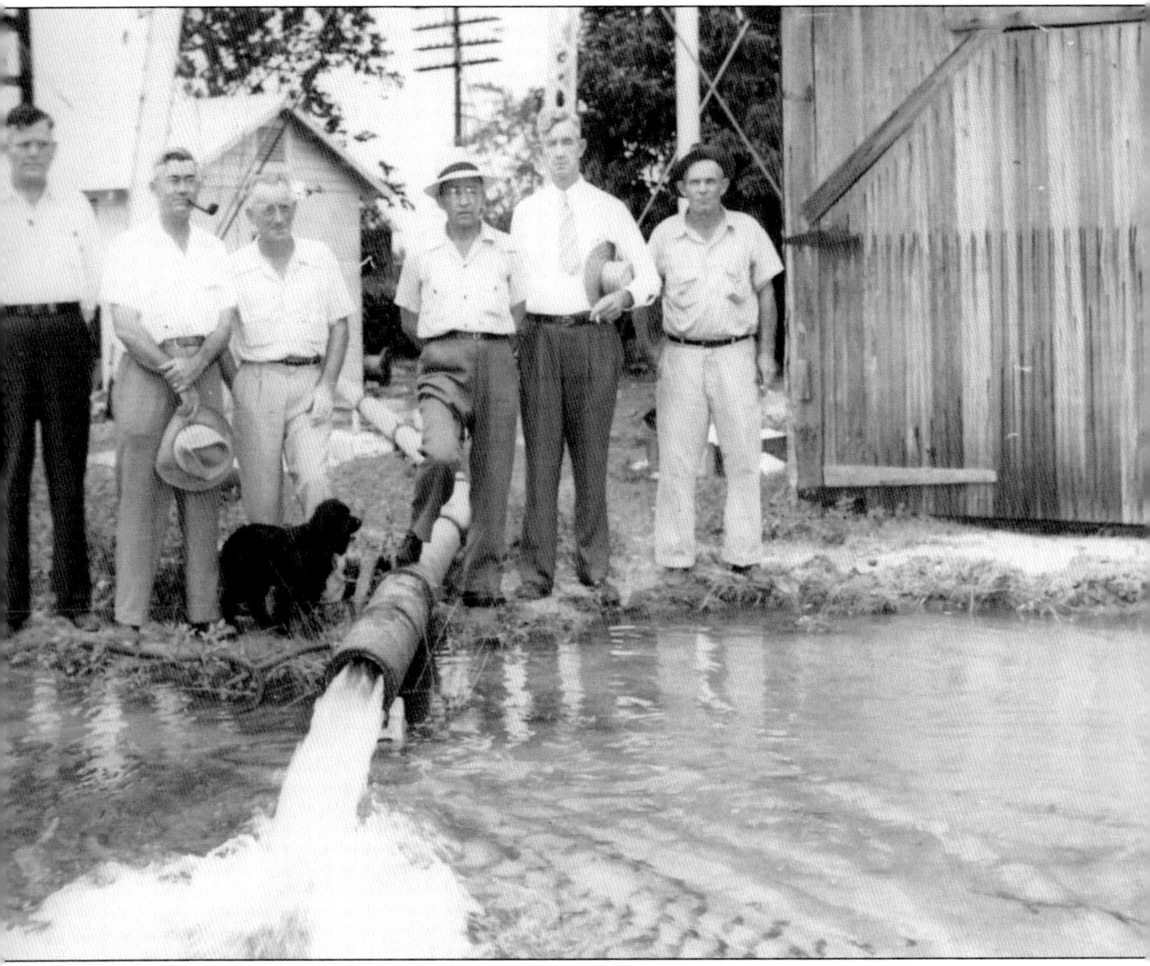

In 1923, the town government approved money for a water system to supply running water to residents. A well was drilled, and a pump was installed to push the water up into a water tower. Pictured here from left to right, citizens Alton Mims, Harry Corneal, Frank Burcham, Harry Penn, Jim Anderson, and Curtis Dansby inspect the flow of water.

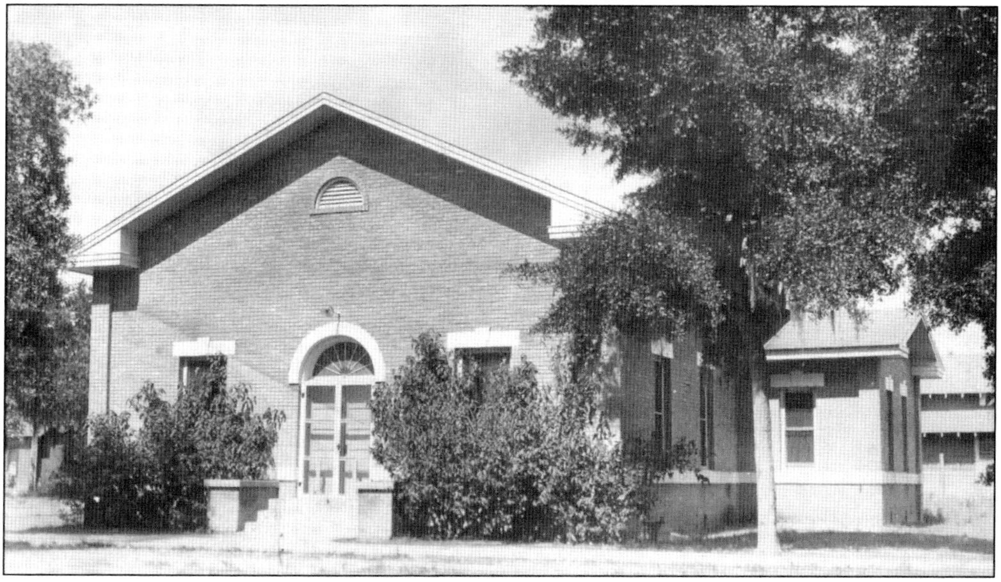

The Methodist church was organized in 1921 on the northwest corner of Bridgers Avenue and Main Street. Charter members were Bessie Braddock, Mamie and Marion Denton, Ethyl and Renus Olson, Mary and William Kimbrough, Carrie and Millard Jones, I.E. and Nettie Davis, Julia and Percy Hall, and Kate and Elam Stevenson.

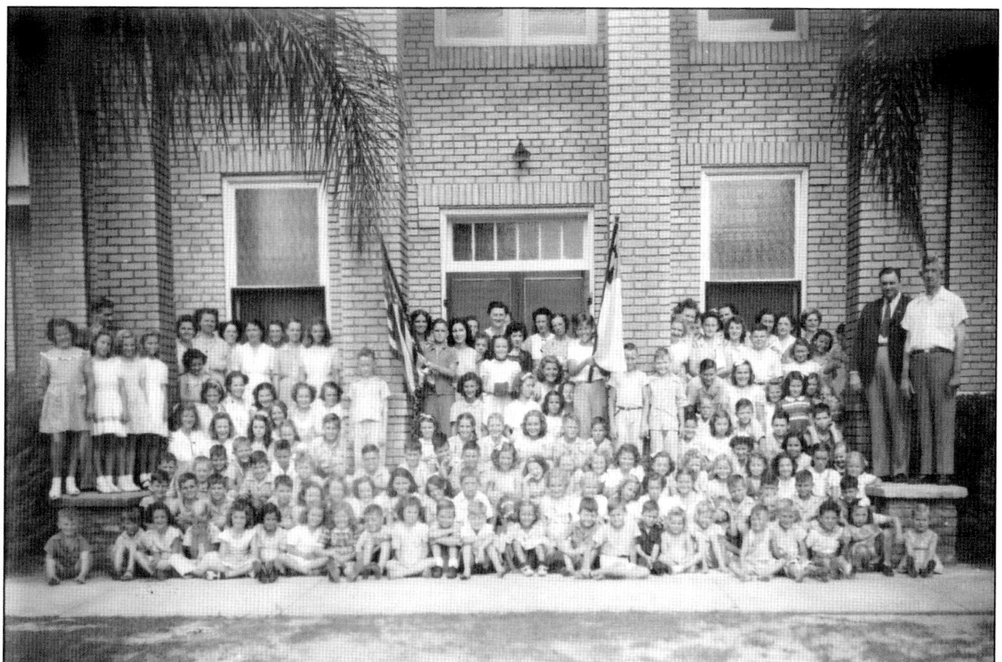

The Baptist church began in a tent revival in 1920. The church was on the southwest corner of Bridgers Avenue and Main Street. Charter members were L.L. Smith, Ella and William Coffman, Hannah and David Pearson, Mr. and Mrs. Jimmy Kelly, Mr. and Mrs. Draughty, and Tecoy Mims.

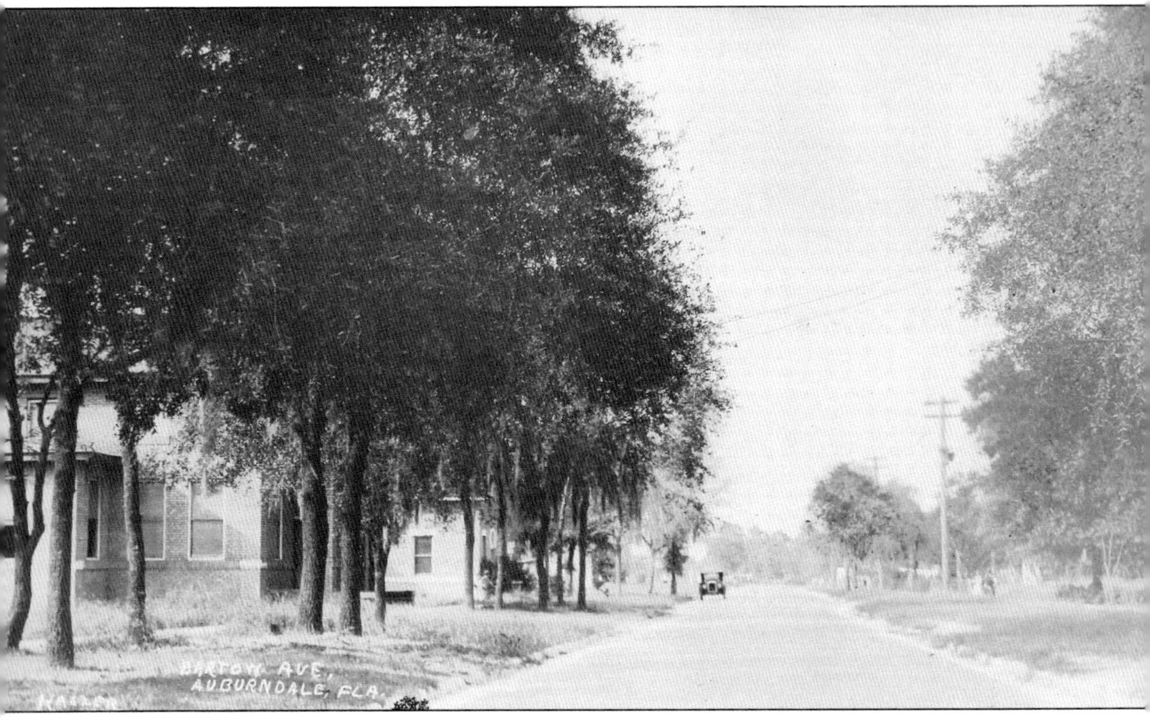

This is Bartow Avenue looking north about 1925. The Methodist and Baptist churches are visible through the trees on the left. There are no cross streets yet, and the park is straight ahead in the distance. The car on the road belonged to Alice Kaszer. Her car was frequently found in her photographs.

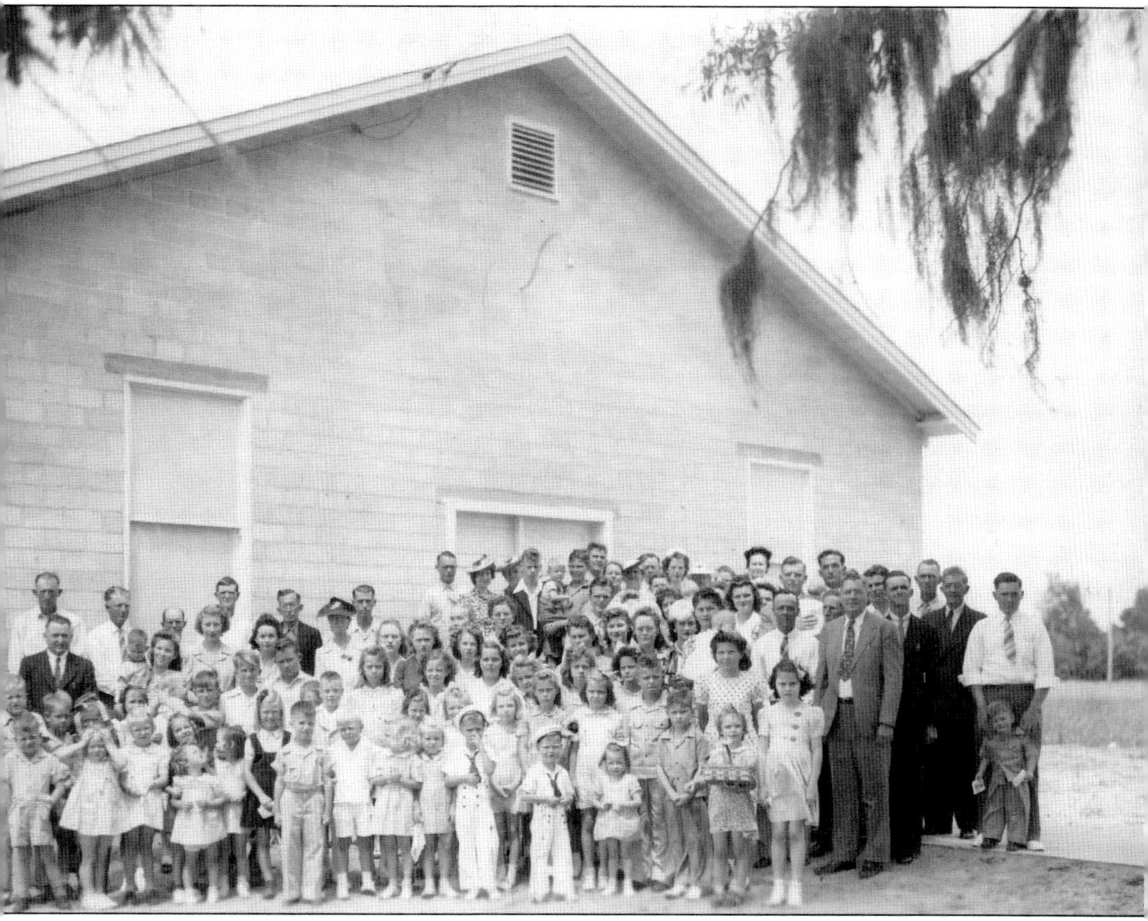

The Missionary Baptist church began in a small church across the street from the 1915 school on Sesaquachita Avenue. When the congregation built its new church on Main Street, this little church was bought by the school board and used for classrooms. It was later torn down.

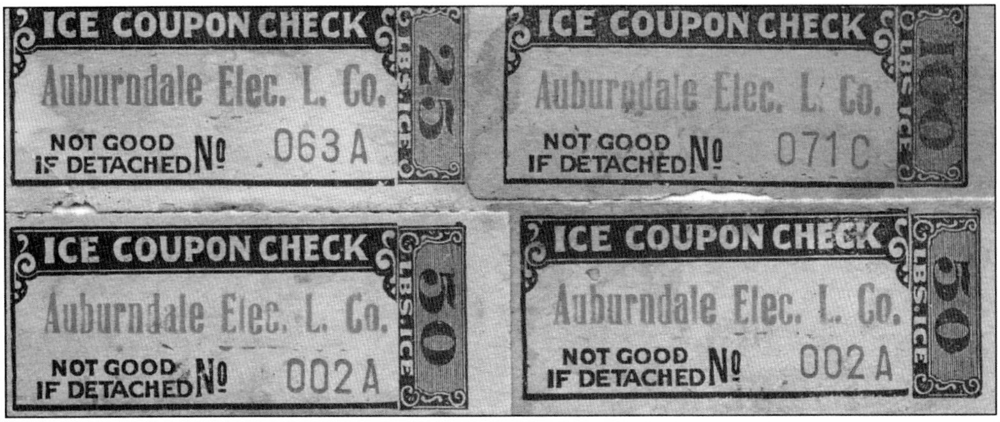

In 1923, Chester Hewitt installed a power plant in Auburndale. It was only in operation part of the day, but streetlights shone on Main Street for the first time. As an inducement to get new subscribers, he offered these coupons for 25 pounds of free ice at the Wilcox ice plant.

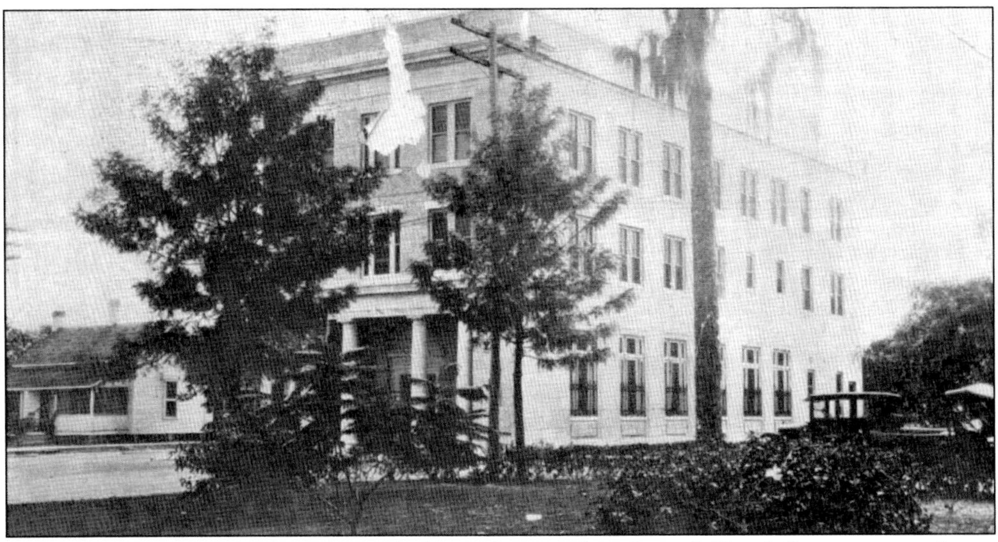

In 1926, the First National Bank was built on the site of the Patrick Hotel. Patrons entered past massive cement pillars into the stone and granite lobby room on the ground floor. The second floor was divided into offices, and the third was a meeting/ballroom. The house to the left was the first office of the Peninsular Telephone Company. There were fewer than 70 telephones in town, mostly in businesses.

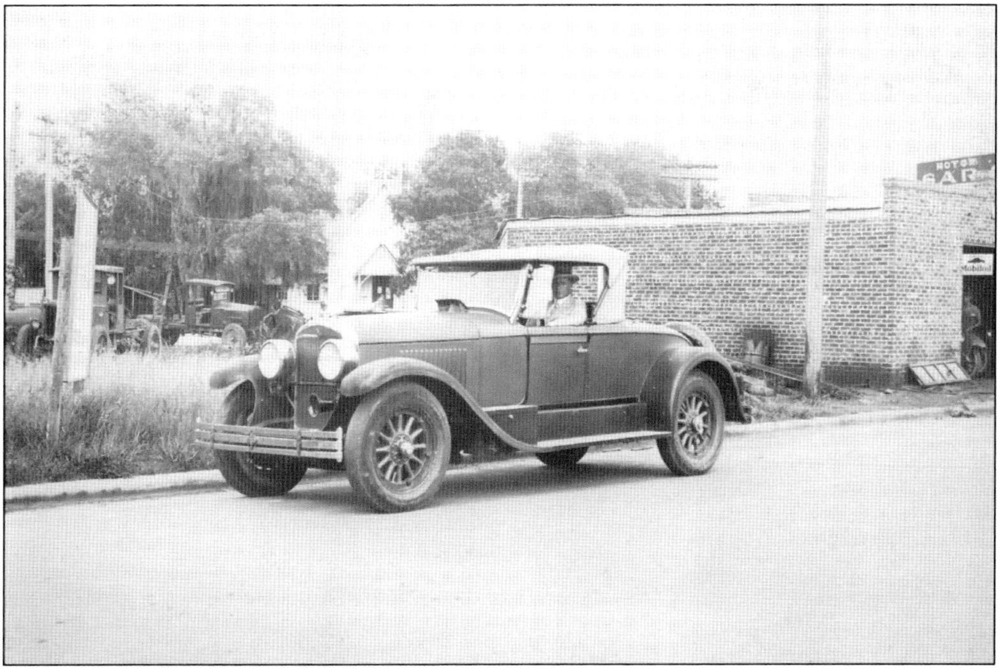

No one noticed this suave young man who took up residence in Auburndale for a week—no one except the young ladies, that is. After all, it was a boom time in 1927, and new people appeared daily. But, residents noticed when Marvin Miller, the self-professed "best bank robber in the business," failed at his craft and was attempting to escape in his snappy roadster. He was shot dead by Deputy Marshall Jim Glover in front of city hall.

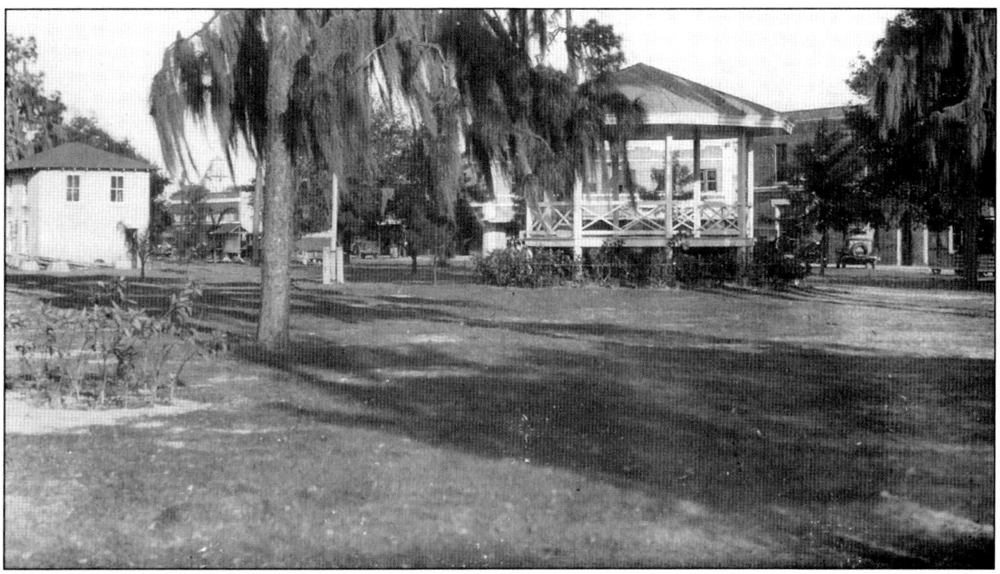

When the new city hall was completed in 1927, the jail remained in the city park. It is the white building to the left of the gazebo. By 1946, an addition was made to the back of city hall for two jail cells and a desk for the officer. Since the Auburndale crime rate was low, the cells were usually reserved for the occasional over-imbiber who got a little rowdy.

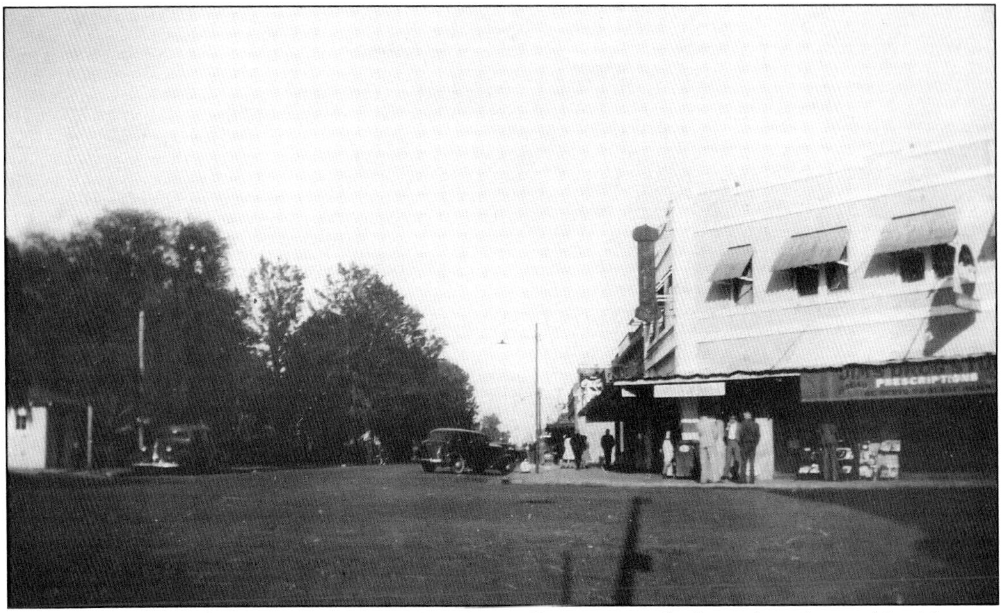

The police station for Auburndale's single police officer was a telephone booth–sized building in the city park. It is shown here on the far left. The officer had to stand to do his paperwork. There was a telephone in the booth in case of an emergency. The park had a half-moon drive here. There was usually a checkers game or two going on at one of the picnic tables in the circle.

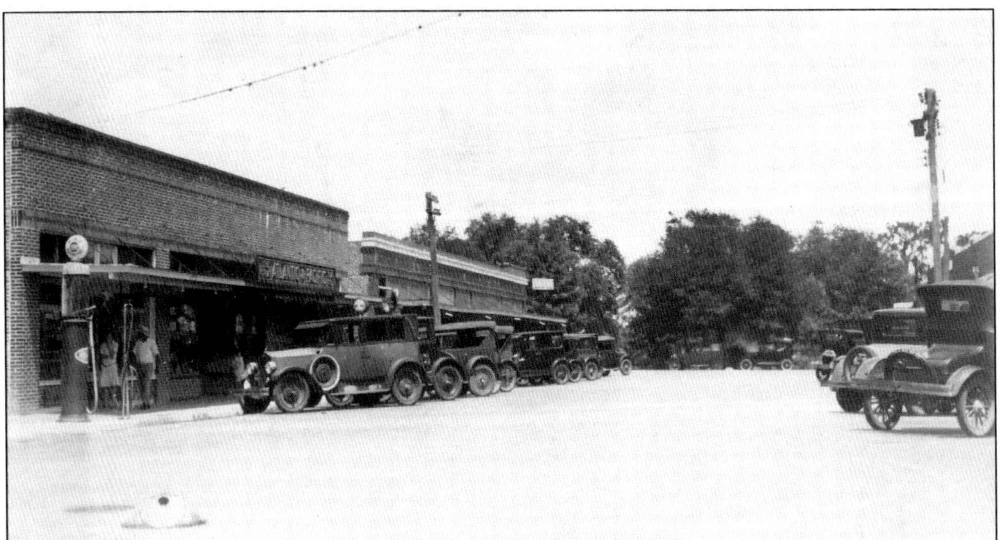

In 1927, West Lake Avenue was bustling: the street was paved, and streetlights were on. The Edgar Williams gas station is on the left, next to it is the Atlantic and Pacific Tea Company, and the Auburndale Pharmacy visible in the background. Later, Don Hancock's Five and Dime Store was in this building. The Hudson Hotel is across the street on the right.

Seven

What Goes Up Must Come Down

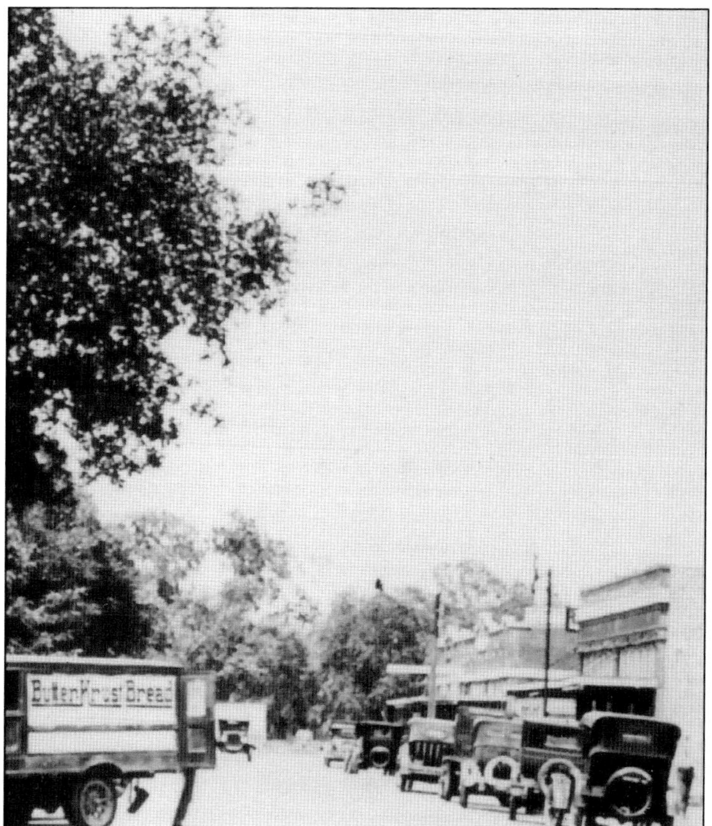

By 1930, the impact of the Great Depression that devastated the United States had reached Auburndale. The boom was over, and Auburndale was deflated. The city had a debt of more than $110,000. Projects like the water system were unfinished, but the money was gone. The city defaulted on bonds. Some blamed city manager Dan Thorp. He was fired, and Auburndale went back to the mayor form of government.

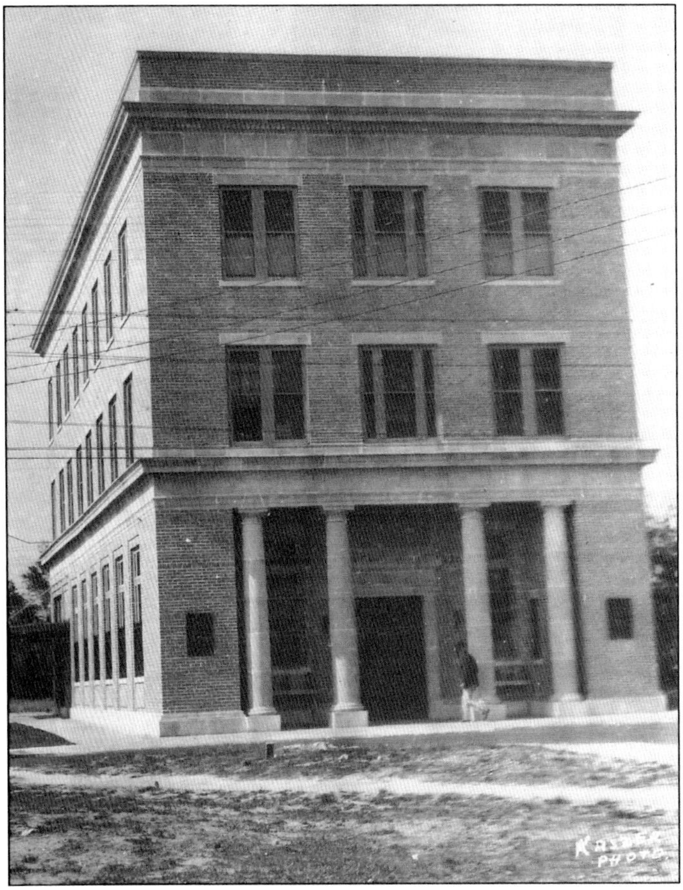

During the Great Depression, the First National Bank (at left), like banks all over the country, failed and suddenly closed its doors. There was no deposit insurance, so anyone who had money in the bank lost it. Even children lost the pennies they had been saving to improve their school. Agents of the federal comptroller put the bank up for sale, and it was bought by C.F. Smith. On August 5, 1939, the Peoples Bank of Auburndale opened (below). The vice presidents were Henry Smith, C.V. McClug, and C.W. Palmore. Julia Hall and H.C. McCollum were cashiers. This bank building was torn down when the new Sun Trust was erected. The small brick building in front was used for city business before the completion of city hall.

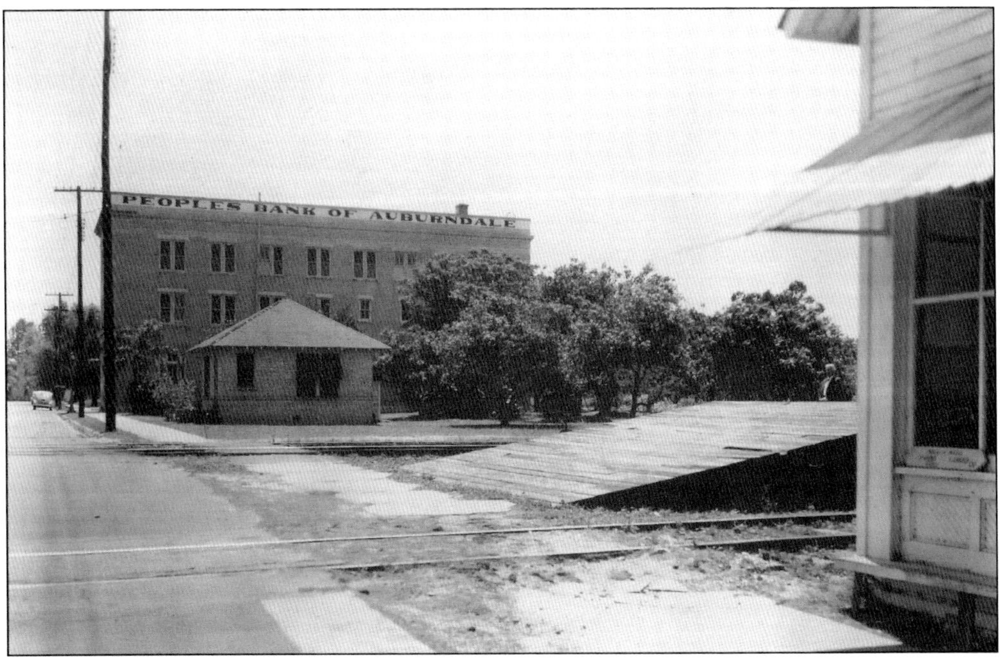

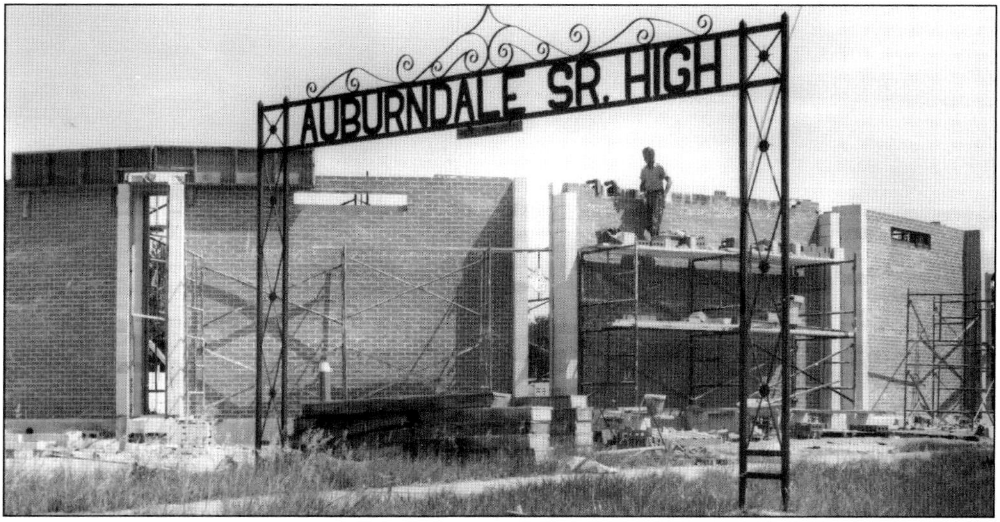

Auburndale High School was built in 1954 on part of the Patterson homestead. A New Jersey man planned a community with homes, shops, and a multifloor hotel. Paved streets and sidewalks were completed when the developer went bankrupt. The school board bought the property by paying the taxes. Land could be had anywhere in town by just paying the taxes, but the city had stopped foreclosing on property because it was just too costly to file the papers. (Courtesy of the *Auburndale Star* archives.)

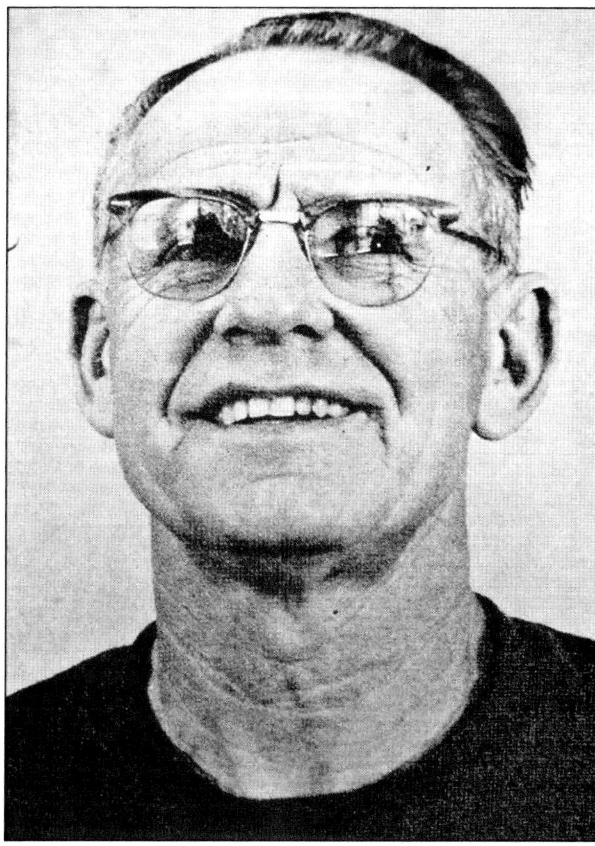

Percy Watts began working for the school board in 1936. He was hired as a custodian and bus driver, but he did not stop there. If something needed cleaning, Watts cleaned it. If it needed painting, he painted it. He made props for every school play. And he did it all with a song; he had a beautiful voice, and he could be heard singing as he worked.

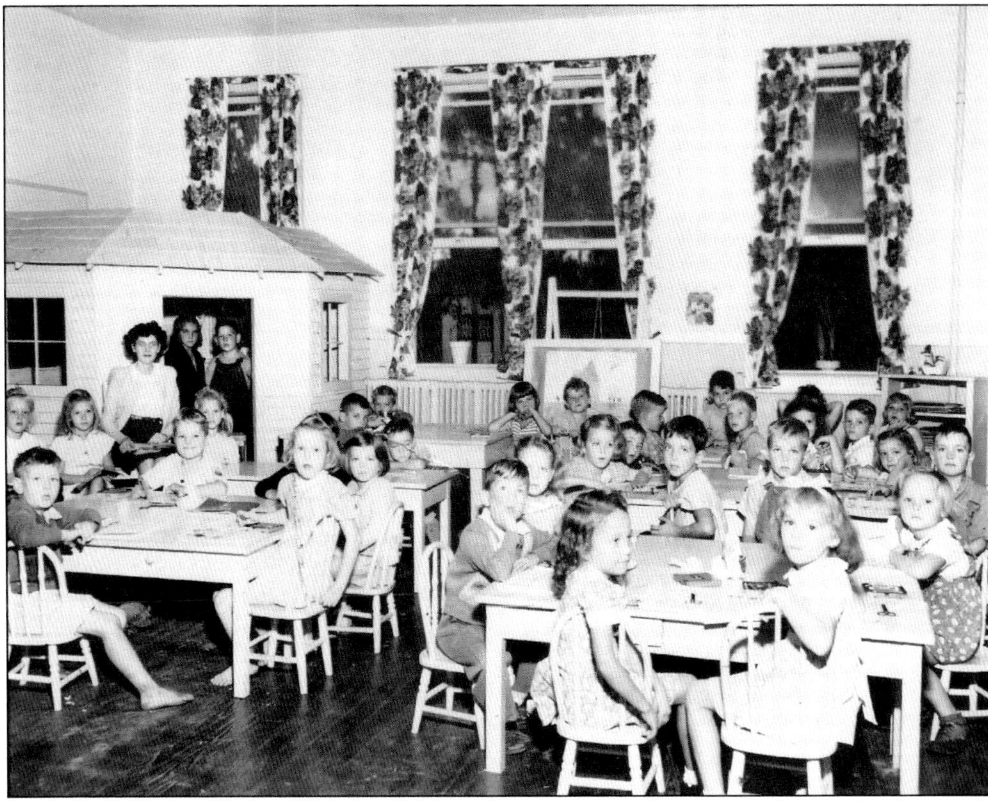

This 1945 classroom shows the full-sized playhouse that Percy Watts built for the first-grade schoolroom. On cold mornings, he got up early to stoke the furnace to make sure the children arrived to a warm room—except on those days when the school had to be closed because there was no money for the $8 a day it cost for heat. The teacher was Virginia White Mears.

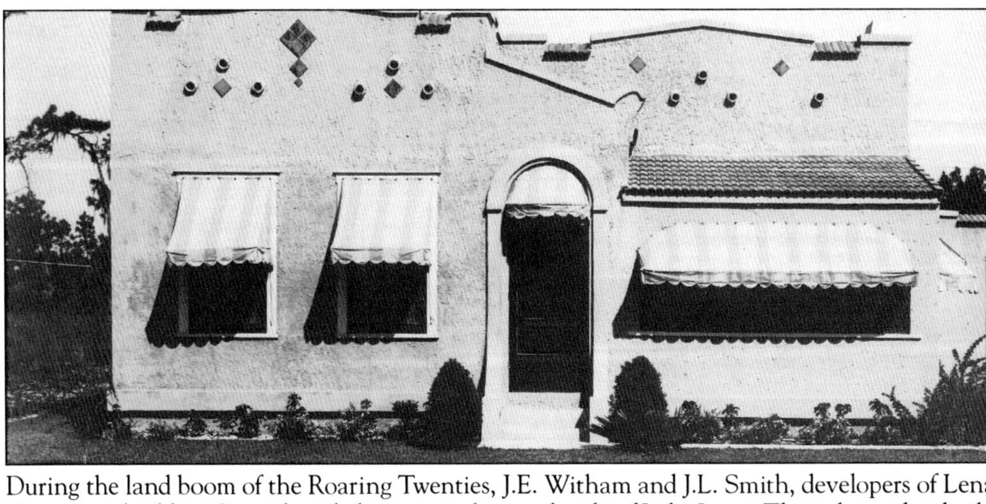

During the land boom of the Roaring Twenties, J.E. Witham and J.L. Smith, developers of Lena Vista, were building Spanish-style homes on the north side of Lake Lena. They planned to build a hotel between Lakes Lena and Ariana. Paved streets and nine houses were completed when their Maine Development Company went bankrupt. Foundations and houses in various stages of completion were left to the elements.

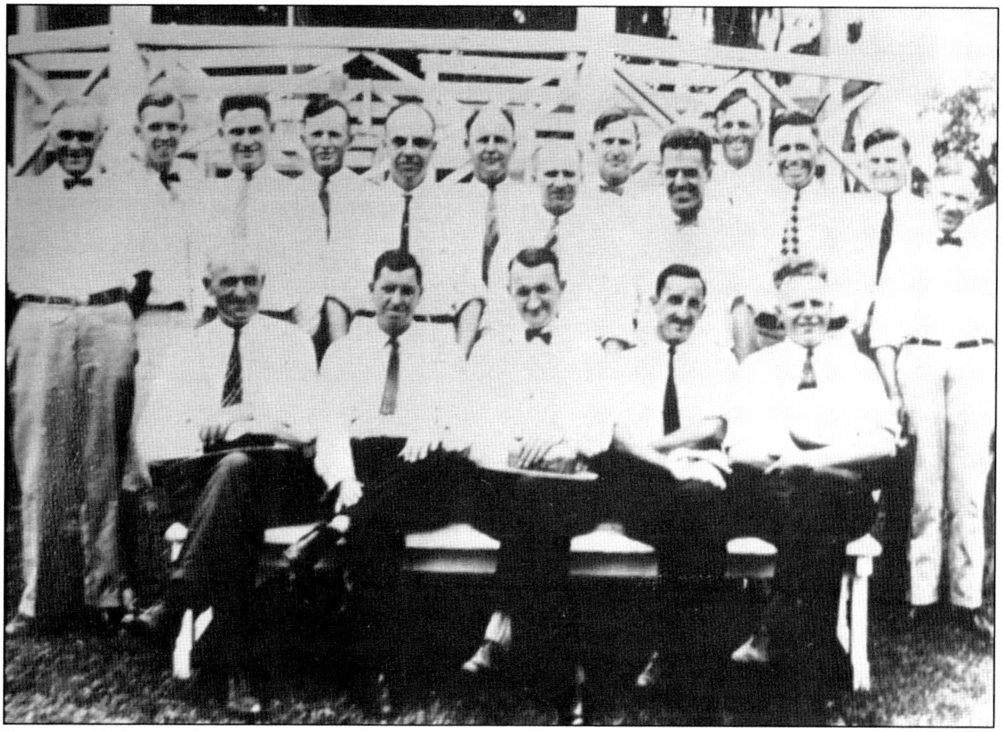

Rotary Club members pose for a portrait in 1925. The officers were James Morton, president; Harold Dearing, vice president; LeLand DeGraaf, secretary; Chic Scheible, treasurer; and Frank Nelson, sergeant-at-arms. Charter members were Ralph Allen, Willis Bancroff, Douglas Black, Reid Bryan, Bill Carmichael, E.B. Crackle, Harold Dearing, O.D. Eger, Dean Hickman, George King, James Metcalf, William Mackey, Clifton Moore, Charles Scheible, R.U. Nelson, Rev. E. Schwab, William Sinclair, Jere Stambaugh, Worthy Stanford, A.E. Strong, Dan Thorp, and Howard Trescott.

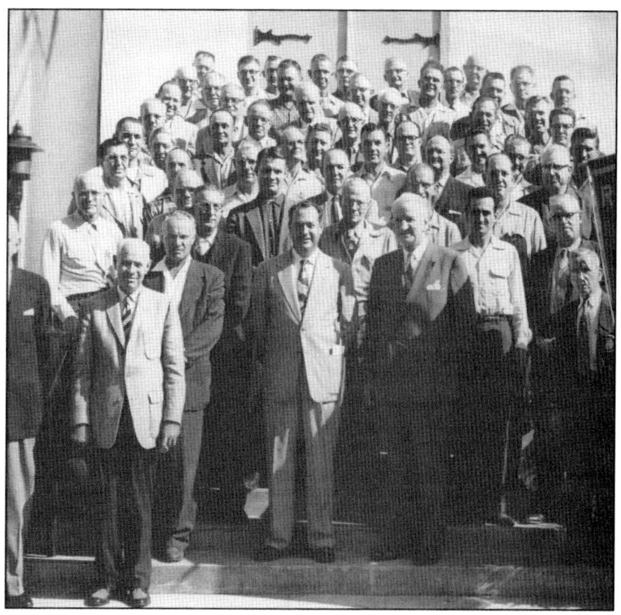

Twenty-five years after its founding, the Rotary Club was still active and had doubled in size. It was meeting at the Presbyterian church, where the women of the church prepared lunch for club members. The club was a close-knit service organization that met on a weekly basis.

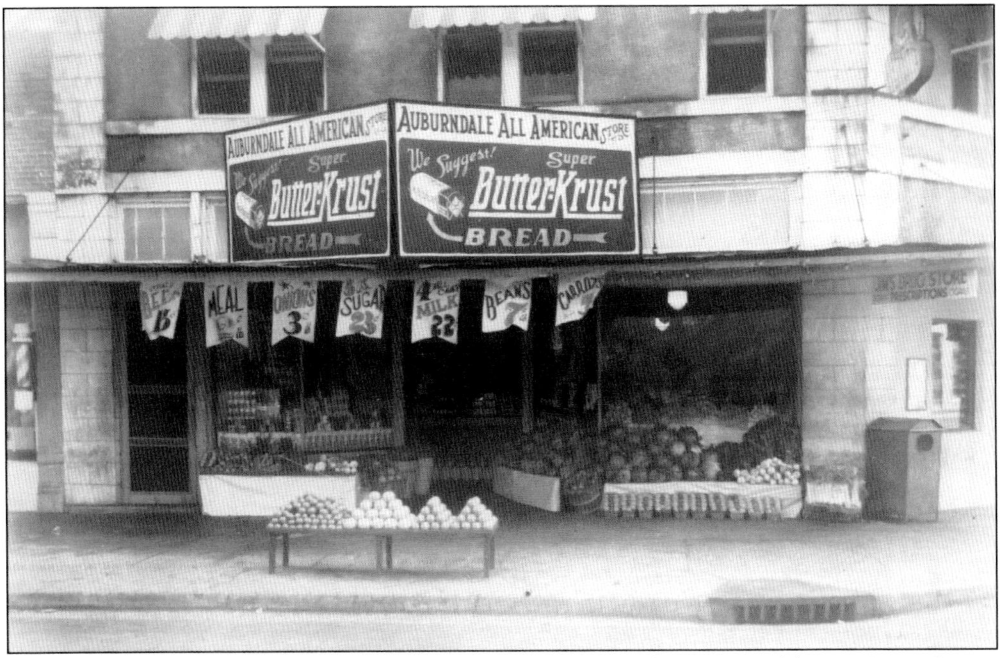

During the Depression, the All American Store was located in the Jones Building on Main Street. Herman McLain, nephew of Louis McLain, who designed the depot, was manager. In 1945, George Jenkins built his first Publix Super Market. That same year, he bought the All American chain, including the one in Auburndale, and renamed them Publix. In 1951, he closed this store and opened his modern Publix Super Market on South Main Street.

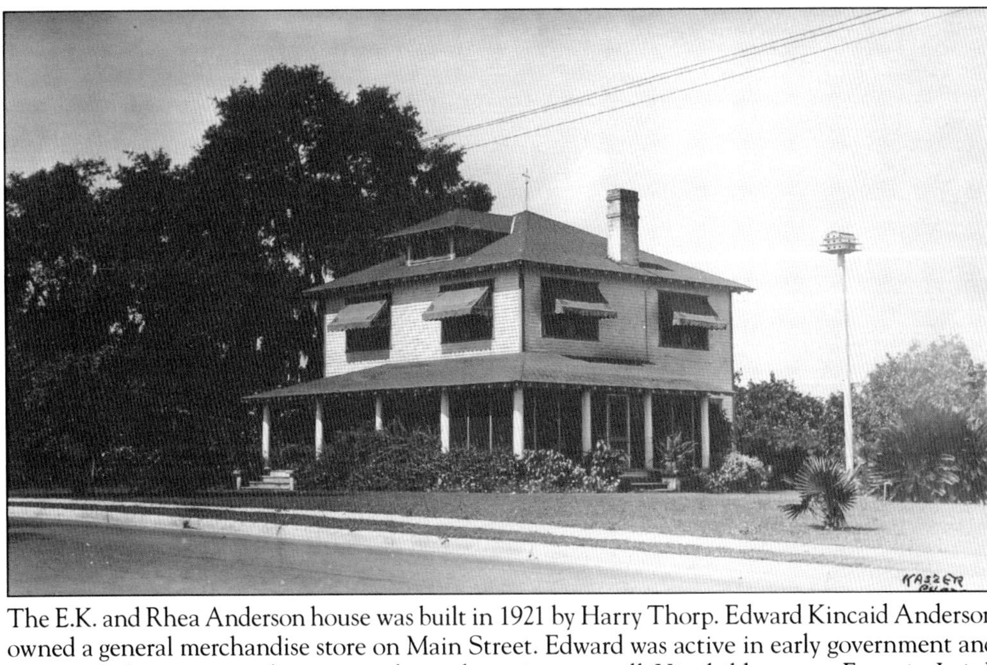

The E.K. and Rhea Anderson house was built in 1921 by Harry Thorp. Edward Kincaid Anderson owned a general merchandise store on Main Street. Edward was active in early government and was mayor three times and city councilman three times as well. His children were Eugenia, Laird, and Edward Jr.

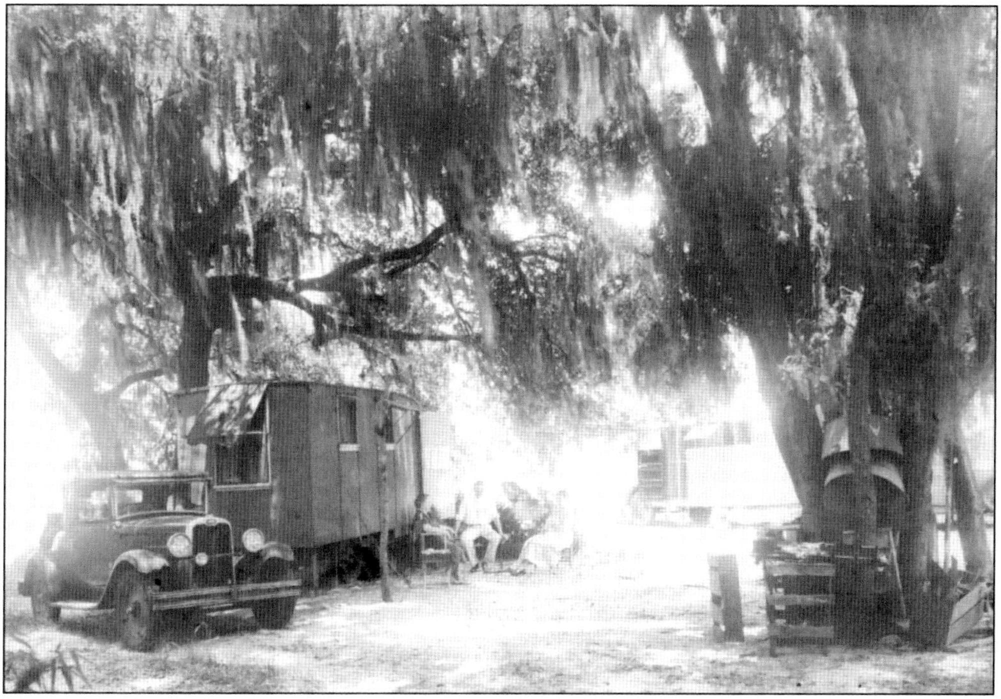

Grace and Arch Anderson came to Auburndale in 1931 towing their "house car" behind their Model A. They parked their homemade, wooden mobile home on a lot on Bartow Avenue and added to it until it was completely enclosed. They set up movie equipment on a vacant lot on Main Street, owned by the Pattersons. For 10 years, during the height of the Depression, local merchants financed the free movies they flashed on the exterior wall of the I.E. Davis store next door.

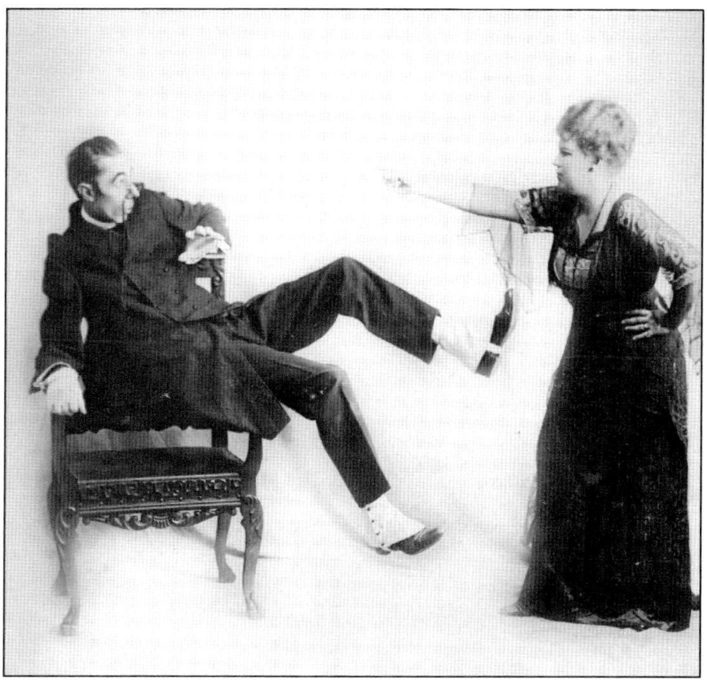

People walked for miles, sat on the ground, and battled ants and mosquitoes to see the flicks Grace and Arch turned out with their hand-cranked projector. Before arriving in Auburndale, the Andersons had been actors. They are shown here in one of their burlesque comedy skits. They worked in vaudeville and silent movies and once appeared in a stage show with Edwin Booth, brother of John Wilkes Booth.

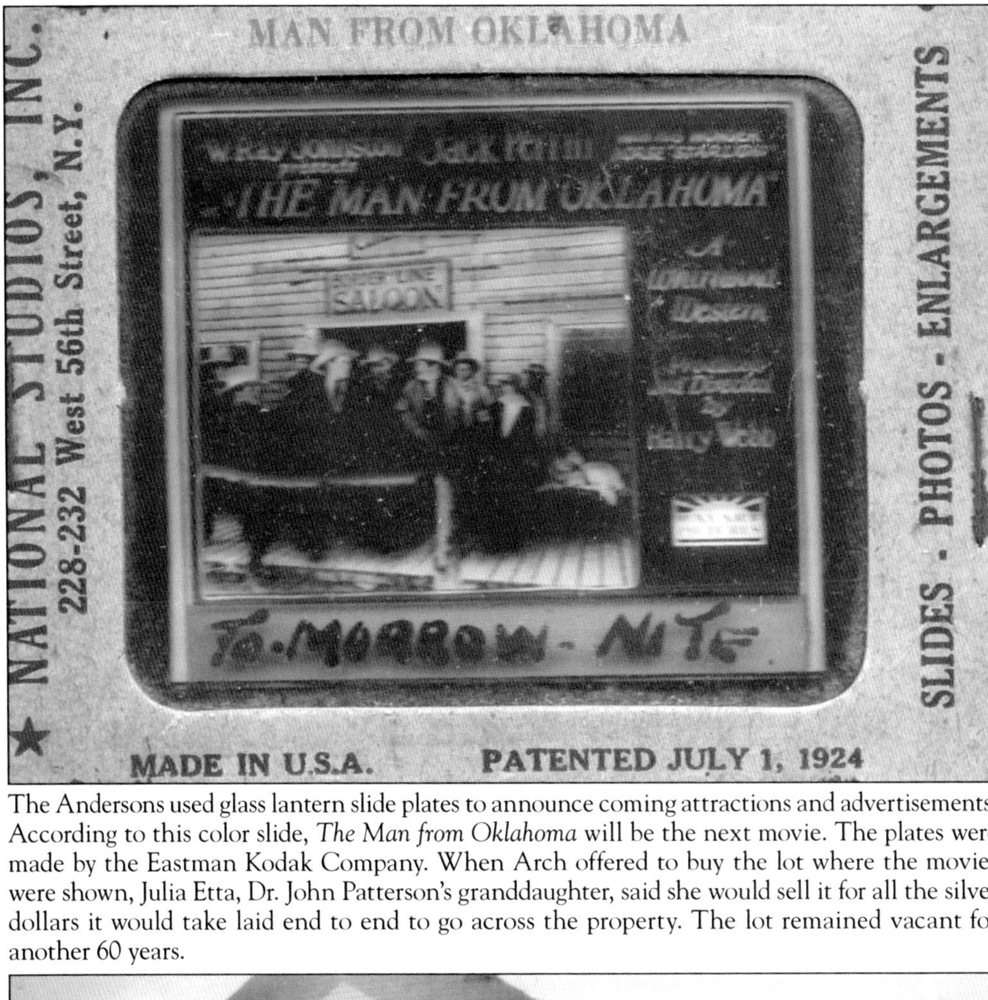

The Andersons used glass lantern slide plates to announce coming attractions and advertisements. According to this color slide, *The Man from Oklahoma* will be the next movie. The plates were made by the Eastman Kodak Company. When Arch offered to buy the lot where the movies were shown, Julia Etta, Dr. John Patterson's granddaughter, said she would sell it for all the silver dollars it would take laid end to end to go across the property. The lot remained vacant for another 60 years.

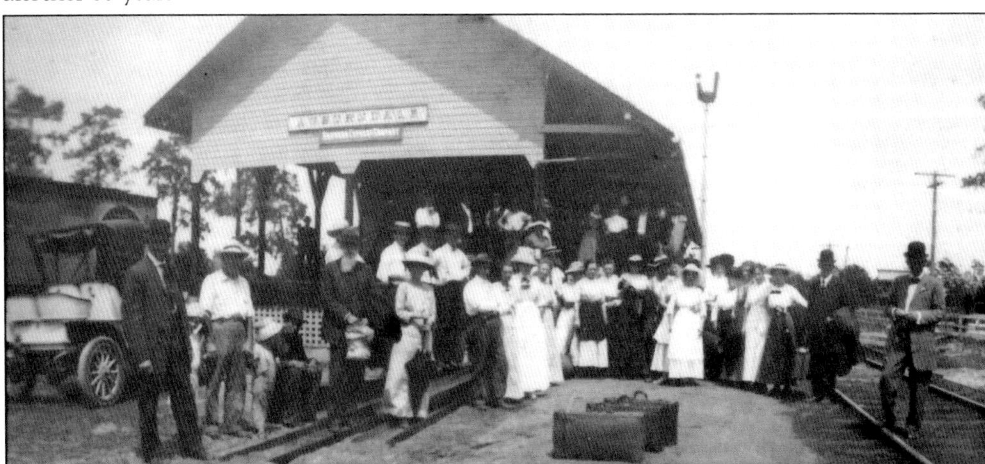

A group of Auburndale residents waits at the depot to depart on a train excursion. It must have been a special occasion, as the ladies are dressed in their finest hats, and the gentlemen are wearing business suits. Alice Kaszar's car is on the far left.

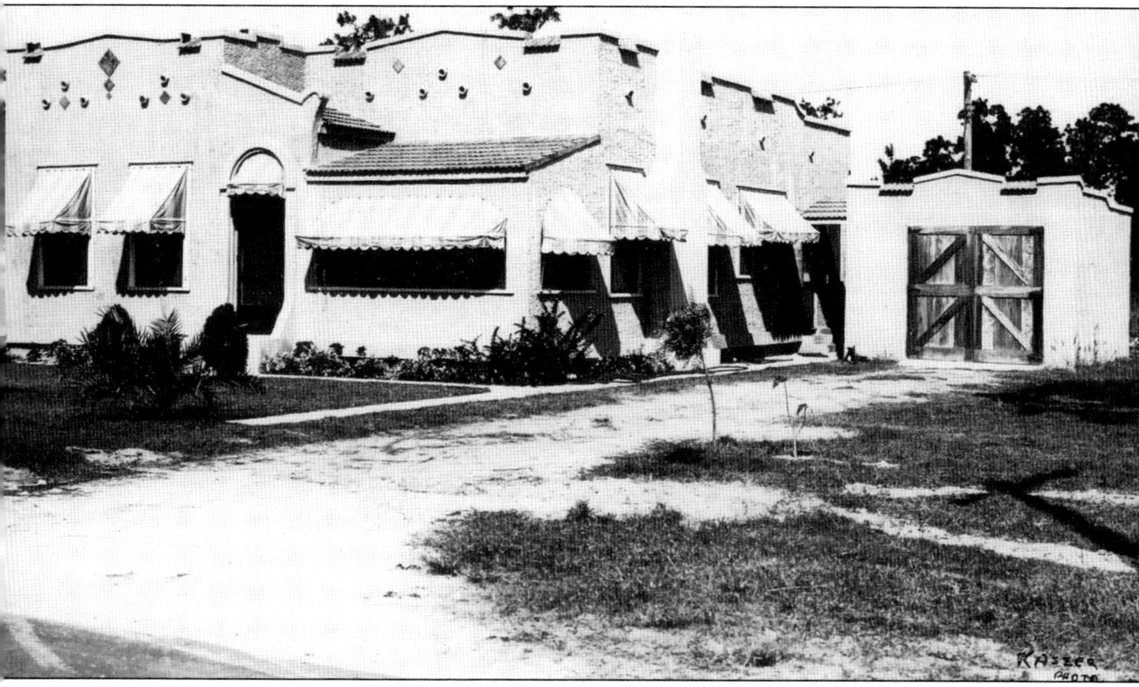

Dr. Thomas Simmons and Sue Jane lived in this house after coming to Auburndale in 1925. Dr. Simmons and Dr. Charles Deal shared an office in the State Bank Building until Dr. Deal was killed in an auto/train crash in 1936. Dr. Simmons moved his office to the second floor of Peoples Bank and then into a house behind the bank.

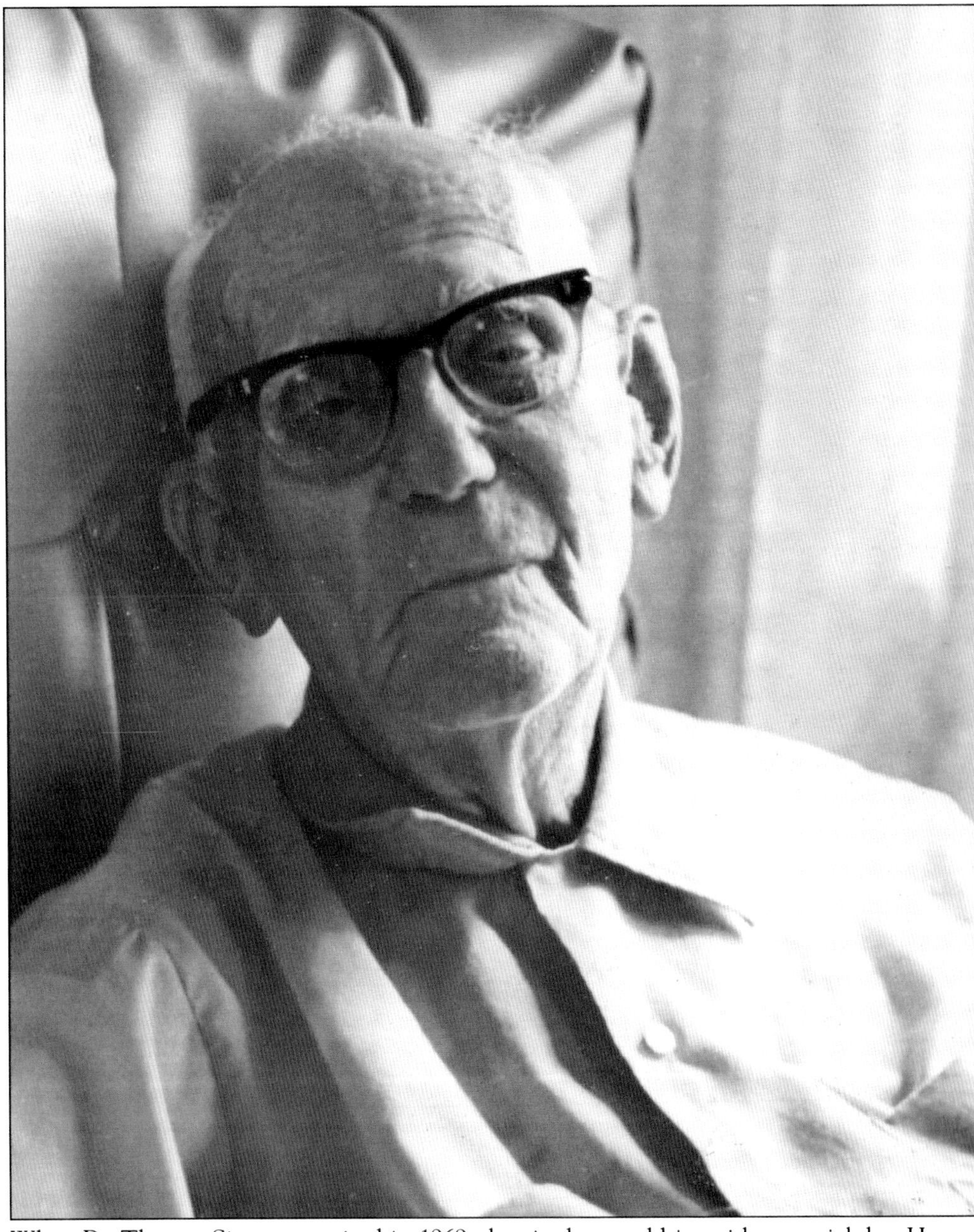

When Dr. Thomas Simmons retired in 1969, the city honored him with a special day. He and Dr. E.R. Morlan, whose office was in the Jones Building, were Auburndale's only physicians for more than 30 years. Dr. Simmons made house calls and delivered numerous babies at home. He raced to accidents and was an EMT (emergency medical technician) before anyone knew what that meant.

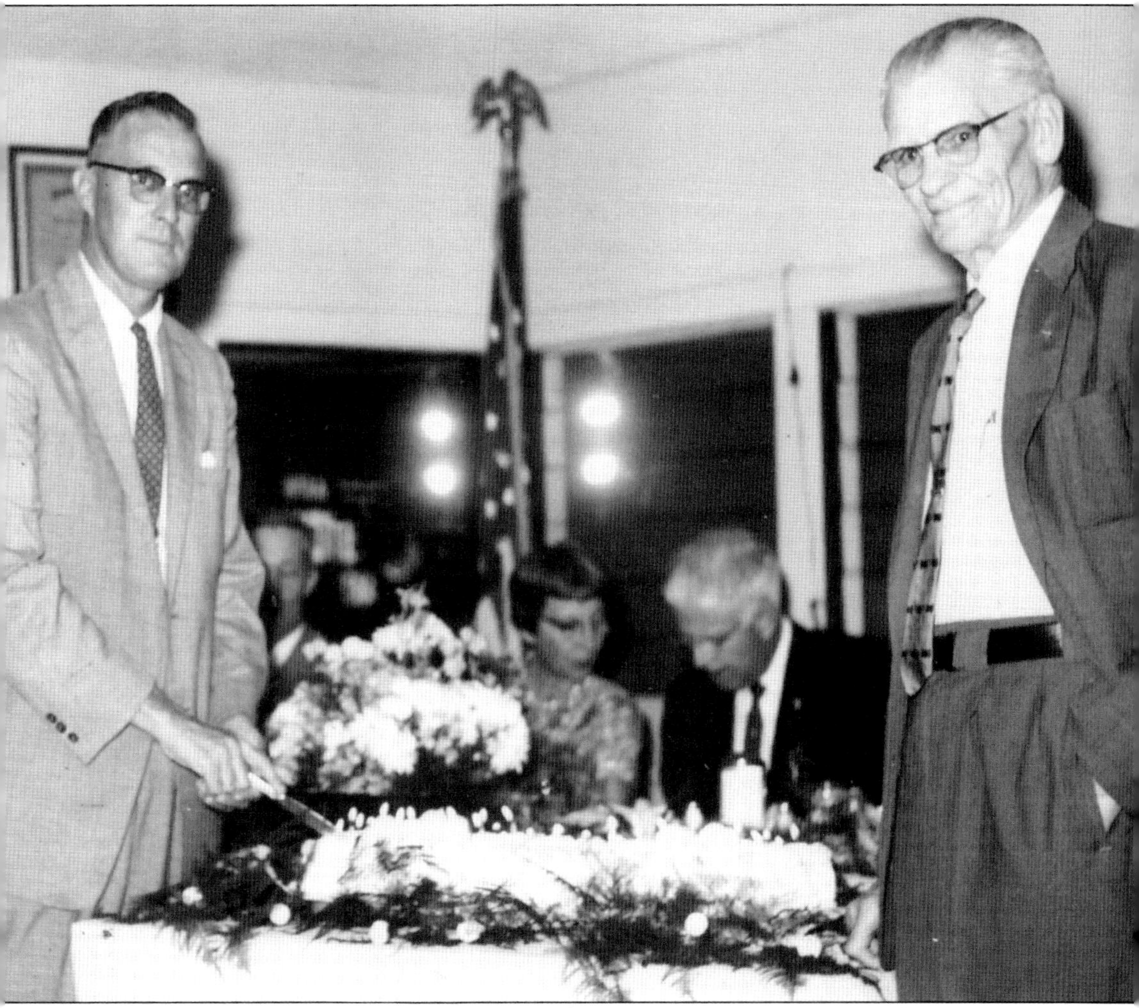

Dr. E.R. Morlan, on the far right, had his office on the second floor of the Jones Building. He and Dr. Simmons took care of the town's medical needs during the Depression. Babies were delivered at home with little prenatal care. More often than not, the doctors either did not get paid or were paid in food or other items. Their very sick patients were sent to Winter Haven Hospital or the county hospital at Bartow. Jim Crews is seen on the far left.

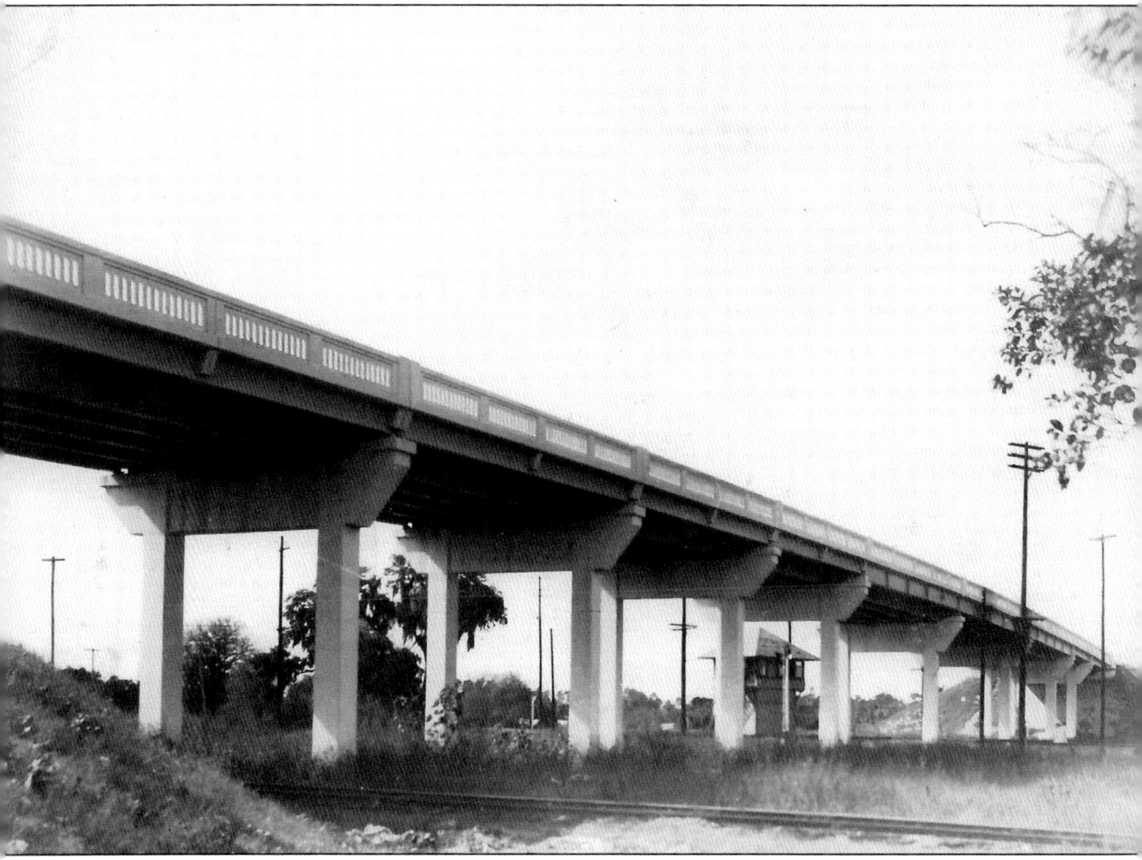

Two main railroads, the east-west Atlantic Coast Line and the north-south Seaboard Air Line, crossed in Auburndale. At this point, a room was built high on stilts, and a watchman was hired to sit in the house and watch the tracks. Later, an overpass was built over the crossing. This must have been successful as there were no recorded accidents.

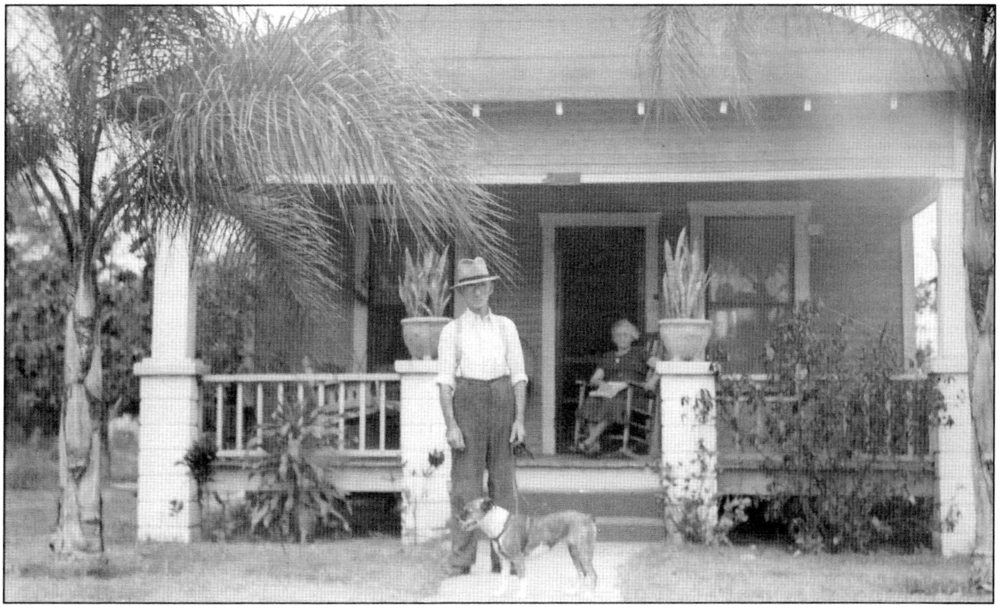

Auburndale, unlike some US cities, grew in population during the Depression. People in neighboring states heard there were jobs to be had in the citrus industry, so they came. Housing, however, was a major problem. Almost everyone in town rented out rooms in their homes, garages, and even converted chicken coops. This unidentified couple rented out their front porch for someone to sleep on. If a family managed to rent a house, their extended family members moved in with them.

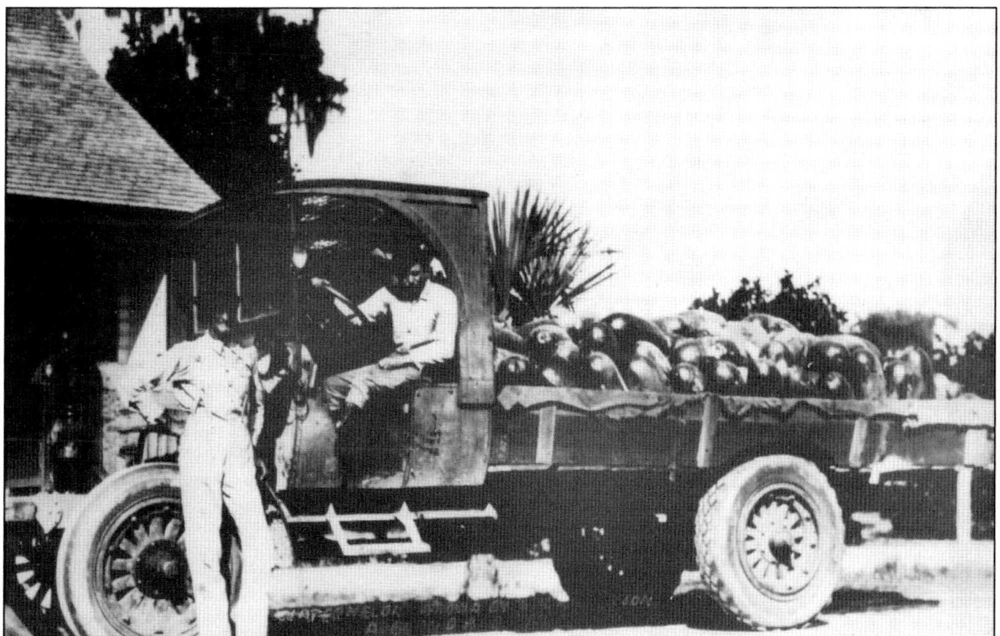

Truck farming around Auburndale was profitable, as America was hungry. Watermelon grew well in the sandy soil. Auburndale became known for the oversized melons its farmers produced and was called the "Watermelon Capital of the World." Here, William F. Allen (left), father of Auburndale historian Carl Allen, and Arnold Winn take a truckload of watermelon to the market.

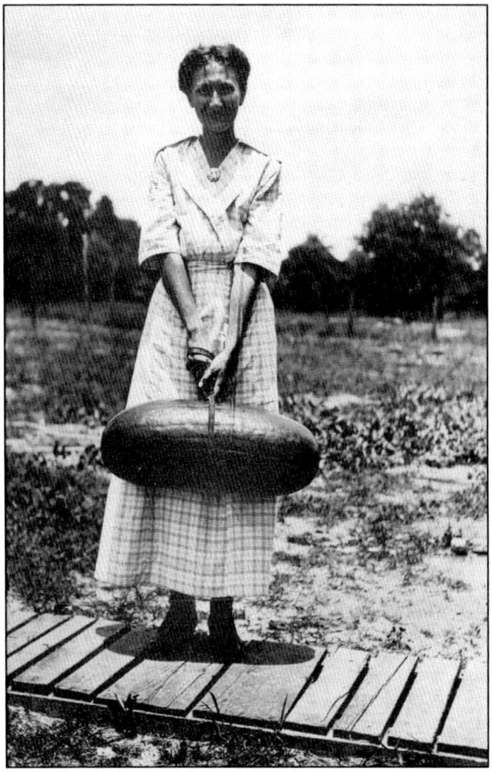

Photographer Alice Kaszer holds a watermelon almost as big as she is. The Rattlesnake watermelon was named for the stripes on its skin that resembled a big snake, and they grew to enormous sizes. During the Depression years, watermelons were shipped out of Auburndale daily by train to help feed hungry Americans.

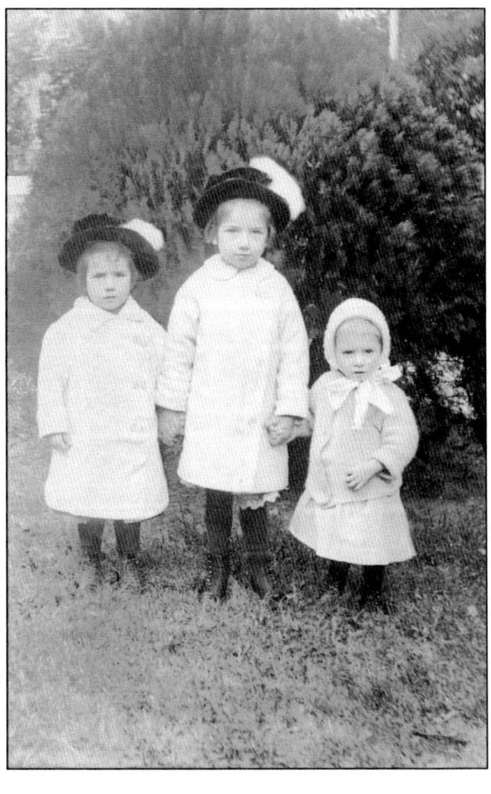

The children of Andrew and Emma Driver, from left to right Elsie, Edna, and Wilfred, are pictured here in 1914. Elsie and Edna would become teachers. Edna Driver Adams taught in Auburndale and became principal of Central Elementary School. Wilfred "Casey" was president of the Peoples Bank of Auburndale. He married Annie Gladden, whose family owned the Seminole Club. Annie also taught in Auburndale.

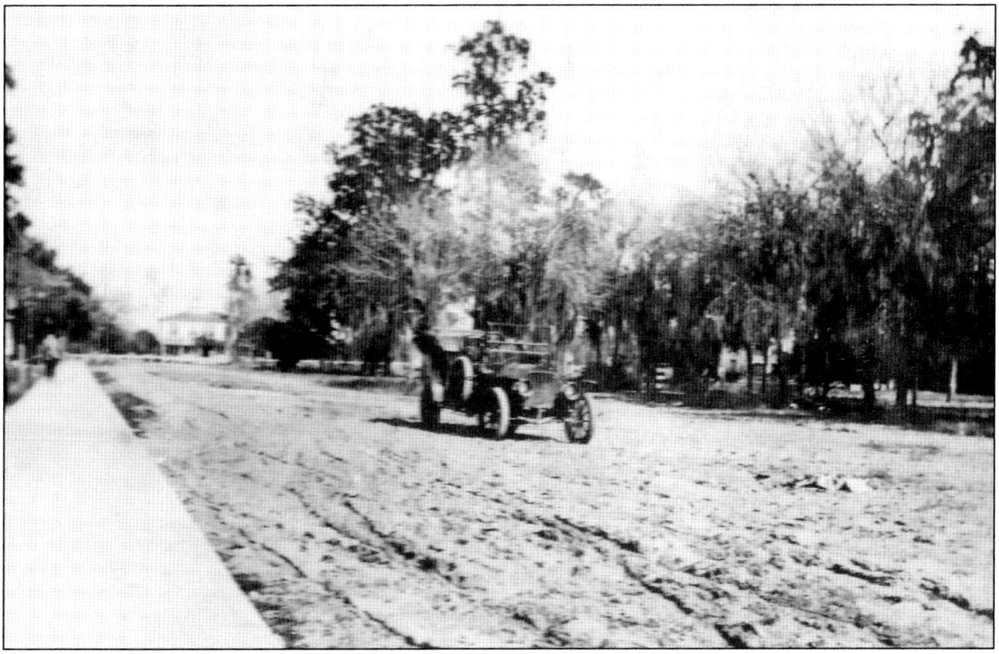

Seen here in 1918, West Park Street is being tilled in preparation for being paved; the sidewalk is already finished. On the right is the park. The Hampton House/Ariana Hotel can be seen at the end of the street. The house on the left belonged to Alfred C. and Naomi Thorp. This house was once the Auburndale Post Office, and Naomi was the postmistress.

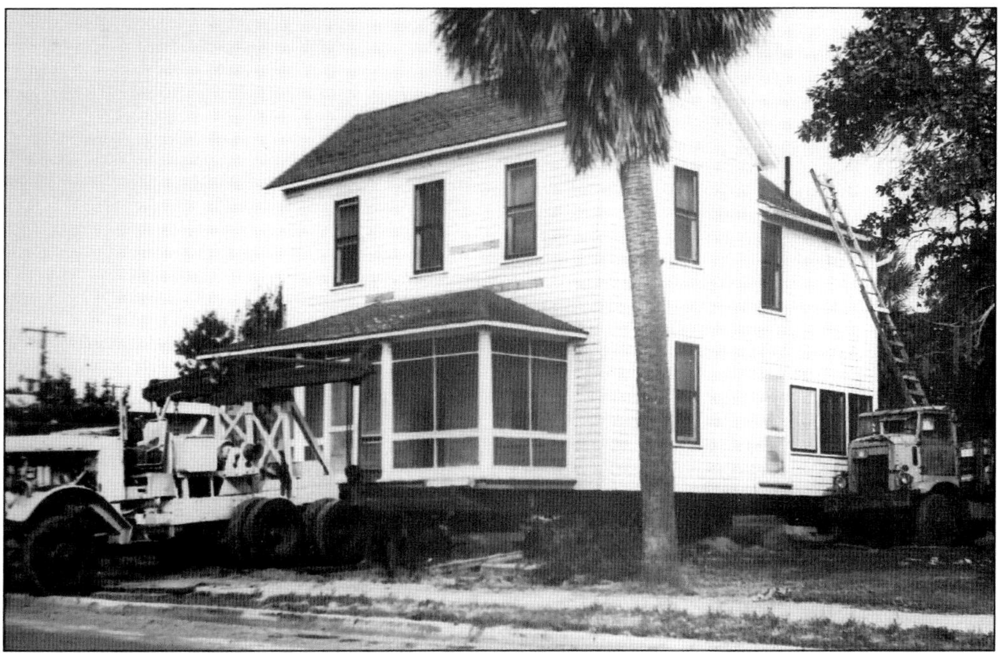

In 1962, the A.C. Thorp house was moved from the corner of East Park Street and Lake Avenue to make room for the Auburndale Parks and Recreation. Alfred Thorp and his son Harry were home builders. Among others, they constructed both of E.M. Baynard's houses. Harry and his wife, Glenn Anna, had a home on Bay Street.

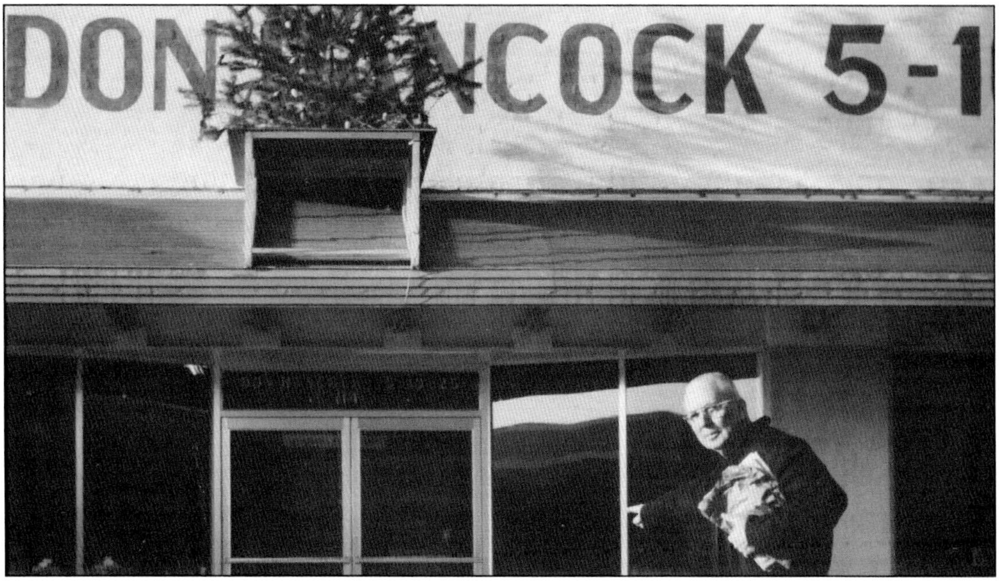

Don Hancock, shown here waving customers into his store for Christmas specials, owned a Five and Dime Store on East Lake Avenue. He and his wife, Frances, bought out an existing general merchandise store. They sold everything from candy to fabric. The store eventually expanded to include the whole block. In 1952, they added a smaller variety store on Magnolia Avenue. Don died in 1965, and Frances elected not to keep the store open.

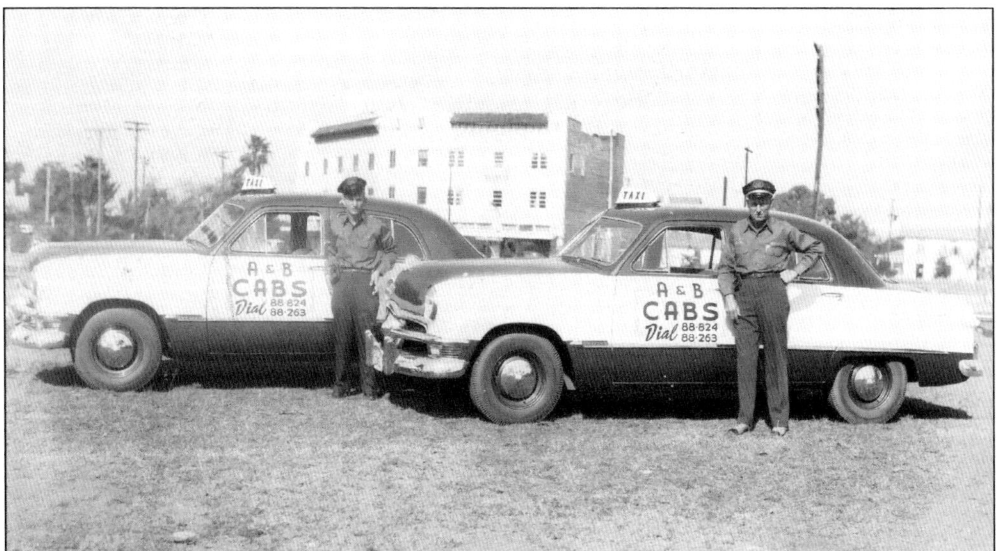

In 1956, Auburndale had two taxicabs. The company was owned by Clayton "Split" and Dale Spivey. The Spiveys had just renovated the Paul Smith/Ariana Hotel, turning the rooms into apartments. The dance hall on the third floor was two apartments. They had a restaurant on the first floor.

This is an unidentified Auburndale World War I solider dressed in his Doughboy uniform. In 1916, Lt. James Van Fleet and Auburndale residents William McLain, Gordon Winter, and Josh Burbage were sent to New Mexico to pursue Pancho Villa after he killed 16 Americans. Two weeks after returning to Auburndale, they were sent to Europe for World War I. The selective service had gone into effect, and Auburndale boys were being drafted.

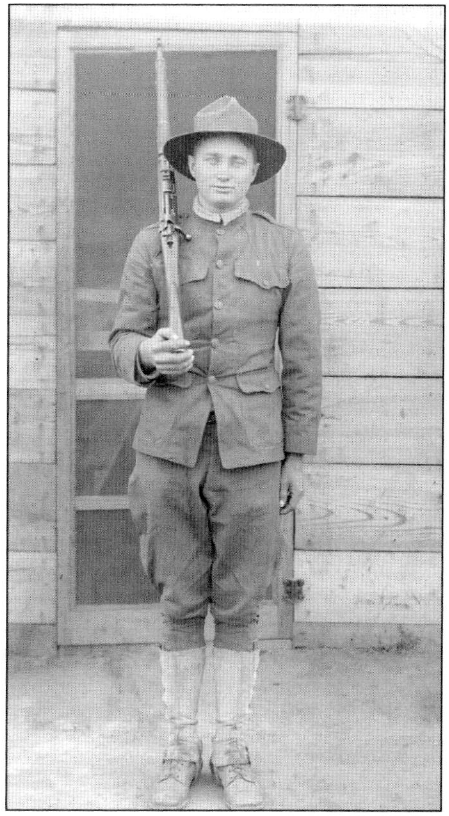

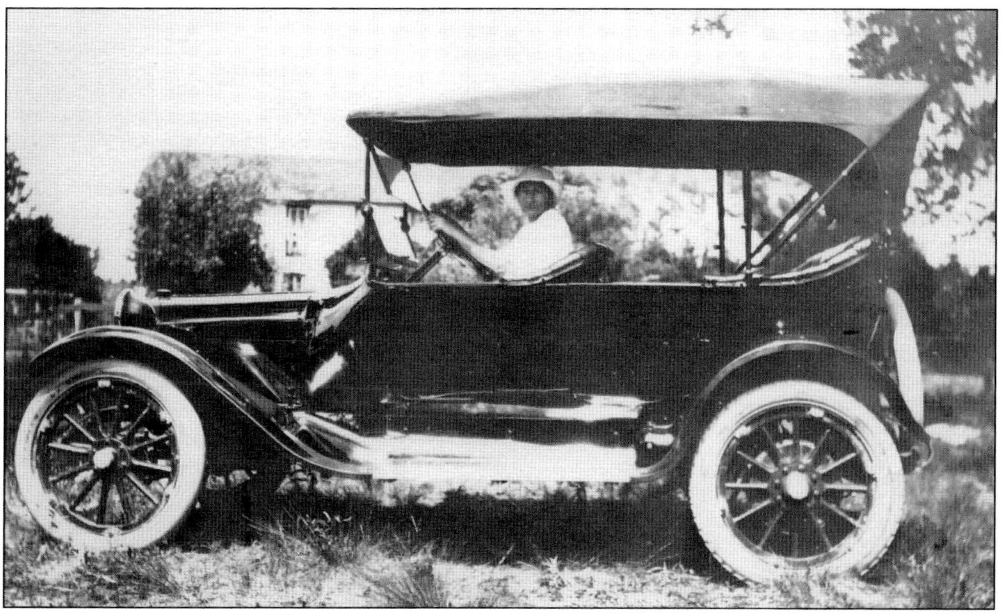

On June 30, 1917, Alice Kaszer, her mother, and two other ladies left Auburndale for a visit back to Pennsylvania in her 1910 Buick. There were no maps or road signs. The ladies had to ask for directions. Auto-repair shops were scarce and motels had not been invented yet. They stayed in boardinghouses along the way.

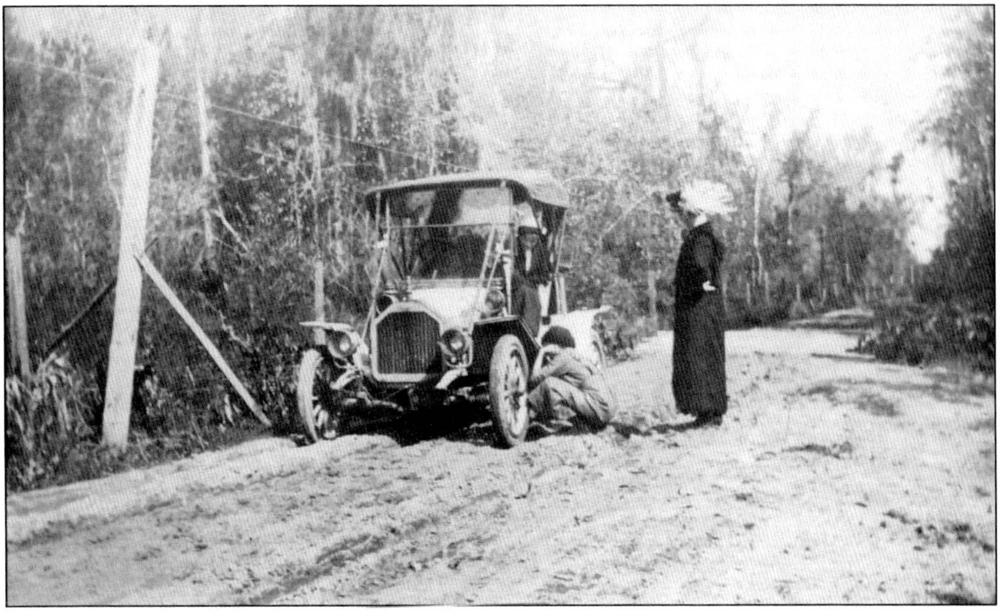

Outside Richmond, they were given wrong directions, and the car became stuck. Two boys pulled them out of the mud with horses. They asked for $3 for their trouble. Alice thought it was too much, so she gave them $2. The women had traveled 1,576 miles without a car breakdown and without a man on board.

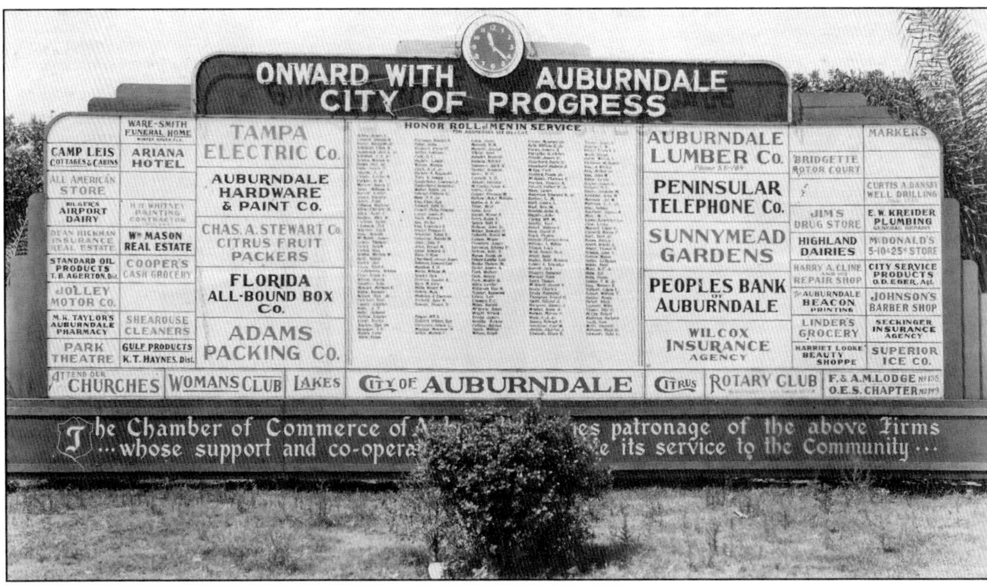

This sign, painted by Harry Cline, contains the names of all Auburndale service people. It stood in the park during World War II. Harry added names as needed and added a star beside those killed in action. At the end of the war, there were eleven stars: Hayes Bessinger, Leslie Childs, Alton Clark, Ross Clem, George Colton, Laverne DeBerry, Jack Hancock, Scott "Sub" Jordan, Raymond Ready, Ralph Sonanstine, and Robert Stetson.

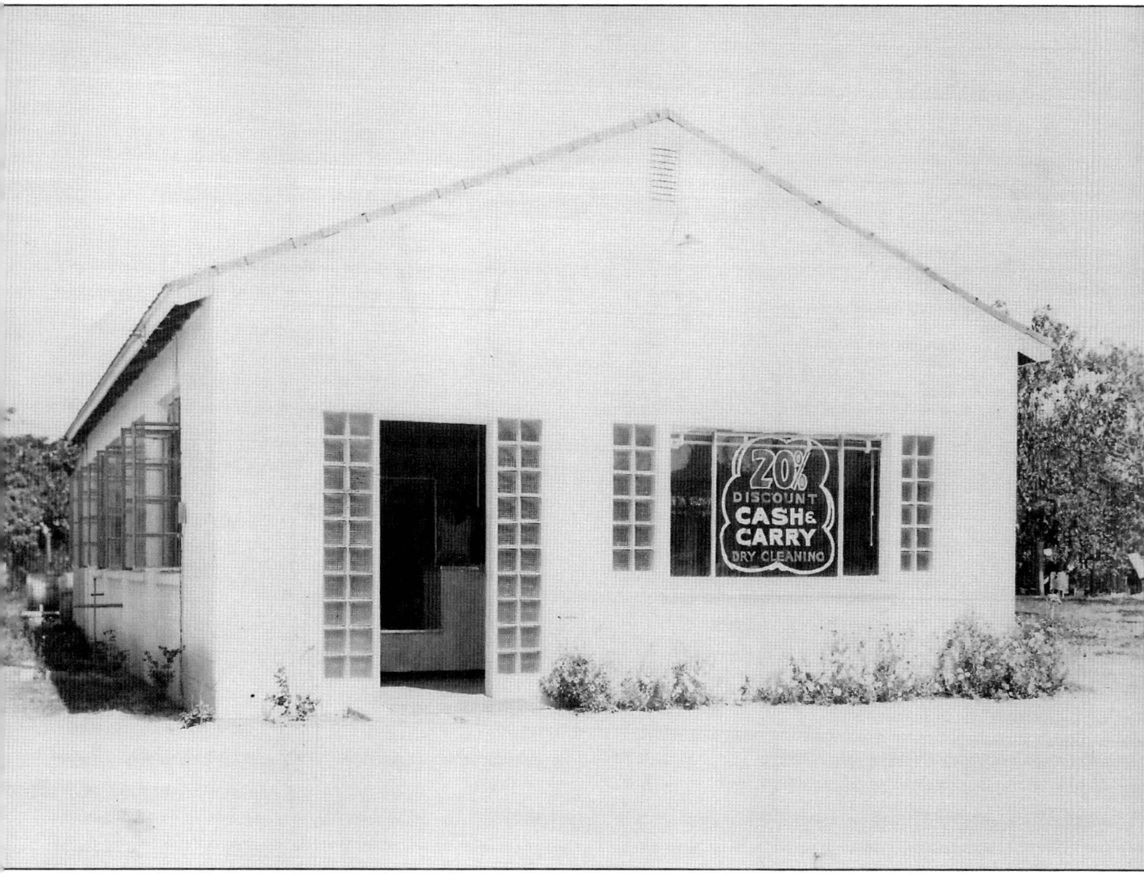

This dry-cleaning business, located on Bartow Avenue (Main Street), was owned by Clara Mae and Herbert Forsythe. Clara Mae Brewer came to Auburndale in 1920 with her family from Arkansas. She and Herbert graduated from Auburndale High School in 1929 and 1930, respectively. After they were married, they operated Forsythe's Dry Cleaners for about 35 years. The building has since been torn down.

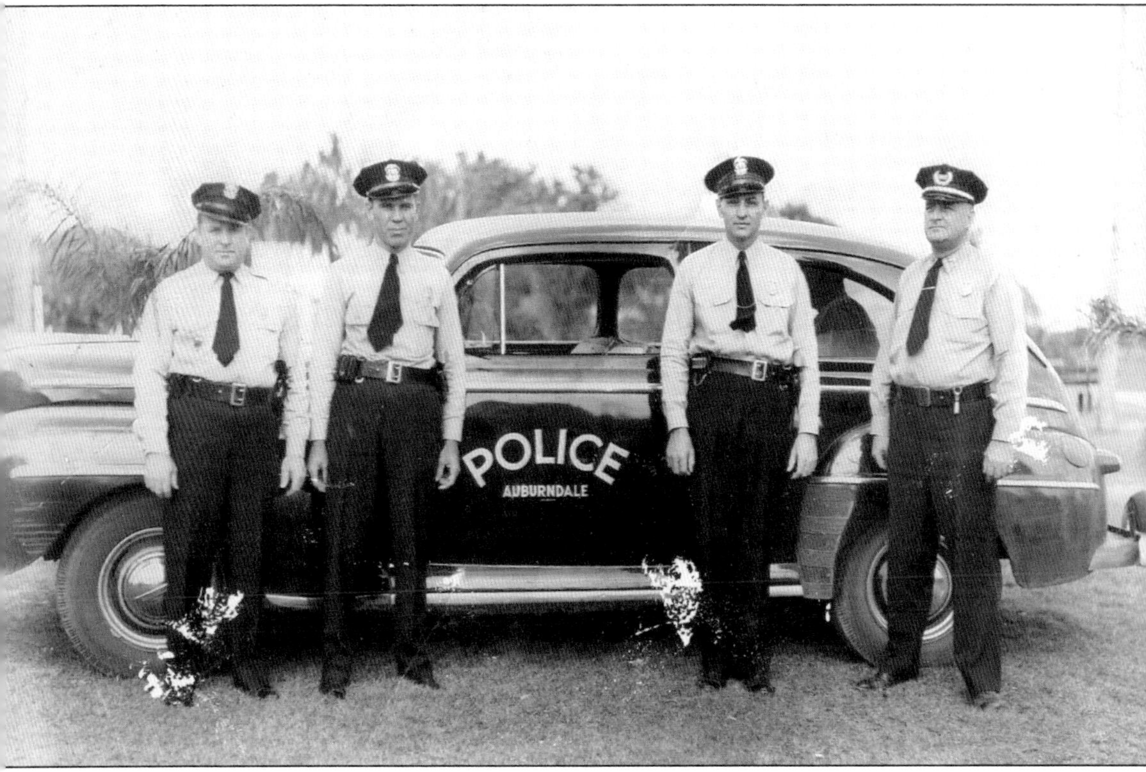

Auburndale's finest are pictured here around 1950. The Auburndale Police Force consisted of one car. The police station was in a small room addition to the rear of the city hall with two cells and a desk. From left to right, Bryant Joiner, Lawrence Lewis, Clarence Duncan, and Chief Ralph are the officers.

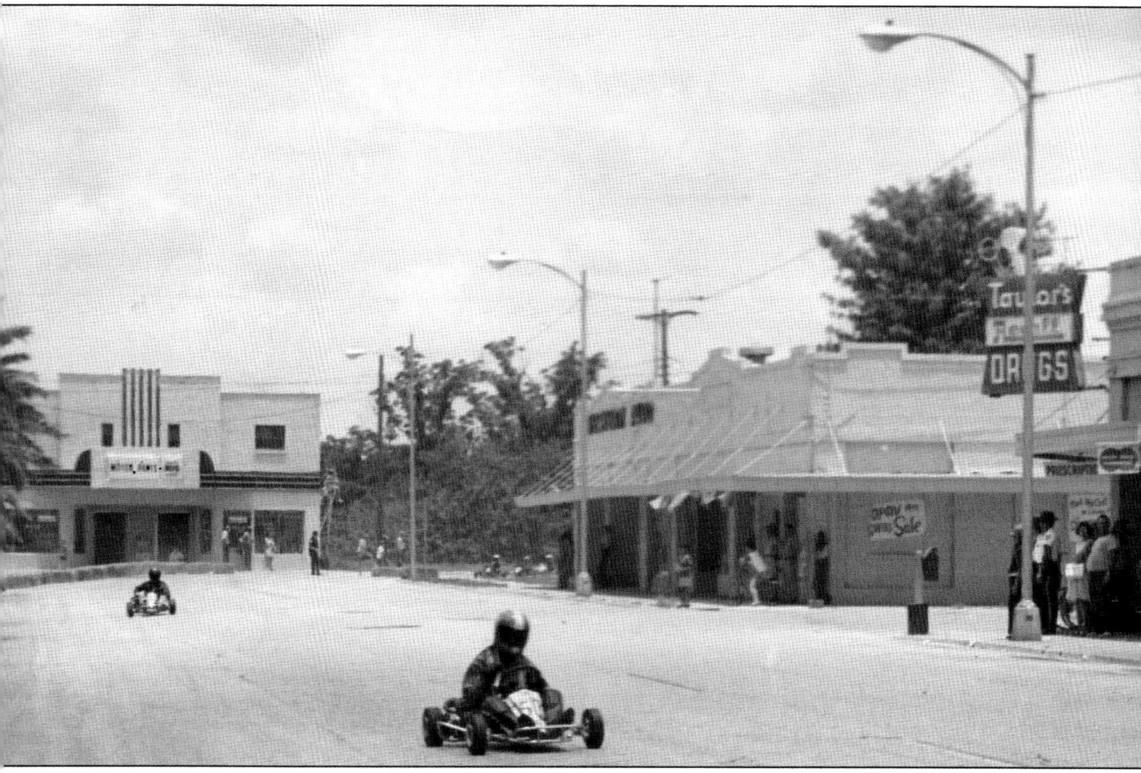

This photograph was taken during downtown go-cart races. The Auburn Theater, in the background, opened in 1948. The modern movie house showed first-run films. Inside, there was a separate smoking room and a soundproof room for noisy young children. The seats were padded, and the building was air-conditioned. The companion to the Auburn, the Dale Drive-in, was located on Berkley Road. Maurice Hensler owned both theaters.